JURY DECISION MAKING

MW01039953

PSYCHOLOGY AND CRIME SERIES

GENERAL EDITORS
Brian Bornstein, University of Nebraska, and Monica Miller, University of Nevada, Reno

The Perversion of Youth: Controversies in the Assessment
and Treatment of Juvenile Sex Offenders
Frank C. DiCataldo

Jury Decision Making: The State of the Science
Dennis J. Devine

Jury Decision Making

The State of the Science

Dennis J. Devine

NEW YORK UNIVERSITY PRESS
New York and London

NEW YORK UNIVERSITY PRESS
New York and London
www.nyupress.org

References to Internet Websites (URLs) were accurate at the time of writing.
Neither the author nor New York University Press is responsible for URLs that
may have expired or changed since the manuscript was prepared.

Library of Congress Cataloging-in-Publication Data

Devine, Dennis J. (Dennis John)
Jury decision making : the state of the science / Dennis J. Devine.
p. cm. — (Psychology and crime series)
Includes bibliographical references and index.
ISBN 978-0-8147-2018-9 (cl : alk. paper)
ISBN 978-0-8147-2019-6 (pb   )
ISBN 978-0-8147-2522-1 (ebook)
ISBN 978-0-8147-0498-1 (ebook)
1. Jury—United States—Decision making. 2. Jury—United States—Psychological aspects.
I. Title.
KF8972.D48 2012
347.73'752—dc23

New York University Press books

Manufactured in the United States of America
c 10 9 8 7 6 5 4 3 2 1
p 10 9 8 7 6 5 4 3 2 1

*This book is dedicated
to all those working to understand
and improve juries throughout the world.*

CONTENTS

ACKNOWLEDGMENTS

I want to express my thanks and appreciation to many individuals who helped make this book a reality. My editor at NYU Press, Jennifer Hammer, convinced me to submit a proposal for this book and was then unflaggingly cheerful and patient throughout the long writing process. Supportive inquiries about the status of the book from my parents and family served to enhance my resolve to complete what at times seemed to be an overwhelming task. I might never have developed a passion for conducting research on juries without the generous assistance of Judge Grant Hawkins of the Marion Superior Court in Indianapolis. Scott Billingsley assisted in conducting the first stage of the literature search and provided contagious doses of anticipatory enthusiasm. Several colleagues took time out of their busy lives to provide very helpful comments on drafts of selected chapters or the entire manuscript—David Caughlin, Mark Costanzo, Steven Penrod, Dennis Stolle, and one other anonymous reviewer.

On the home front, thanks to Talking Heads and David Byrne for providing musical background during much of the writing process, and Jon Stewart and Stephen Colbert for supplying late-night comedic relief from book-related consternation. Jessica and Eric Devine instigated many pleasant distractions from writing and helped me find humor in going "back in the box" during the long stretch run. Finally, I am especially grateful for the help and support of my wife, Julie Devine, who displayed her exceptional writing and project management skills in helping me to wrap this up. Most notably, I am indebted to her for a close reading of the entire manuscript, multiple rounds of proofreading, assistance in taming the references, and graciously tolerating many (many) conversations where my mind was somewhere else.

Thank you one and all!

LIST OF ABBREVIATIONS

ALI	American Law Institute
ATCLS	Attitudes Toward the Criminal Legal System
BJW	Belief in a Just World
BWS	Battered Woman Syndrome
CJP	Capital Jury Project
ELM	Elaboration Likelihood Model
G	Guilty
GBMI	Guilty but Mentally Ill
ICIE	In-court Inadmissible Evidence
IDA-R	Insanity Defense Attitudes-Revised
IE	Inadmissible Evidence
JBS	Juror Bias Scale
LE	Laboratory Error
LIC	Lesser Included Charge
LOC	Locus of Control
NC	Need for Cognition
NCSC	National Center for State Courts
NG	Not Guilty
NGRI	Not Guilty by Reason of Insanity
NORC	National Opinion Research Center
NP	Not Proven
P	Prosecution/plaintiff
PC	Probability of Commission
PJAQ	Pretrial Juror Attitude Questionnaire
PTP	Pretrial Publicity
RD	Reasonable Doubt
RLAQ	Revised Legal Attitudes Questionnaire
RMP	Random Match Probability
SDS	Social Decision Schemes
SES	Socioeconomic Status
SIS	Social Interaction Sequence
SJS	Scientific Jury Selection
SOE	Strength of Evidence
STS	Social Transition Schemes
SVF	Serious Violent Felon

"So, do you think there is anything we can know for certain?"

The question was directed at me by one of the prosecuting attorneys. We were in the midst of voir dire, and I happened to be one of the twelve persons seated in the jury box at the start of juror selection. Moments before, having looked over the responses on my juror information card, the D.A. had probably noticed that I was a professor, and his question likely reflected a concern that no amount of evidence presented by the state of Indiana would be sufficient to convince me of the defendant's guilt. I don't recall exactly what I said in response to his question about knowing anything with certainty, something along the lines of "maybe gravity." Whatever it was, it did not get me kicked off the panel. I sat on a twelve-person jury that decided a case involving an SVF (Serious Violent Felon) charged with possession of a firearm. The evidence was entirely circumstantial—no one actually saw the defendant with a gun. According to the arresting officer, the defendant was chased into a house and challenged while coming out of a bedroom. He refused to show his hands, backed into the bedroom, closed the door, then came out a moment later with hands raised. A gun was found in the room, and the defense could not account for its presence. We ended up convicting, and the whole experience was kind of surreal. I drove downtown in the morning, sat through an entire jury trial, deliberated for a couple hours, sent someone to prison, and arrived back home in time for a late supper. Every once in a while, I think about that case and hope that we made the right decision. I mean, no one actually *saw* the guy with a gun.

This book is about juries—specifically, how they make decisions. Unlike most books on juries, this one is not focused on how a particular jury reached a particular verdict. There is a "journalistic" model of jury research that attempts to do this—often in the wake of a high-profile case where the jury outrages the general public by inexplicably acquitting—but that is not the approach taken here. We in the community are always curious to learn what happened in the jury room of a major trial and draw our own conclusions about whether the jury "got it right"—and there is no harm in that. However, if we want to learn something about juries in general, we need to look beyond what an isolated jury does and consider the patterns that emerge across *many* jury decisions.

Over the last several years, when asked what this book is about, I invariably replied something to the effect that it summarizes the research on jury decision making and offers a theory based on that research. By *research*, I mean formal studies conducted by professional scholars using social science methods; by *theory*, I simply mean a thorough yet concise explanation of how juries operate. Considerably more scholarly attention has been devoted thus far to conducting empirical research than tying together the results. Relatively few efforts have been made to gather the many findings about juries and synthesize them into an overarching theoretical framework. Accordingly, that is the primary goal of this book and, as such, it differs from other scholarly books on juries that mostly represent critiques of the jury system or reviews of the empirical research in a specific domain. Books of the first type provide an evaluative perspective on the jury system; books of the second type aim to extract conclusions from a relatively well-defined body of research on a particular topic or question (e.g., the effectiveness of Scientific Jury Selection). In a nutshell, this book is more "saturated" in the empirical research than those of the first type and broader in scope than those of the second.

In terms of structure, this book is divided into three sections. The first section provides a methodological and theoretical foundation for the subsequent chapters. Chapter 1 offers an overview of jury research, including how it is done, how much is out there, what makes for a good empirical study, and some of the major milestones in the study of juries. Chapter 2 presents a comprehensive summary of existing theories that address the decision making of juries. This includes theories of how individual jurors arrive at their opinions as well as how juries as a whole make decisions.

The second section of the book summarizes what has been learned about juries from social science research. Each of its five chapters addresses research on a different set of variables that may influence jury decisions: jury-related trial practices (chap. 3), the trial context (chap. 4), characteristics of jurors and defendants (chap. 5), the evidence (chap. 6), and the deliberation process (chap. 7). All forms of research relevant to the behavior of jurors and juries are considered, including studies of individuals and interacting groups, simulated trial situations and real trials, and civil as well as criminal matters. Most major lines of research on juries are covered somewhere in these five chapters. In this section, I aim to distill and present the major *findings* that emerge from the literature on juries, highlighting selected individual studies that represent some of the best "flagship" research available along the way.

The final section of the book contains two chapters that present and discuss a new theory of jury decision making. Chapter 8 offers an integrative "Multi-Level" theory of juror and jury decision making that builds on existing theory and major findings from the empirical literature. Chapter 9 discusses the contributions of the theory in terms of its implications for advancing our understanding of juries and applications in the courtroom.

This book is aimed primarily at students and jury scholars but should also be of interest to legal professionals. It will be especially useful to those who study juries, as well as those who work with them on a daily basis (e.g., judges, attorneys, and court staff). For jury scholars and students, this book provides a good overview of the field, many testable research ideas, and jumping-off points for literature reviews. For legal professionals, it offers numerous insights into how juries operate and associated practical implications for the conduct of trials. Throughout the book, I have minimized the technical aspects of the research presented in favor of emphasizing the bottom line regarding what we have learned about juries—you definitely do not need to be a scientist to get something out of it. Accordingly, this book may also be of interest to general readers who just want to find out what science has learned about the jury system.

One last thing: This book does not offer a sweeping conclusion about the merits of the jury system. Like all human institutions, the jury system is not perfect—the research clearly shows that jurors are sometimes affected by "extralegal" variables, which should ideally have no impact. But the research also shows convincingly that juries are heavily influenced by the evidence and, in most trials, their decisions are consistent with the weight of it. There is certainly no foolproof alternative when it comes to making legal decisions—human judgment will always be involved, and so error will always be possible. Thus, the overarching goal of this book is to call attention to the known limitations of human information processing in the context of jury decision making so that, going forward, a pretty good system can be made even better.

1

The Lay of the Empirical Land

How many jury trials would you guess occur in the world each year? Ten thousand? One hundred thousand? A million, maybe? Well, no one knows for sure, but the number is certainly large. The first systematic attempt to estimate the number of annual jury trials *in the United States* appears to have been made by researchers associated with the Chicago Jury Project, who tried to determine the number that occurred in 1955. Obtaining a precise tally proved much more difficult than expected, as some jurisdictions didn't keep records, others didn't keep good records, and still others didn't respond to the query. In the end, after more than a year of sleuthing, Kalven and Zeisel (1966) estimated that 55,670 jury trials were completed in the United States during 1955, with perhaps another 20,000 initiated and terminated. Since then, other estimates have been offered that range from 150,000 to 300,000 (Abramson, 1994; Hastie, Penrod, & Pennington, 1983; Kassin & Wrightsman, 1988).

The best and most recent estimate of the number of annual jury trials in the United States, though, comes from a massive study conducted by the National Center for State Courts (NCSC). Based on data from the "State-of-the-States" survey research project collected from all fifty states and the

District of Columbia, researchers estimated that 148,558 jury trials were held in state courts in 2006 along with an additional 5,463 in the federal district courts (Mize, Hannaford-Agor, & Waters, 2007). Combining these two numbers yields a total current estimate of about 154,000 jury trials each year in the United States. Of these, about 47 percent appear to be for felony crimes, 19 percent for misdemeanor crimes, and 31 percent involve civil lawsuits, with 4 percent listed for "Other." These jury trials involve around 32 million summons for jury duty and more than 1.5 million empaneled jurors. Although some commentators have lamented the perceived decline of the American jury, these numbers do not suggest that juries are going the way of the dinosaur any time soon.

In addition, many jury trials occur each year outside the United States. A handful of countries use juries composed entirely of laypersons as is done in the United States (e.g., Australia, Canada, England, New Zealand, Russia, and Spain). A few others use a mixed "escabinado" system in which juries are composed of both laypersons and judges or magistrates (e.g., France, Germany, Italy, Japan, and Poland). Unfortunately, we have no good estimate of their frequency, with numbers notably absent from the most comprehensive source of information on world jury systems (Kaplan & Martin, 2006). It isn't clear how many jury trials occur in these various countries each year, but the number is certainly much smaller than the corresponding figure for the United States (perhaps several thousand). Regardless of the precise value, it is important to keep in mind that juries are not unique to the U.S. and the number of jury trials taking place outside the United States each year is not inconsequential.

Jury Research 101
How Many Jury Studies Are Out There?

A jury study is viewed here as a formal, quantitative analysis of data collected systematically from a large sample of participants for the purpose of yielding broad generalizations about juror or jury decision making. Just as there are challenges associated with obtaining a precise estimate of the annual number of jury trials, there are obstacles to getting an accurate tally of the number of jury studies in existence. For starters, there is some question as to what should be counted. Some data collection efforts yield multiple publications; is each of these publications a study, or is it just one big study with its results divided up? This is not a critical question given the relatively small number of datasets that turn up in multiple publications, but my view is that jury studies should be defined by their datasets. There are other challenges beyond what to count, though. Scholars and scientists who study juries operate in a variety of professional disciplines and publish their research in a large number of professional outlets, including some two hundred law journals and more than fifty social science journals. Any effort to identify (much less collect) every published study of juries is bound to miss some. Many jury studies are also never published for one reason or another, including suspect methodologies, prosaic findings, or lack of author inclination. Finally, like New York City, jury scholars never seem to sleep—the number of jury studies is growing all the time.

All the same, a ballpark estimate of the number of existing jury studies would be useful for conveying some sense of the magnitude of the existing literature and the rate at which it is increasing. An early count by Bray and Kerr (1979) yielded seventy-two studies involving mock jurors, sixty of which were published after 1970. Most of these early studies were done in laboratory settings (70%) using written (54%) or audiotaped (29%) trial materials, and about half featured deliberation (52%). Two decades later, Nietzel, McCarthy, and Kerr (1999) tallied all studies involving jurors or juries that appeared in ten leading U.S. journals (most of them in the social sciences) between 1977 and 1994. They identified 265 studies published in this eighteen-year interval, or an average of about fifteen studies per year. Two journals accounted for nearly two-thirds of the publications—*Law and Human Behavior* (40%) and *Journal of Applied Social Psychology* (25%). The vast majority of studies (89%) dealt with criminal as opposed to civil matters, and the most frequently studied topic was the performance of witnesses (20%).

These search results were updated and extended by Greene et al. (2002), who examined two additional years of content (i.e., 1998 and 1999) in the ten journals surveyed by Nietzel et al. and also cataloged the contents of an unspecified number of additional journals that published jury research for the entire 1977–99 period. This added a sizeable number of studies to each year's total, sometimes doubling (or more) the number found in just the ten leading U.S. journals. Greene et al. did not report the total number of publications they found but provided a three-dimensional graph that shows a clear upward annual trend and suggests (by my reckoning) that about 825 studies of juror or jury decision making were published between 1977 and 1999.

Merging the results of these literature surveys, and assuming that some were missed, it would seem that there were about 850 studies on juries published before 2000. Using the mean number of annual jury studies published in the last few years of the time span covered by Greene et al. (2002) as a starting point (51) and adding a few more per year for good measure, approximately 650 jury studies would have been published between 2000 and 2010. All told then, 1,500 is a plausible estimate of the number of published jury studies by the end of 2011. This value is doubtless an underestimate of the total number of formal jury studies conducted, with perhaps as many as half of those never published. Nonetheless, two things are very clear: (1) There is a great deal of existing research on juries available to consider, and (2) Efforts to conduct a comprehensive review of jury research are doomed to failure. Some level of selectivity will be required for any review.

Types of Jury Studies

Jury studies vary along many dimensions, including: (1) research design (experimental v. nonexperimental); (2) research setting (e.g., laboratory v. field); (3) participant type (e.g., students, community members, actual jurors); (4) trial format (e.g., case summary, edited transcript, audiotape, videotape, actual trial); (5) realism (e.g., inclusion of opening statements, jury instructions, deliberation); and (6) level of analysis (i.e., juror or jury). The various combinations allow for a dizzying variety of study profiles, but in practice only a few configurations occur with much frequency. Specifically, most jury studies fall into one of five categories: (1) analyses of archival data representing compilations of jury decisions across time and/or jurisdictions; (2) post-trial surveys of ex-jurors, attorneys, or judges collected via paper-and-pencil or the Internet; (3) post-trial interviews with real jurors; (4) field experiments assessing the impact of some procedural rule or instruction on actual juries; and (5) laboratory experiments that simulate a real trial and employ undergraduate students or community members as mock jurors. The first four categories represent different forms of field research based on real trials, whereas the latter two involve experiments that feature the manipulation of independent variables and (usually) random assignment of participants to study conditions. Of the jury studies published thus far, at least two-thirds represent mock jury experiments. The remaining third are based on actual trials, with about half of those representing some form of archival analysis and most of the rest involving post-trial surveys. Only a few studies feature in-depth interviews with real jurors or true field experiments with actual juries, primarily because they are so difficult to do.

Outcome Variables

The focal outcomes used in jury studies can be grouped into three major categories based on their chronological ordering: *predeliberation, deliberation,* and *postdeliberation*. Predeliberation outcomes correspond to the cognitive states of jurors before any group interaction. The flagship variable in this category is the juror's preferred verdict immediately after exposure to the trial-related materials. *Verdict preferences* are often measured in terms of discrete choices (i.e., guilty v. not guilty) but sometimes using a continuum of culpability or responsibility. When aggregated to the jury level, individual verdict preferences yield a distribution of jurors who favor different verdict options prior to deliberation (e.g., nine who favor guilty, three who favor not guilty). One characteristic of a juror's preferred verdict is the degree of confidence associated with it. *Verdict confidence* measures typically feature continuous response scales involving a subjective probability estimate. Other predeliberation variables include the extent to which jurors can recall case facts and the degree to which jurors comprehend their legal instructions. Recall and comprehension are often measured using a multiple-choice test but occasionally with open-ended short-answer items.

A second category of outcomes is associated with what happens during deliberation. One cluster of variables has to do with the *foreperson*—how this person is selected, when the selection takes place, and his or her demographic characteristics. A second cluster concerns the *participation* of jurors during discussion. Participation can be measured in various ways, including the number of times a juror speaks, the cumulative number of words spoken during deliberation, or the relative proportion of speaking acts or words accounted for by each juror. A third cluster corresponds to the assessment of individual opinions of members during deliberation via *polling* (i.e., "voting"), particularly the timing of the first poll, the number of polls taken in total, and whether polls are conducted openly or in some anonymous fashion. These variables are measured retrospectively by asking respondents to report what was done by the jury, or by videotaping simulated jury deliberations. A fourth cluster of deliberation variables pertains to the *content of the jury's discussion*. Various coding schemes can be used to categorize what jurors say, and then counts can be obtained for each category and relative proportion measures created by dividing the number of statements of each type by the total number of statements made by the jury. Yet another cluster of deliberation variables is associated with *jury performance*—how well the jury fulfills its focal task of deliberating. Measures of deliberation quality include: (1) the thoroughness of the jury's review of the evidence, (2) how well the jurors understand their instructions, (3) the extent to which deliberation is characterized by broad participation and input from members, and (4) the degree to which a positive, constructive atmosphere characterizes the jury room. Although it has not received a great deal of attention from researchers thus far, jury performance is important because of the strong relationship it should have with accuracy—in other words, juries that deliberate better should be more likely to reach the correct decision.

Postdeliberation outcomes represent a third category of variables relevant to jury research. Far and away, the most frequently studied variable in this category is the *verdict* reached on one or more charges (or claims) against the defendant, with probably 95 percent of the studies conducted on jury behavior employing verdicts as the focal outcome. In civil trials where the defendant is found liable for *damages*, juries also determine the amount of money to be awarded to the plaintiff for compensatory and (occasionally) punitive purposes. In criminal trials involving capital crimes, juries also decide the punishment or *sentence* as well (i.e., death v. life in prison). Separate from the party favored by the jury's decision, another important outcome that has received surprisingly little attention from scholars is whether the jury's decision is accurate—in essence, whether the jury "gets it right." *Accuracy* from a legal perspective amounts to whether a jury arrives at the decision that would be legally appropriate given the relevant case facts and correct application of the relevant law. Of course, it is difficult if not impossible to determine jury accuracy with certainty in most real-world trials, but it can be approximated through various means. For instance, jury decisions can be compared with the opinions of objective legal experts such as the presiding judge or an appellate court. Another proxy indicator of accuracy is whether jury decisions can be viewed as legally defensible by objective legal experts given the most favorable interpretation of the facts established at trial.

Study Quality

Two primary criteria serve as benchmarks for assessing the value of any study: the degree to which accurate conclusions can be drawn about what causes what (causality), and the degree to which observed effects or relationships can be expected to hold in other settings (generalizability). These two criteria have been referred to as *internal validity* and *external validity* (respectively), and a number of considerations affect inferences about causality and generalizability in studies of jury decision making.

The ability to draw accurate conclusions about causality is primarily a function of a study's research design. Basically, stronger inferences are warranted when independent variables are manipulated effectively, when participants are randomly assigned to levels of the independent variable, and when a high level of *control* exists over known or suspected extraneous (confounding) variables. Control can be achieved by either holding constant the potential confounding variables or, less optimally, by measuring them and removing their effects statistically during the analyses. Whether achieved via the design or the statistical analyses, the purpose of control is to rule out alternative explanations for the observed findings that do not involve the independent variables. A study's *sample size* is also an important determinant of quality. In essence, a large number of observations (either individual jurors or juries) is needed to minimize sampling error, or the discrepancy between the numbers obtained from a sample and what is true in the overall population of jury trials. Sampling error occurs to some extent in any research study where the entire population is not examined but, other things being equal, the smaller the sample used in a study, the more the sample value can deviate from the true population value. As a result, larger studies are more trustworthy than smaller studies. Finally, the quality of a study's manipulations and measures is also a critical determinant of internal validity. If study variables are conceptualized loosely, manipulated weakly, or measured poorly, it is simply difficult to interpret *any* findings (or non-findings) that emerge.

Likewise, several factors affect our confidence that a study's results will generalize to other settings (e.g., real-world trials, or trials in other jurisdictions). Two important determinants of generalizability with regard to jury studies are *realism* and the *type of participants* involved. Realism basically concerns the degree to which a study incorporates elements of an actual jury trial, with the most important of these being a visual medium, opening and closing statements by the attorneys, a question-and-answer format for presentation of the evidence, cross-examination, formal jury instructions, and the opportunity to deliberate and reach a group decision. Research findings are usually more generalizable when they are based on real trials and actual jurors, although studies based on simulated trials involving mock jurors can offer a high degree of generalizability under some circumstances. Even when a study involves real trials and actual juries, observed findings cannot be assumed to hold automatically in other jurisdictions, as unique influences may be operating in the setting where the data were gathered. Thus, generalizability is usually greatest when real juries are studied across multiple jurisdictions and trial types (i.e., focal charges), which limits the possibility that study findings are restricted to a particular locality, court system, or kind of trial.

Trade-Offs

No study is perfect; all have some weakness. Of special note, the ability to draw causal inferences and the ability to generalize study findings are inversely related to one another. Essentially, the high degree of control needed to rule out alternative explanations and achieve good internal validity usually comes at the cost of lowering the realism of a study and thus reducing external validity. In particular, tightly controlled experimental studies that allow strong causal inferences must usually be conducted in laboratory settings with simulated trial materials and mock jurors. Any findings associated with these "unnatural" environments could be due to the unique experimental context. In contrast, nonexperimental field research typically features much less control over the research context but greater realism. The primary weakness of most field studies with real juries is the possibility that observed results are due to the nature of the case, the characteristics of the participants, or (most critically) the quantity and quality of the evidence presented as opposed to the focal variables. It is very difficult to attain both high control and high realism in the same study, so researchers usually must choose their poison. The inherent trade-off between internal and external validity highlights the importance of conducting multiple studies with complementary strengths and offsetting weaknesses.

Quality Continuum

While no study is perfect, they are not all equal either—some are better than others. Indeed, the many studies on juries fall on a continuum of study quality, with a distribution roughly bell-shaped in form. There are a few fantastic studies, some that are quite good, many that are moderate in quality, some with value but constrained by notable limitations, and a few that would better serve the field if they had never been done.

There are also some general tendencies with regard to the quality of different types of studies. Case studies focusing on one jury are at the low end of the quality continuum, at best leading to working hypotheses about how juries in general do things. Somewhat higher on the quality continuum are archival studies that involve compiling and analyzing distributions of jury verdicts or damage awards in one or more jurisdictions over some period of time. These studies have the benefit of involving real jury decisions, but usually suffer from poor (or missing) measures of important variables and are subject to alternative explanations associated with extraneous variables. The majority of jury studies—and those exhibiting the greatest range of quality—involve simulated trials and mock jurors. Many of these studies have only modest value due to a conjunction of undesirable attributes—abbreviated trial materials (e.g., case summaries), student mock jurors, and no deliberation. However, there are also some very good laboratory experiments that feature excellent control along with realistic trial depictions, representative participants (e.g., community residents, actual venirepersons, or jurors), and a deliberation component. These high-quality mock jury studies allow for strong inferences about focal independent variables, and their relatively high realism affords some confidence that their results will apply to real juries. All other things being equal, though, field experiments represent the best jury studies in that they combine high levels of experimental control and realism. Indeed, if there is an "ideal" jury study, it would probably be a field experiment with a large sample of real juries from multiple jurisdictions where one or more focal variables (e.g., trial practices) was manipulated and juries were randomly assigned to study conditions. Unfortunately, this ideal is very difficult to achieve, although a few research teams have come remarkably close (e.g., Diamond, Vidmar, Rose, Ellis, & Murphy, 2003; Heuer & Penrod, 1988; 1989; 1994a; 1994b).

Meta-Analysis

Social scientists have long been aware of the dangers of expecting any individual study to definitively answer a research question and instead have sought to base conclusions on a body of research. Originally developed in the 1970s, meta-analysis represents a quantitative compilation of the results of existing empirical studies. One is performed by first conducting an extensive search of the literature to identify and obtain all possible studies that measured the focal independent and dependent variables and reported their statistical association. The results from each primary study (often called "effects") are then mathematically averaged to obtain an estimate of the relationship between the focal variables in the larger population (e.g., all jury trials), the idea being that the errors associated with individual studies will tend to cancel out and provide a better overall value than any single study would allow. Meta-analyses can be done using a variety of statistics, but most involve calculating the average observed difference in means on the outcome measure for different levels of a categorical independent variable (i.e., the d statistic), or the average correlation between two continuous variables (i.e., the r statistic), across the set of obtained studies. In general, for the d statistic, values of near .2 correspond to small (or weak) effects, values near .5 represent medium (or moderate) effects, and values larger than .8 represent large (or strong) effects (Cohen, 1992). For the r statistic, the corresponding reference values are .1 (weak), .3 (moderate), and .5 (strong). Sometimes the focal statistics are weighted based on their sample size or rated quality prior to the averaging process in order to allow the better studies to have more impact. Regardless of the specific procedures employed, however, it is important to keep in mind that meta-analyses do not yield "perfect" estimates of true relationships—their results are constrained by the amount and quality of the primary studies they are based upon. Nonetheless, they represent a major step forward in the synthesis of knowledge in all areas of the social sciences, and upcoming chapters will highlight meta-analytic findings whenever they are available.

Summary

The many empirical studies of juries consist primarily of five general types. No study is perfect and most involve a trade-off of internal and external validity, but some studies warrant more attention than others. Study quality tends to be highest for field experiments and realistic mock jury studies that involve participants from the community, and lowest for case studies of single juries and archival studies with limited information about trials and juries. Ultimately, we hope to observe consistent findings across studies that employ a variety of different research designs and to estimate the strength of true effects using meta-analysis. To the extent this occurs, we can be more confident of drawing accurate conclusions about jury decision making in general.

A Brief History of Jury Research
Prior to 1950

Although juries have been used for hundreds of years, they have not been studied scientifically until fairly recently. Indeed, systematic efforts to collect data on juries go back less than one hundred years, with the earliest "studies" taking the form of judges keeping track of jury verdicts and comparing them with their own view of the appropriate verdict (summarized by Kalven & Zeisel, 1966; pp. 521–523). For instance, in the 1920s, Judge Philip J. McCook of the Supreme Court of New York recorded his personal belief about the correct verdict in 114 civil jury trials that occurred in his court over ten terms and reported agreeing with the jury's verdict regarding liability in 72 percent of the cases. Similarly, in 1949, Judge Richard Hartshorne of the Court of Common Pleas in Newark, New Jersey, calculated agreement rates of 89 percent for 270 criminal jury verdicts and 85 percent for 253 civil jury verdicts, whereas Judge Emory Niles of the Supreme Bench of Baltimore City reported an 83 percent concordance rate between his personal view and the verdicts of his civil juries in 1952. Anticipating later findings, these early court-specific tallies provided preliminary indication that judges and juries generally agree on the correct verdict at trial.

Mock juries made their first appearance between the two world wars, with Marston (1924) given credit for being the first to use them (Ellsworth & Mauro, 1998) but Weld and his colleagues (Weld & Roff, 1938; Weld & Danzig, 1940) apparently the first social scientists to publish research on mock jurors in a psychology journal. The latter were interested in studying a question long pondered by attorneys: When do jurors come to a personal decision regarding the appropriate verdict during a trial? Taking multiple measures over the course of a mock trial, they observed something important that now seems rather intuitive—jurors did not wait until the end of the trial to form opinions about the evidence (and the corresponding appropriate verdict), but rather tended to form beliefs early on and then adjust them over the course of the trial as the evidence accumulated. This observation led to the development of the sequential weighting model of juror decision making in which jurors presumably begin a trial in a neutral or agnostic position regarding the appropriate verdict, then update their belief as they encounter each new piece of evidence. On the whole, however, research on juries was rare and isolated before the mid-point of the twentieth century.

The 1950s

The systematic study of jury decision making began at the University of Chicago in 1953 about the time Cubs fans were beginning to wonder if there was something wrong with their team. It was then that a group of researchers received a $400,000 grant from the Ford Foundation to study juries using social science methods. Such an event seems mundane now, but it was unprecedented at the time. The research team included a statistician and sociologist (Hans Zeisel), a social psychologist (Fred Strodtbeck), and a law professor (Harry Kalven), along with many of their graduate students. With such a diverse group, we can only imagine the frustration and eye-rolling that must have occurred during those early project meetings.

In any case, the researchers knew they were involved in a groundbreaking initiative, and their research program was appropriately ambitious. Their overall goals were to identify and summarize what had been learned about juries to date, and then add to that knowledge using social science empirical methods. To accomplish the latter, they initiated a number of studies using various methodologies that have since become standard tools in the study of juries, including interviewing and surveying jurors and legal professionals after trials, and observing mock juries. The most well-known study associated with the Chicago Jury Project involved a national survey of all U.S. trial judges in which recipients were asked to indicate their agreement with recent jury verdicts in their courtroom. This massive effort eventually yielded judge–jury agreement data from 555 judges on 3,576 criminal trials and approximately 4,000 civil trials that still serves as a benchmark today.

One research initiative associated with the Chicago Jury Project inadvertently led to the first experimental use of mock juries after touching off something of a national scandal. It started out innocently enough with an observational study designed to shed light on what juries do during deliberation. Specifically, in 1955, the deliberations of five civil juries in federal district court were audiotaped in Wichita, Kansas. Permission to do so was obtained from the judge and attorneys on both sides, but the jurors were not consulted or informed. When the *L.A. Times* ran a story on the project, uproar ensued over the apparent violation of the sanctity of the jury room. The event made national headlines in the summer of 1955 and led to a special hearing by the Senate Judiciary Committee at which some of the project researchers were subpoenaed to testify. The researchers were basically told they would not be allowed to stick their noses in the jury room again. When all was said and done, direct observation/recording of deliberation was censured by the U.S. Attorney General and the American Bar Association, and a majority of states passed legislation prohibiting the direct observation or taping of jury deliberations. This essentially barred the door to the jury room for research purposes—a door that remains closed to this day. Clearly stung by the furor and showcasing the wit that characterizes their writing, Kalven and Zeisel facetiously awarded their project a Purple Heart and proceeded to use mock juries to study the effects of varying the weight of the evidence, knowledge of the defendant's insurance status, and the legal definition of key terms (i.e., "negligence" in civil trials and "insanity" in criminal trials).

Looking back, the Chicago Jury Project represents a landmark in the scientific study of juries. Among other things, the project yielded estimates of the number of jury trials in the United States, the frequency of hung juries, the extent of agreement between judges and juries regarding the appropriate verdict, and the "success rate" for majority factions during deliberation. A slew of journal articles were published in the late 1950s and 1960s along with several books, including probably the most well-known book ever on juries, *The American Jury* (Kalven & Zeisel, 1966). Despite this, at least one large chunk of project data was never thoroughly analyzed. In the introduction to *The American Jury*, Kalven and Zeisel tantalizingly mentioned that another book was in the works summarizing their survey research findings on nearly 4,000 civil juries—but apparently nothing was ever done with this massive dataset beyond calculating an overall agreement rate. These data are probably still resting peacefully at the bottom of the scholarly ocean in the archives of the University of Chicago Law Library.

The 1960s

The 1960s are notable for many things, but jury research is not one of them. Aside from the 1966 publication of *The American Jury* summarizing Chicago Jury Project findings from the 1950s, research on juries consisted primarily of a few analyses of archival data published in scattered law journals (e.g., Bullock, 1961), along with a handful of early mock jury studies (e.g., Boehm, 1968; Kline & Jess, 1966; Landy & Aronson, 1969) and one of the first surveys of ex-jurors (Reed, 1965). Although the period was one of sweeping change within the legal system stemming from several landmark Supreme Court decisions (e.g., *Witherspoon v. Illinois* in 1968), it was a quiet decade with regard to research on juries.

The 1970s

The placid landscape of jury research changed dramatically in the early 1970s when the Supreme Court managed to both agitate and inspire social psychologists via major rulings on requirements related to jury size and unanimous verdicts. Over several cases, the Court determined that juries could legally have fewer than twelve members but at least six (*Williams v. Florida*, 1970; *Colgrove v. Battin*, 1973), and that non-unanimous jury verdicts were acceptable in some cases (*Apodaca v. Oregon*, 1972; *Johnson v. Louisiana*, 1972). These rulings provoked a flurry of empirical research designed to examine the Court's assumptions about the non-effects of jury size and decision rule on jury performance and verdicts. Another major spark came in 1973 in the form of James Davis's work on social decision schemes. Social decision schemes (SDS) are "rules" that aim to capture the implicit social process by which individual preferences are transformed into a collective decision (e.g., "majority rules"). Davis and his students began using mock juries to examine the effects of various trial practices on group decision processes and verdicts, aiming to identify the SDS that best reflected what actually happens in juries. Much of the research on juries during the 1970s and into the 1980s had its origins in the SDS approach. The first large-scale research on juries outside of North America also took place during this period in England (Baldwin & McConville, 1979; 1980; McCabe & Purves, 1972; 1974). The year 1977 stands out as noteworthy as well, marked by the inaugural issue of the flagship journal publishing research on juries

(*Law and Human Behavior*) as well as publication of the first extensive literature reviews of empirical research on juries (Davis, Bray, & Holt, 1977; Gerbasi, Zuckerman, & Reis, 1977). Another milestone was achieved in 1979 when the first special issue on juries appeared in *Law and Human Behavior*.

The 1980s

For the reasons noted earlier, research on juries mushroomed in the 1980s. The study of jury size and decision rule continued, and the investigation of several additional trial-related practices began in earnest (i.e., death qualification, bifurcation, and severance/joinder). The 1980s also witnessed the beginning of systematic examination of jury instructions, especially the impact of trial complexity on juror instruction comprehension and various practices intended to improve comprehension. In the wake of the Supreme Court's upholding of capital punishment (*Gregg v. Georgia*), researchers began using large archival datasets to investigate the possibility of racial bias in cases involving the death penalty. Particularly noteworthy was the work of David Baldus and his colleagues, widely considered to be some of the best research of its kind. Foreshadowing a surge of attention given to civil juries in the 1990s, researchers at RAND began analyzing a huge archival database of civil jury verdicts obtained from San Francisco and Chicago (Cook County) over nearly twenty years. Reflecting the growing body of empirical research, several influential scholarly books on juries were also published, including *Inside the Jury* (Hastie, Penrod, & Pennington, 1983), *Judging the Jury* (Hans & Vidmar, 1986), and *The American Jury on Trial* (Kassin & Wrightsman, 1988). The first book summarizes in exhaustive detail one of the best empirical studies based on mock juries, whereas the latter two were some of the first to systematically assess and critique the performance of juries using the empirical literature. Finally, the first meta-analyses relevant to jury decision making appeared in the 1980s (MacCoun & Kerr, 1988; Tanford, Penrod, & Collins, 1985).

The 1990s

Research on juror and jury behavior continued to accelerate throughout the 1990s, with the number of topics under study increasing as well. For the first time, concerted attention was also given to civil juries. It *might* have been possible to do a comprehensive review of the research on civil jury decision making in the early 1990s, but certainly not by the end of the decade. In the wake of burgeoning research in several domains, additional meta-analyses appeared based on studies of juror and/or defendant characteristics (Mazzella

& Feingold, 1994; Narby, Cutler, & Moran, 1993; Sweeney & Haney, 1992), jury size (Saks & Marti, 1997), pretrial publicity (Steblay, Besirevic, Fulero, & Jimenez-Lorente, 1999), and trial practices (Nietzel, McCarthy, & Kerr, 1999). Continuing the trend established in the previous decade, a number of excellent books on juries were also published. Some were intended primarily to advance theory and research for scholars (e.g., *Inside the Juror*, Hastie, 1993), but a growing number targeted a broader audience of legal practitioners as well as the general public, including *We the Jury* (Abramson, 1994) and *The Jury: Trial and Error in the American Courtroom* (Adler, 1994). A notable feature of these latter books was their use of research findings to address questions about jury performance. In turn, reviews of work by social scientists also began to appear in law journals toward the end of the decade (e.g., Saks, 1998; Vidmar, 1998).

2000 and Beyond

Research in the first decade of the twenty-first century continued at a blistering pace on a wide and ever-expanding range of topics. A highlight of this period is the excellent field work on real juries conducted by multidisciplinary research teams. Two such studies resulted from the Arizona Supreme Court allowing researchers to evaluate the impact of permitting civil juries to discuss their cases before the end of the trial. In both studies, researchers were able to conduct field experiments involving the random assignment of juries to study conditions, an exceedingly rare event. In the first experiment, extensive post-trial questionnaire data were gathered from presiding judges, attorneys, litigants, and jurors associated with 172 civil jury trials (Hannaford, Hans, & Munsterman, 2000). The second experiment represents one of the most comprehensive examinations of real juries ever conducted (Diamond et al., 2003). In addition to videotaping fifty civil jury trials from start to finish, project researchers were allowed to videotape the deliberations of each jury and collect post-trial questionnaire data from judges, attorneys, litigants, and jurors. Judges have very rarely permitted jury deliberations to be recorded under *any* circumstances, and this is the only large-scale scientific study to accomplish the feat. Around that same time, another team of researchers associated with the National Center for State Courts conducted a major field study of jury decision making focusing on the frequency of hung juries and jury nullification (Hannaford-Agor, Hans, Mott, & Munsterman, 2002). This research team collected extensive case and questionnaire data on 382 jury trials held in four different metropolitan areas, ultimately obtaining 366 responses from presiding judges as well as data from 576 lead attorneys and 3,497 jurors. Finally, the long-running Capital Jury Project, conducted by a consortium of jury scholars

at several universities, represents the best research yet conducted on jury decision making in death penalty cases. Over a number of years, project researchers conducted three-hour structured interviews with nearly 1,200 jurors from
354 capital juries in fourteen different states. The time, resources, and energy
required to undertake such research is considerable—as is the contribution
made to our understanding of jury decision making.

Another notable occurrence in the current period is the growing consoli-
dation of knowledge about jury decision making. Numerous reviews were
published in the last decade (e.g., Devine et al., 2001; Diamond & Rose, 2005;
Greene et al., 2002; Levett et al., 2005; Schuller & Yarmey, 2001; Winter &
Greene, 2007). In addition to continuing efforts by legal scholars to ground
book-length reviews and critiques of the jury system in empirical research
(e.g., Jonakait, 2003; Vidmar & Hans, 2007), professional associations such
as the American Psychology-Law Society and the American Psychological Association sponsored several books featuring thorough reviews of the
empirical literature on selected topics such as the determination of damages
in civil trials (Greene & Bornstein, 2003), the death penalty (Haney, 2005),
and Scientific Jury Selection (Lieberman & Sales, 2007). This promising
trend toward amassing accumulated knowledge relevant to specific domains
within the jury decision making literature seems likely to continue.

A Look Ahead

Jury research continues to be conducted at an increasing rate, and the quality
of the work—once easily dismissed by the courts—has risen as well. New technologies and a grudging appreciation of scientific research by the courts are
opening up exciting opportunities to better understand how juries operate. Via
the Internet, detailed post-trial information can now be obtained quickly and
easily from large samples of judges, attorneys, and jurors from a wide variety of
jurisdictions. In addition to overcoming the constraints imposed by geography,
the Internet allows for data to be collected on real jury trials cheaper, faster,
and more accurately than ever before. The growing availability and acceptance
of handheld electronic devices also allows for the possibility of studying jurors
in something close to real time. Increased video access to the courtroom is also
facilitating the creation of more realistic trial stimulus materials. Most promising of all, the door to the jury room may be starting to swing open just a bit. As
legal professionals become more familiar and comfortable with social science
research, they are more likely to allow social science researchers to get high-
quality data through direct observation of actual jury deliberation. More than
ever, those who wish to understand jury decisions have reason to be optimistic.

2

Models of Juror and Jury Decision Making

As long as juries have existed, people have probably wondered how they make their decisions. In the short history of scientific study of juries, scholars have given this question a good deal of attention as well. Numerous theoretical models have been offered addressing how jurors reach their individual decisions about the appropriate verdict—whether the defendant should be convicted or the plaintiff awarded damages. These models differ along a variety of dimensions, with one of those being their focal level. Some models focus on how individual jurors reach their decisions, whereas others concentrate on how the jury as a whole reaches a collective decision. The jury-level decision process has the potential to be considerably more complex than the individual-level process, although at least group interaction can be observed directly. This chapter examines the various models identified by social scientists to account for and explain both juror-level and jury-level decisions.

Models of juror and jury decision making differ in terms of their primary purpose as well. *Descriptive* models attempt to capture what jurors and juries actually do as they make decisions. The ultimate test of a descriptive model is whether it reproduces (or explains) known outcomes. In contrast, *prescriptive* models specify the way decisions should logically be made using formal mathematical algorithms that identify relevant variables and the optimal manner of their combination. For example, if a theory says that the attractiveness of a verdict should be the product of A*B, then jurors told that A = 5 and B = 2 should report an attractiveness level of approximately 10 for that verdict. To the extent that jurors indicate an attractiveness value that differs from 10, the theory suggests they are making suboptimal decisions. Thus, prescriptive models also provide a benchmark for evaluating how well jurors actually make their decisions.

Juror-Level Models

Pennington and Hastie (1981) and Hastie (1993) provide excellent summaries and critiques of the different approaches that have been taken to model juror thought processes. This section is heavily indebted to their work.

Bayesian Model

The Bayesian model is an individual-level prescriptive model based on the work of Thomas Bayes, a member of the British clergy interested in developing mathematical algorithms to evaluate evidence for the existence of God. Essentially, the model he proposed involves a set of formulas featuring two perceived probabilities: an initial "a priori" belief in the probability of some event and a final (or updated) "a posteriori" probability belief in the event's likelihood. The Bayesian model specifies how an existing probability belief regarding some event should be combined with new information to yield an updated probability belief regarding that event. In the context of juror decision making, the initial probability corresponds to the perceived likelihood that a defendant is guilty of some crime or liable for damages at a set point in time (e.g., the beginning of a trial). "New" information then arrives in the form of evidence presented at trial.

As each new piece of information comes in via witness testimony, demonstrative exhibits, etc., the model predicts how the initial probability belief will be updated. Specifically, Bayes's model specifies a *multiplicative* combination of the initial probability belief in guilt/responsibility and a likelihood ratio capturing the diagnostic value of the new evidence. Diagnosticity is seen as a function of the likelihood that such evidence would exist if the defendant were truly culpable relative to the likelihood that the evidence would exist in the event of innocence. Thus, if a juror believes initially that there is a 60 percent chance the defendant is guilty of some charge and then hears the testimony of a witness who provides information deemed to be very unlikely unless the defendant really did commit the crime, then Bayes's model predicts that the updated perceived probability of guilt will be higher than 60 percent. By obtaining measures of initial probability belief and the diagnosticity of isolated evidentiary items from study participants (sometimes at multiple points in time), Bayes's model can be used to generate precise predictions of the updated probabilities that jurors *should* report.

We are not yet to a decision, however. When it comes to choosing a verdict, Bayes's model implies a juror's final probability belief will be compared to a threshold (cutoff) value representing the individual's personal level of certainty required to justify a verdict of guilt/liability. This threshold value will vary across jurors and is presumably determined by the nature of the instructions given to the juror (particularly the wording surrounding the standard of proof to be applied), as well as the juror's own personal values regarding the utility of the different decision options. Ultimately, if the final updated probability value exceeds the threshold cutoff value, the juror would be predicted to find the defendant guilty/liable.

The Bayesian model is attractive for its basis in probability theory and formal mathematical elegance. Its primary limitation as a model of juror decision making is its rather optimistic assumptions about what jurors can do in their heads. In essence, the Bayesian model specifies a set of cognitive operations that are not very plausible—it is certainly doubtful that any real-life juror has ever described his or her thought process in terms that sound even remotely like Bayes's model. The model assumes jurors process the evidence in an elemental fashion, updating their perceived probability beliefs as they go. As each new piece of evidence is acquired, a new probability is supposedly calculated, which then serves as the initial probability for the next calculation. One troubling question that has yet to be adequately addressed is what constitutes a "piece" of evidence, and whether jurors vary in their parsing of the evidence into elements. As a result, the Bayesian model is useful as a prescriptive benchmark for determining the logical implications of the evidence and, in particular, specifying how jurors *should* combine their evaluations of it in reaching their decisions—even though few would argue that it provides an accurate account of how they *actually* do make their decisions.

Algebraic Models

The processing and evaluation of evidence could be represented mathematically in many different ways, but one particular approach that has appealed to jury scholars is the use of algebraic equations (Hastie, 1993). Within this approach, *weighted linear models* have proven to be most promising. This model of decision making essentially involves jurors' summing (or averaging) the diagnostic values for a set of evidentiary cues that have been "weighted" according to some criterion (e.g., their relevance, importance, or credibility). These models are quite popular in the social sciences and similar in some respects to the Bayesian model. Two well-known lines of research that rely heavily on a linear combination of weighted information cues are Anderson's (1981) theory of information integration and Brunswik's lens model (Brunswik, 1947). Ostrom, Werner, and Saks (1978), as well as Moore and Gump (1995), demonstrate how weighted linear models can be used to guide empirical research on juror decision making.

Similar to the Bayesian model, weighted linear models begin with an initial belief regarding the defendant's culpability, which is then modified based on the evidence. At trial, jurors are exposed to various pieces of evidence through the testimony of witnesses and the presentation of exhibits. The model presumes these evidentiary elements can be isolated and assigned a probative (diagnostic) value that has implications for the defendant's culpability (e.g., larger values for items that strongly suggest or negate culpability). The probative value of each piece of evidence is then assigned a weight that reflects the trustworthiness or credibility of the source, with more reliable sources assigned larger values. The informational value of a given piece of evidence is then assumed to be the *product* of the probative value and the credibility weight value. For example, if a juror hears an expert witness conclude the DNA found at the crime scene matches the defendant's, this piece of information might be assigned a large probative value consistent with a strong indication of guilt (e.g., +9 on a scale ranging from -10 to +10). However, if the juror thinks that the DNA expert may have done the test incorrectly, a very small credibility weight may be assigned (e.g., .10 on a scale of 0 to 1.00). Multiplying the large probative value by the small credibility weight yields the item's informational value, which in this instance would be relatively minor (+.9, or near zero).

According to the weighted linear model, a juror's overall evaluation of the evidence is an additive function of the informational value of the various pieces of evidence. Weight values across all the items are seen as summing to a fixed value (e.g., 1.00) and thus will vary according to how much evidence is presented at trial. If a great deal of evidence is offered, resulting in many elements to consider, the weight assigned to any one particular element will be relatively small. In contrast, if there are only a few pieces of evidence offered at trial, the weights assigned to each item will be relatively large. This mechanism allows weighted linear models to explain how a given item of evidence may be more or less important depending on the other evidence presented.

As with the Bayesian model, jurors are theorized to generate a final probability belief about the defendant's guilt/liability after the evidence is weighted and summed, and then compare this final probability value to a cutoff that corresponds to the subjective certainty required to find the defendant culpable. If the perceived evidence of culpability surpasses the certainty threshold, the juror should prefer a verdict of guilty (or liable). If the value does not exceed the threshold, the juror should favor not guilty (or not liable). Overall, although there are some notable differences, weighted linear models have many of the same strengths and weaknesses as the Bayesian model. They are "rational" in nature, can be expressed quantitatively (at least in general form), and have some predictive utility—they just aren't very psychologically plausible (Hastie, 1993).

Stochastic Models

The underlying premise of stochastic models is that some aspects of juror decision making are not completely understood and thus best represented as probabilities. As such, different jury decisions are seen as possible from a given starting point and, although we may not be able to forecast which outcome will occur in a specific instance, we can estimate the chance that each will result. Similar to the models described already, stochastic models feature an initial belief about the defendant's culpability which is then adjusted based on the evidence and ultimately compared to a certainty threshold.

A key distinguishing characteristic of stochastic models, though, is the incorporation of *time*. Jurors are assumed to sequentially process the evidence they encounter at trial, extracting the evaluative implications along the way, but at some point a critical event occurs that halts the decision process. This could be one of several things, including a particularly diagnostic piece of evidence, fatigue, or cognitive overload. Regardless of the cause, the end result is that the juror disengages from the evidence evaluation process and any evidence presented after that point will have little or no impact on the juror's thinking. The chance of a critical event freezing the accumulation of information is modeled as a random variable that will differ across jurors. In other words, jurors will vary in terms of the amount of time they spend evaluating the evidence. Similar to previous approaches, when a juror stops processing, the perceived weight of the evidence is viewed as an additive function of the elements in memory which is then compared to a subjective threshold value. Because there is variation with regard to the valuation of the evidence as well as how long the process goes on, some jurors will exceed their cutoff whereas others will not. Stochastic models further assert that the confidence a juror has in his or her decision is a linear function of the distance from the threshold cutoff. In other words, the greater the absolute difference between the perceived weight of evidence and the cutoff, the more confident jurors will be with regard to their decision.

One well-known application of the stochastic approach is the work of Thomas and Hogue (1976). They identified and tested six different models containing stochastic components and found there to be a clear winner in terms of being most consistent with empirical results. An interesting feature of the best-fitting model was that it included two separate random distributions with regard to evidence against the defendant, one for "evidential" factors encountered at trial, and one for "nonevidential" factors encountered outside the courtroom. The occurrence of critical events was seen as responsible for stopping the processing of each of these sources in a separate fashion, with the overall perceived weight of evidence being the sum of the two component values. Kerr and his colleagues (1978; Kerr, Harmon, & Graves, 1982) have also used stochastic models to represent the process by which jurors reach their decisions.

On balance, stochastic models have some advantages, such as capturing the importance of temporal ordering and being able to account for variations in verdict preferences even though jurors are exposed to the same evidence at trial, but their heavy reliance on probability to represent jurors' decision processes limits both their prescriptive and descriptive value.

Story Model

The Story model represents a marked departure from the previous models of juror decision making. Most notably, it involves no formal mathematical modeling or mental arithmetic; instead, it offers a compelling *verbal* account of how jurors reach their decisions. In a nutshell, the Story model presumes that jurors make sense of the evidence at trial by imposing a chronological narrative organization on it. Trials are viewed as complex, information-rich phenomena that are difficult for jurors to comprehend given the ambiguity of underlying events and the choppy, disjointed manner in which the evidence is elicited. A critical assumption of this model is that jurors are active information processors rather than passive registers. Instead of simply absorbing a flood of information and storing it verbatim, jurors are seen as sifting through the mass of evidence presented to them, focusing on some elements, and discarding others. Another key assumption is that jurors rely heavily on their existing knowledge and beliefs in creating their stories, using them to fill in gaps in the evidence, resolve contradictions, and determine plausibility. Much of this stored information is accessed via existing cognitive structures such as *scripts* that involve common sequences of events and *stereotypes* that link categories of people or objects with typical attributes.

In essence, stories represent a causal chain of connected actions with an episodic structure. Actions are viewed as the product of intentions, with consequences governed by the laws of the physical world. Episodes consist of initiating events, psychological states, goals, actions, and consequences (Pennington & Hastie, 1986; 1993). Initiating events produce psychological reactions and/or goal states that are seen as the immediate causes of action. Actions have consequences that may lead to further actions in a cascading sequence. For example, David insults Sheila at a bar (initial event), leading her to become upset (psychological reaction) and pick a fight with David outside the bar later on in order to gain revenge (goal). The fight (action) results in David being soundly thrashed and suffering a broken jaw from a hay-maker punch (consequence). Such a story could be employed by jurors to explain the events behind a civil lawsuit in which David is suing Sheila to recover the cost of his hospital bill.

According to the Story model, jurors must fundamentally do three things: (1) process the evidence and construct one or more alternative stories, (2) learn the verdict categories and legal requirements of each decision alternative, and (3) reach a decision by matching the preferred story with the most appropriate verdict category. Jurors are assumed to use information from two sources in constructing their stories: case-specific information acquired during the trial, and existing knowledge and beliefs. In other words, as jurors process the evidence at trial, they make inferences based on their existing knowledge and beliefs. Jurors would have an easier task if the attorneys and witnesses on both sides worked together to generate a single story, but of course this is not what happens at trial. Instead, each side usually attempts to lead jurors to a different story. Jurors may also arrive at their own stories as they contemplate the evidence presented in light of their own personal life experiences.

Regardless of how they come to be, the Story model assumes that multiple stories will often exist and identifies three criteria for evaluating and choosing among competing story alternatives: coverage, coherence, and uniqueness. *Coverage* is the extent to which a story can account for the various pieces of evidence presented at trial. It can be thought of in quantitative terms as the proportion of relevant facts that can be explained. A story that could explain nineteen out of twenty case "facts" would exhibit high coverage; a story that could only account for two of the twenty facts would display low coverage. *Coherence* refers to a story's logical resilience and is presumably a joint function of three elements: consistency, completeness, and plausibility. Consistency corresponds to freedom from internal contradiction; plausibility concerns the extent to which a story is in accord with a juror's understanding of the way the world works; and completeness refers to whether a story has all its parts and leaves no gaps in the causal chain. In a nutshell, coverage and coherence boil down to whether a story accounts for the "facts" and makes sense, and they are used to evaluate stories in isolation. In contrast, *uniqueness* is a function of the number of stories that satisfy some minimal threshold of coverage and coherence; it determines the confidence a juror has in any given story. To the extent that multiple acceptable stories exist, a juror's confidence in any one story will be lower. Uniqueness is greatest when only one story provides good coverage and coherence.

In addition to constructing stories that give meaning to the evidence, jurors must make legal decisions (e.g., choosing a verdict, deciding on a damage award). In keeping with the cognitive nature of the Story model, verdict options are seen as mental categories defined by critical features regarding the identity of the perpetrator, his or her mental state, the circumstances surrounding the alleged crime, and the actions taken by those involved. Jurors learn about the verdict categories and construct their mental representations based primarily on their understanding of the jury's instructions as given by the judge, along with their beliefs about crime categories. They then decide on their belief about the appropriate verdict by engaging in a matching process. Specifically, jurors are presumed to compare the identities, actions, psychological states, goals, and consequences of the actors in their best-fitting story with the legal requirements of the different verdicts, and then choose the verdict that best aligns with their story.

Although stories have been with us forever, Bennett (1978; 1979) and his colleagues (Bennett & Feldman, 1981) appear to have been the first to apply the notion of narrative story construction to legal decision making. Their pioneering work was noted by Pennington and Hastie (1981), who then formalized the Story model and presented empirical support for it in the form of the analysis of verbal protocols from twenty-six venirepersons who showed up for jury duty, were co-opted to watch a videotaped mock murder trial, and were asked to "think aloud" as they arrived at a verdict (Pennington & Hastie, 1986). Further support emerged from a series of experiments in which predicted story-driven effects were observed on the evidence recall and global judgments of mock jurors (Pennington & Hastie, 1988; 1992). A primary conclusion from this work was that the Story model was better able to explain juror decision processes than Bayesian or linear models. Since then, research by other jury scholars has provided further support for the existence of stories in other contexts (e.g., Huntley & Costanzo, 2003). At this point, the Story model has emerged as the leading model in the juror decision-making literature (see Pennington & Hastie, 1993, for a cogent summary in their own words).

Social Cognitive Models

The models considered thus far have been focused on how jurors use the evidence, and have little or nothing to say about how trial-related information interacts with existing knowledge and beliefs. Two theoretical frameworks help to answer this question. The first, *Commonsense Justice*, was developed in the 1990s by Norman Finkel and Jennifer Groscup (Finkel, 1995; 2000; Finkel & Groscup, 1997). The second, *Generic Prejudice*, stems from the work of Neil Vidmar (Vidmar, 1997; 2002; 2003).

Commonsense Justice (CJ) is centered on the notion that jurors develop their own intuitive understanding of many legal concepts through everyday life experiences, and these personalized understandings are not necessarily in accord with the "black-letter" (i.e., written) law. A particular focus of Finkel's work has been on the perception of fairness, but other legally relevant concepts such as insanity (Skeem & Golding, 2001) and murder (Wiener et al., 2002) have been examined as well. In general, this research shows that the prototypical associations that people have with regard to legal concepts can have a notable influence on their evaluations of the evidence in a case— sometimes more than the legal definitions provided.

Vidmar's work on prejudice begins by distinguishing several forms of extralegal bias. One of these is a classic form of prejudice ("specific") that occurs when jurors have a strong opinion about the case at hand as a function of the issues or parties involved. Exposure to pretrial publicity (PTP) could result in this type of prejudice. Another form of prejudice ("interest") results from a juror having some stake in the outcome of the trial (e.g., the defendant is a friend). Both types of prejudice have long been recognized by the courts and could serve as cause for dismissal if discovered during voir dire. However, Vidmar also identified two other types of prejudice that are more insidious: conformity and generic. "Conformity" prejudice is viewed as a source of pressure arising from salient community values and their corresponding implications for the appropriate jury decision. "Generic" prejudice represents the focus of Vidmar's work and is seen as an extralegal influence stemming from jurors' stereotypes about the case and/or the defendant. For example, a case involving the charge of terrorism may elicit expectations of a defendant of Middle Eastern descent with extreme religious views who believes that random acts of violence are a legitimate tool to use in subverting opposing nations.

The Commonsense Justice and Generic Prejudice frameworks complement earlier models of juror decision making by identifying important individual differences related to the evaluation of trial evidence and story construction. Both frameworks highlight the fundamental role of cognitive *schemas*—mental structures related to categories of people (e.g., defendants) and events (e.g., crimes) that include beliefs about likely features and characteristics of category exemplars. Schemas develop over time and are essential for efficient cognition in serving to activate, encode, retrieve, and comprehend task-relevant information (Wyer, Jr., 2007). There is now overwhelming support for the existence of these cognitive structures—including their influence on juror judgments in trial situations (e.g., Smith, 1991a, 1993; Smith & Studebaker, 1996; Stalans, 1993). Despite the negative connotation associated with the influence of stereotypes, it is important to recognize how fundamental and important they are to human cognition (jurors included), as well as their potential for informing our understanding of how jurors make decisions by providing "grist" for the story "mill."

Jury-Level Models
Social Decision Schemes

Based on the work of Lorge and Solomon (1955), James Davis made a major contribution to the study of jury-level behavior in 1973 with his influential treatise on Social Decision Schemes (SDS). The SDS approach represents a general conceptual framework for analyzing how groups make collective decisions. It does not attempt to model the fine points of group interaction but instead focuses on identifying the probabilities of different decision outcomes based on an initial distribution of member preferences. At the core of the SDS framework is the notion of an implicit decision rule—a social decision scheme—that captures how juries go about reconciling the divergent verdict preferences of their members when some minimum level of agreement is required (e.g., unanimity). The SDS framework can be represented visually in terms of a matrix that crosses every possible distribution of initial member verdict preferences with every possible verdict option. Each cell of the matrix contains a probability that represents the likelihood of a particular verdict given an initial preference distribution. Davis' SDS model is stochastic in nature in that an initial distribution of verdict preferences will not necessarily result in a particular verdict with absolute certainty. In other words, two juries with the same distribution of member verdict preferences might arrive at different verdicts. For instance, a six-person jury that begins deliberation with four members favoring guilt and two favoring acquittal might generally be expected to eventually convict but occasionally such juries return a "not guilty."

A focus of SDS investigation has been the search for formal rules (i.e., decision schemes) that quantitatively summarize the social combination processes underlying a jury's decision. These rules can be represented numerically in terms of a set of probabilities that reflect the likelihood of each possible jury verdict *given* an initial distribution of juror verdict preferences. In other words, for every possible split in member verdict preferences at the start of deliberation (e.g., five favoring guilty and seven favoring not guilty), some probability can be identified that the jury will ultimately choose each of the possible verdicts (e.g., 25% chance for conviction, 50% for acquittal, and 25% for "hung" in a criminal trial). Various decision schemes have been proposed in the literature, including a *simple majority* (the verdict preferred by the initial majority has a very high probability of being the jury's final verdict), *proportionality* (the probability of a given verdict is equal to the proportion of jurors initially favoring it), and *equiprobability* (all verdict options are equally probable). Some decision schemes even have primary and secondary elements wherein the primary scheme identifies the operative rule under most conditions, and the secondary scheme applies when the conditions for the primary rule are not met (e.g., proportionality if there is a clear majority in the jury, otherwise equiprobability).

Researchers seeking to identify the decision scheme(s) operating in juries have compared the predictions of various schemes with the verdict distributions of mock juries (or, occasionally, actual juries). These efforts have not produced a clear winner, but all SDS studies show a "strength-in-numbers" effect where the probability of a faction "winning" (i.e., getting the jury to choose its preferred verdict) is directly proportional to the initial number of members in the faction (i.e., faction size). In particular, the decision schemes that have fared best feature a high probability of success for factions that contain a simple majority of members. This has been referred to as the *majority effect*. Meta-analyses of SDS studies by MacCoun and Kerr (1988) and Devine et al. (2001) further indicate the chance of a faction winning in the end is not only a function of its initial size but also which verdict it favors. In essence, in criminal trials where the burden of proof is clearly on the prosecution, the experimental research shows evidence of a *leniency effect* such that, for any given faction size, pro-acquittal majorities are more likely to win than their corresponding pro-conviction majorities. This leniency effect serves to lower the probability of guilty verdicts for all verdict preference distributions relative to what would be expected if conviction and acquittal were equally attractive as verdict options (MacCoun & Kerr, 1988).

Social Transition Schemes

The Social Transition Schemes (STS) model extends the SDS model by incorporating shifts in the distribution of verdict preferences over time. Whereas the SDS model is concerned with the relationship between the final verdict and the initial state of the jury as captured by the distribution of verdict preferences, the STS model addresses the movement of juries in and out of the various possible states (i.e., distributions) on the road to consensus. Similar to the SDS model, the STS model can be represented visually with a matrix that presents all possible verdict preference distributions at any given time (e.g., Time 1) in rows, and all verdict preference distributions possible at some future point in time (e.g., Time 2) in columns. The values in this matrix correspond to the probability that a jury will shift from any particular verdict preference distribution (i.e., "state") at one time to any other one in the future. STS models can be further delineated based on their unit of analysis. *Shift* models specify the probabilities of transition from one state to another *given* that a change occurs in the distribution of member preferences. For example, if six jurors favor conviction and six favor acquittal in the current state, a shift model would specify the probability that the jury would move to each of the other possible states (i.e., other than 6–6) the next time one or more members change their preferred verdicts. *Rate models* identify the probability of a change in the verdict preference distribution *given* a fixed unit of time that passes (e.g., five minutes). Here, the entries in the matrix reflect the likelihood of the jury being in each of the various possible distributions at Time 2 given its distribution at Time 1. With rate models, it is possible for a jury to remain in the same state (distribution) at both times. In essence, STS matrices identify the probabilities that juries will move from one verdict preference distribution to another given that a transition occurs (shift models) or some amount of time passes (rate models).

Research on the STS model has examined the impact of several variables that could influence transition probabilities, including polling method (e.g., Davis, Stasser, Spitzer, & Holt, 1976), deliberation time limit (e.g., Kerr, 1981), polling interval (e.g., Kerr, 1982), and jury size (e.g., Kerr & MacCoun, 1985).

Some attention has also been devoted to testing two assumptions about the fundamental nature of preference change during deliberation. The first, *stationarity*, holds that the transition probabilities are fixed and do not change over time. In other words, one set of probabilities will capture the likelihood of movement regardless of how far the jury is into deliberation. The second assumption, *path independence*, asserts the likelihood of a transition from one state to another is independent of the path that the jury took to get to the current state. Put differently, there is no effect of "history" on the transition probabilities—the current distribution of verdict preferences is the only one that matters, not the distributions that the jury moved through to get to the present one. A study by Kerr (1981) suggests these two assumptions may not hold, however. He observed a slight *momentum effect* in which movement towards a verdict led to increased probability of continued movement in the same direction (e.g., a shift from 7–5 to 8–4 produces a heightened probability of the next shift being to 9–3 as opposed to back to 7–5). Kerr also noted a stronger majority effect toward the end of discussion in that movement in the direction of unanimity (i.e., defection from the minority) was more probable later in deliberation than earlier. Combining these two trends suggests that once juries move from their initial distribution toward a verdict, they tend to keep moving toward that verdict and pick up speed as they go along.

Social Interaction Schemes

According to the SDS and STS models, jurors have only one noteworthy characteristic—a preferred verdict. Similar to how the STS model extends the SDS model by adding time, the Social Interaction Sequence (SIS) model adds to the STS model by introducing an individual-difference variable—a juror's confidence in the preferred verdict. As articulated by Garold Stasser and James Davis (1981), the SIS model treats verdict confidence as a dichotomy involving two levels: certain or uncertain. In a trial with only two possible verdicts, there are four possible cognitive states that fall on an underlying certainty continuum: (1) certain-guilty, (2) uncertain-guilty, (3) uncertain-not guilty, and (4) certain–not guilty. According to the model, jurors can move among these states but only to adjacent states. Those who favor a particular verdict but are uncertain about it (i.e., the middle two states) are in a state where they could be converted to a preference for the other verdict option *or* move to a state of certainty regarding their current preference. Jurors who feel certain of their preferred verdict at any given moment (i.e., the end states) can switch their preference, but only *after* confidence in their currently preferred verdict has eroded from certain to uncertain.

At the heart of the SIS model is a complex influence function that models juror movement between "adjacent" mental states on the continuum. In keeping with the literature, faction size is a key parameter. One of the interesting characteristics of the SIS influence function is that faction size is seen as affecting verdict choice differently than verdict certainty. Stasser and Davis (1981) argued that changes in verdict certainty were the product of informational influence, or the influence resulting from the articulation of facts and arguments supporting the verdict in question. The more advocates favoring a verdict, the more information presumably produced during deliberation to support that verdict. In contrast, verdict preference changes were viewed as a joint function of informational influence and normative influence. Normative influence arises from our desire to be in accord with others and not stand apart from the rest of the group. Put simply, normative influence is peer pressure.

Consistent with these expectations, Stasser and Davis (1981) observed a linear relationship between the number of mock jurors favoring a particular verdict and reported movement into and out of certainty states. In other words, changes in certainty (i.e., moving between certain-guilty and uncertain-guilty or between uncertain–not guilty and certain–not guilty) were best predicted by a linear function of the number of jurors favoring the associated verdict. In contrast, movement between the two adjacent uncertain states was better predicted by an exponential function containing the number of jurors favoring the other verdict. So, focusing on a single juror who favors acquittal but is not certain in a jury in which seven other members favor conviction and four others favor acquittal, the "uncertain-guilty" state would have a "drawing power" of forty-nine (i.e., 7^2), whereas the drawing power of the "certain–not guilty" state would be only four. Our uncertain, pro-acquittal juror could move to either adjacent cognitive state, but the SIS model predicts a much greater likelihood of movement to the "uncertain-guilty" position.

The SIS model essentially builds upon the earlier STS model by incorporating differences in the extent to which jurors are cognitively committed to their preferred verdicts. The computer program that implements the SIS model begins with "inputs" in the form of an initial distribution of verdict preferences, a group size parameter, an explicit set of distinguishable verdict alternatives, an assigned decision rule (i.e., minimum concurrence on verdict), and a maximum discussion time. Like STS, the program uses an iterative approach and keeps track of the jury's current group-level distribution of preferences as well as the preferred verdict and certainty of each individual juror. In what appears to be the only study that explicitly adopted the SIS approach (Stasser & Davis, 1981), a series of potential influence functions were tested using data from mock juries. Predictions for the influence functions were based on formal algorithms specifying different mathematical relationships involving the current group-level distribution of verdict preferences and each individual's current mental state. The results suggested that movement between *certainty states* for a particular verdict (i.e., between "certain" and "uncertain") was primarily due to information exchanged during deliberation, whereas change in *preferred verdict* was due to both information exchange and peer pressure (i.e., normative influence).

DICE and JUS

In 1979 Penrod and Hastie published a critical review of jury-level models in one of the leading psychology journals. Dissatisfied with existing models, they decided to create a new group-level model of jury decision making and formalize it in a computer program. The DICE model (Penrod & Hastie, 1980) was named for the blindfolded Greek goddess often portrayed holding the scales of justice in one hand (and a sword in the other—just in case). JUS, in turn, represents an extension of DICE.

In many ways, DICE (and later JUS) is similar to the SIS model developed by Stasser and Davis around the same time. Penrod and Hastie sought to develop a model that could account for the existing empirical data on juries, and recognized that the complexity of the model would benefit from formal implementation using a software program. Early versions of DICE were compared to real data and new parameters were added to better align simulation results with real-world empirical observations. As with the STS and SIS models, transition matrices between distinguishable group-level verdict preference distributions are at the heart of the DICE model. The DICE simulation is a fixed-rate program, assessing the verdict preferences of all jurors at regular time intervals. Based on existing data, the transition matrices used in DICE are stationary but not path independent. As with STS, DICE also models an individual-difference variable relevant to whether an individual juror will change preferences. However, rather than modeling juror certainty as a dichotomous cognitive state, jurors in the DICE model are assigned a *persuasion resistance* value that reflects their willingness to hold out in the minority; it is essentially analogous to stubbornness. Persuasion resistance was added to the model to capture the notion that some jurors are more likely to change their minds than others.

DICE begins by randomly assigning persuasion resistance values (either from a population or specified subgroup) after specification of parameter values for the time between ballots, the total time allowed for deliberation, and the number of jurors needed for a quorum. The simulated jury is then polled to determine their preferred verdicts, and transition probabilities are applied to determine the verdict preference of each juror after each simulated unit of time. As with earlier models, transition probabilities are based heavily on the number of jurors favoring a given verdict, with an increasingly higher likelihood of change for individuals in progressively smaller minority factions. Similar to SIS, the transition probability function is exponential with regard to the number of advocates within the jury but also takes into account the persuasion resistance value of each individual juror. In order to account for the empirical finding that jurors do not change their verdict preferences very often, persuasion resistance values are incremented each time a juror changes preferred verdicts. Another interesting feature of DICE is that it predicts hung juries as well as legal verdicts. Essentially, deliberation ceases with a hung jury if no individuals change their preferred verdicts in a specified amount of time.

Penrod and Hastie (1980) presented data showing good agreement between the predictions of DICE and empirical results from a number of studies that measured initial verdict preference distributions in mock juries (e.g., Davis et al., 1976; Padawer-Singer & Barton, 1975). DICE was originally configured for trial settings involving only the two traditional verdict alternatives (i.e., guilty or not guilty). In order to use the program with a large new dataset featuring the possibility of conviction on a lesser charge, Hastie et al. (1983) modified DICE to accommodate more than two verdict alternatives. They also gave the revised program a new name, JUS, passing on the opportunity to apply a flashier moniker that would underscore the revised model's intellectual heritage (e.g., LOADED DICE). Aside from expanding the number of potential verdict alternatives and tweaking the distribution of several model parameters, JUS is the same as DICE. In their book *Inside the Jury*, Hastie et al. (1983) devoted an entire chapter to comparing the predictions of JUS to the observed verdicts of sixty-nine mock juries, which again showed very good correspondence. Unfortunately, despite these promising results, this appears to have been the first and last published study involving JUS. By the mid-1980s, interest in predicting final verdicts seems to have waned in favor of gaining a better understanding of the process by which juries reach their decisions.

DISCUSS

Garold Stasser's work on the DISCUSS model represents a major step forward in the modeling of collective choice by groups and also the most recent formal model of *jury* decision making. Unlike earlier models, it moves beyond simulating the output of discussion to actually representing the discussion process as well. At the individual level, the model addresses cognitive processes in a much more sophisticated manner than earlier models. The DISCUSS computer simulation keeps track of the information that members are exposed to, recall, and share with others during deliberation. Like its jury-level predecessors, DISCUSS is iterative in nature. Instead of being based on discrete units of time, though, it models the speaking acts of individual group members. Each iteration simulates the impact of one speaking act by a single person (e.g., juror). Who speaks on any given turn is a function of a participation parameter, which influences the probability of a juror being "chosen" to contribute something to the discussion. Participation scores reflect the empirical finding that speaking during deliberation is not equal across jurors, but instead tends to display a rank-ordered pattern with a fairly constant drop-off between ranks (Stasser, 1988). The content of the juror's contribution is a function of the information in memory at the moment. When a juror speaks, new information is potentially added to the "memories" of other jurors, and their preferred verdict alternative is updated based on this new information.

DISCUSS is configured on the assumption that a juror's preferred verdict is based on a weighted sum (or average) of the information they have available "in memory." The DISCUSS computer simulation begins by accepting a set of task parameters and assigning valences to each item of information for each juror. It then iterates through speaking turns in which the juror "with the floor" contributes an item of information from the contents of their memory while the other jurors update their memories and preferred verdicts. Jurors' verdict preferences at any given time are a function of the information (i.e., evidence) they have in memory, with deliberation serving to "refresh" information that is currently inaccessible (i.e., forgotten), as well as providing additional information. Each item of information is assigned a specific valence with regard to its implications for each of the possible verdicts. Jurors can differentially weight the importance of the various information items, and weights can be modified over time as the result of discussion. Deliberation ends when a sufficient number of jurors are in agreement on the correct verdict, or if a specified number of speaking turns ensue with no new information contributed.

Stasser (1988) characterized DISCUSS as a general model of group decision making aimed primarily at representing informational influence in situations involving *hidden profiles*. Hidden profiles are situations where group members do not all have access to the same information before group discussion, and the distributed nature of task-relevant information becomes an obstacle to identifying the optimal choice. DISCUSS includes two parameters that enable it to better capture the context of jury decisions: whether members act as advocates for their preferred alternative, and whether discussion serves to minimize differences in the way information is weighted by jurors. The advocacy parameter controls the amount of "bias" inherent in member contributions. In advocacy situations, members tend to inordinately share information that supports their preferred alternative; in non-advocacy situations, there is no bias toward sharing information that supports a particular alternative and spoken contributions are presumed to be randomly sampled from memory. The normative influence parameter controls the variability of the weights assigned to information items across jurors. With normative influence allowed, the variability of weighting tends to decrease when items are discussed, reflecting the evolution of a group "perspective" on an item's importance. Stasser, Kerr, and Davis (1989) noted that the allowance of advocacy and normative influence (as implemented by DISCUSS) yields a strength-in-numbers pattern typical of the STS matrices observed with mock juries, as well as a strong majority SDS.

Social Judgment Schemes

As noted earlier, research on civil juries was more or less dormant until the 1990s. This is likely due in part to the obvious relevance and applicability of jury-level models developed for criminal juries to many civil trial contexts. However, civil juries are sometimes required to make decisions that are continuous in nature when they determine the damages to be awarded to plaintiffs. Davis's (1996) Social Judgment Scheme predicts a jury's final decision (award) based on a weighted sum of individual member preferences for that award. An interesting feature of the weighting process is that the influence associated with an individual juror is assumed to be inversely proportional to the "distance" between his or her preferred amount and the amounts preferred by the other jurors. In other words, jurors with highly discrepant views tend to have marginal influence, and jury deliberation dampens the effect of extreme "outlier" jurors. Some research has supported Davis's model (Davis, 1996; Davis, Au, Hulbert, Chen, & Zarnoth, 1997; Hulbert, Parks, Chen, Nam, & Davis, 1999; Ohtsubo, Masuchi, & Nakanishi, 2002), although these studies also provide support for simpler prediction models based on the mean, median, or "trimmed" median preference (i.e., after discounting the largest outlier) of group member preferences. Other research on opinion change in the context of jury damage awards also underscores the attractiveness of final awards that lie close to a majority of members' initial preferred amounts, presumably because they serve a compromise function (Crott & Werner, 1994).

Discussion of Models

The way scholars approach juror and jury decision making has changed considerably over the last fifty years. At the juror level, the so-called "mathematical" models have been largely supplanted by the more plausible Story model. The advent of the cognitive perspective in the 1980s underscored the weakness of mathematical models that have jurors isolating pieces of information, weighing them, and deriving a preferred verdict by summing the products. Judging from the frequency with which it is invoked in the introductions and discussions of published studies, the Story model appears to have become the model of choice when it comes to individual jurors and it's not difficult to see why. It is straightforward, very intuitive, and has growing empirical support. Although there may be times when jurors engage in resource-intensive mental calculations of the sort posed by the mathematical models, the Story model provides a simple, powerful, and compelling depiction of juror decision making in most trial contexts.

At the jury level, psychological models of jury decision making began with the relatively straightforward SDS framework in the early 1970s and continued to grow in complexity and sophistication until DISCUSS arrived on the scene in the late 1980s. Led by several outstanding scholars who have devoted a good portion of their professional lives to the study of juries (i.e., James Davis, Reid Hastie, Nancy Pennington, and Steven Penrod), jury-level models have systematically built upon one another, with each new model adding something to what came before. SDS highlighted the importance of the distribution of verdict preferences in a jury, STS added a time element and change in the verdict preference distribution over the course of deliberation, and SIS and DICE/JUS included juror individual-difference variables in the form of verdict certainty (SIS) and persuasion resistance (DICE/JUS). DISCUSS continued this trend by adding a participation parameter reflecting a juror's willingness to speak.

Looking across the models, a number of observations are warranted. First, all models of *jury* decision making incorporate the well-established strength-in-numbers effect associated with faction size and are consistent with a very robust empirical finding: initial majorities, especially strong ones, tend to prevail in the end. As a result, they all do one thing very well—predict the jury's final verdict from an initial distribution of member verdict preferences. Indeed, the predictive power of the initial majority should serve as some comfort to those concerned with the possibility that jury deliberation is a chaotic free-for-all where anything goes and who knows what will transpire. Second, models of juror decision making have been focused more on how decisions are made than why. Of note, the Story model acknowledges the heavy influence of existing knowledge and beliefs on the creation of a story, and the more recent Commonsense Justice and Generic Prejudice models help to identify particular trial contexts where existing beliefs may play a dominant role. Third, decision-making models have tended to become bigger and more complex over time, particularly when it comes to jury decisions. This is in keeping with our increasing recognition of the many variables relevant to jury decision making. Fourth, there has been relatively little influence of juror-level models on jury-level models. Even the most recent jury-level models retain a dependence on rational modes of calculation that assume the evidence is processed in a spreadsheet fashion. Fifth, existing models are more focused on criminal juries. The volume of research on civil juries has increased markedly since 1990, but no major model of jury decision making tailored to the civil domain has been offered. This may reflect an implicit belief among scholars that civil juries arrive at verdict decisions in primarily the same way as criminal juries. Finally, there has been no effort to specify a comprehensive model of jury decision making in the last twenty-five years that incorporates characteristics of the case, the participants, and the evidence. An effort will be made to do this in chapter 8 using the foundation provided by the theories reviewed in this chapter.

3

Jury-Related Trial Practices

Across the various court systems in the United States, there is considerable variation in the practices and procedures used with juries. This includes how members of the jurisdiction are summoned for jury duty, what they are asked during voir dire, how many individuals will constitute a jury, what jurors can and cannot do during the trial, what level of consensus is needed for a verdict—and the list goes on. Several particular practices attracted the attention of social scientists in the wake of decisions by the U.S. Supreme Court in the 1970s, and trial-related practices continue to garner steady attention from scholars. In general, the considerable research on jury-related trial practices has been driven by a fairly straightforward, practical question—does it make any difference how things are done with jurors and juries? The answers are at times surprising.

Jury Size

Research on jury size was instigated by a 1970 U.S. Supreme Court decision that upheld the use of juries with fewer than twelve people in criminal cases (*Williams v. Florida*, 1970). Citing the work of Kalven and Zeisel (1966) and

Solomon Asch's famous research on conformity, the Court opined that six-person juries were "functionally equivalent" to twelve-person juries. The only problem was that none of the research they cited dealt directly with jury size, leading to a swift denouncement of the Court's assertion by jury scholars (e.g., Zeisel, 1971) and then empirical testing. Four studies directly comparing juries of different sizes were available by the time of the Court's *Colgrove v. Battin* (1973) decision three years later regarding the constitutionality of six-person federal civil juries. Here the Court perceived "convincing empirical evidence" of functional equivalence in the research, provoking more irascible commentary from jury scholars (Lempert, 1975; Saks, 1977; Zeisel & Diamond, 1974). Partial amends were made later in *Ballew v. Georgia* (1978), when the Court essentially drew the line in prohibiting juries with fewer than six members. There have been no major Supreme Court decisions bearing on jury size since *Ballew*, and juries in many states and the federal courts are currently allowed to have fewer than twelve members but at least six. (See Ellsworth & Mauro, 1998, for a good review of legal developments associated with jury size).

Are juries made up of six persons really "functionally equivalent" to twelve-person juries? The best assessment comes in the form of a meta-analysis conducted by Michael Saks and Molli Marti in 1997. They gathered seventeen empirical studies that compared "larger" juries composed of twelve members to "smaller" juries composed of six, along with one study comparing eight-person and twelve-person juries (Munsterman, Munsterman, & Penrod, 1990). The studies varied considerably in terms of the number of juries included (ranging from 16 to 664) and featured a mix of participants (actual jurors or venirepersons and mock jurors), case types (civil and criminal), study designs (i.e., correlational v. experimental), and stimulus formats (e.g., paper materials, videotape, live). Weights were assigned to each study based on the rigor of its scientific design, with tightly controlled experimental studies receiving the highest weight and several studies with serious methodological problems receiving no weight. A variety of outcome variables were examined, including minority representation, deliberation time, frequency of "hung" juries, memory for the evidence, verdicts, and magnitude and variability of damage awards for civil juries.

Although based on a relatively small number of studies, the results of the Saks and Marti meta-analysis suggest several notable differences between six- and twelve-person juries. First, in three field studies of actual juries, larger juries were more likely to contain at least one non-White member. This finding is not surprising, however; Zeisel (1971) pointed out long ago that the statistical likelihood of minority representation is *necessarily* greater in larger juries than smaller juries under most sampling conditions. Second, larger juries took longer to deliberate than smaller juries, with an overall mean difference of about twenty minutes. The mean difference grew to forty-four minutes in the three studies involving actual juries, but larger juries were more likely to be given more complex cases in one of these studies, which may have exaggerated the difference. Third, two small studies with mock juries also suggest trial testimony is discussed more thoroughly in larger juries, with members of larger juries tending to recall more case facts than members of smaller juries, but the data are insufficient to draw strong conclusions about the effect of jury size on deliberation quality. Fourth, with regard to decision outcomes, jury size was not reliably associated with the frequency of pro-defense verdicts. However, when operating under a requirement of unanimity, larger juries failed to reach a decision (i.e., "hung") more often than smaller juries in eleven of fifteen data sets. Finally, in civil trial settings, smaller juries produced larger mean damage awards in three of four studies, and the fourth study was confounded by a tendency for larger juries to receive more complex cases with the potential for larger awards.

There have been only a few studies of jury size since 1997, but they align well with the results of the Saks and Marti meta-analysis. James Davis and his colleagues (1997) had a large number of civil mock juries decide a product liability case and found the mean damage award to be greater in six-person than twelve-person juries. In addition, the best predictor of the jury's award was the "trimmed" median value of the members' predeliberation award preferences (i.e., dropping the member with the most extreme value). The mean damage award was also higher for six-person juries than for twelve-person juries in one of the most recent studies of jury size by Horowitz and Bordens (2002), although this was true only when juries were allowed to take notes during the trial. In addition, there was further indication that larger juries deliberate better than smaller juries in some circumstances. Specifically, the members of twelve-person juries recalled more probative (case-relevant) facts after deliberation when the jury was allowed to take notes, but this pattern did not hold for the members of six-person juries. The damage awards of smaller juries also showed more variability than those of larger juries. Finally, analysis of data from over 11,000 jury trials gathered for the massive "State of the States" project revealed a mean difference of only eighteen minutes between six-person and twelve-person juries in terms of the duration of deliberation (Mize, Hannaford-Agor, & Waters, 2007), suggesting only a modest effect of jury size.

To summarize, larger juries are more likely to contain a minority representative, spend a little more time deliberating, and may yield better recall
of case facts among their members. Conversely, larger juries are also slightly
more likely to end in a stalemate (i.e., "hang"), and the participation rate of
their members is more variable than six-person juries. Jury size does not
appear to systematically bias juries toward a particular verdict outcome, and
there is no reason to expect that it should. Although the limited research to
this point is far from definitive, interest in jury size has waned since 1980.
This is unfortunate, because the issue of "functional equivalence" across jury
sizes has important practical implications, and there is certainly more to be
learned—particularly about the largely unexplored relationship between jury
size and deliberation quality.

Jury Decision Rule

For much of the jury's history in the English-speaking world, jurors have
been required to reach unanimous agreement on a verdict for it to be legally
acceptable (Saks, 2008). In an effort to allow courts to cut costs, increase
efficiency, and accommodate "harmless diversity," the U.S. Supreme Court
upheld the constitutionality of non-unanimous jury verdicts in civil and
criminal trials via their rulings in the *Apodaca v. Oregon* (1972) and *Johnson
v. Louisiana* (1972) cases. Similar to the *Ballew* ruling regarding jury size, the
Court later drew the line on a minimum level of agreement in *Burch v. Louisiana* (1979) by requiring six-person juries to be unanimous in their decisions.
At last count, twenty-six states require unanimity in all jury trials, forty-four
require it in felony criminal trials, and all thirty-five states allowing capital
punishment (as well as the federal government) require it in capital murder
trials (Costanzo & Krauss, 2012). As with jury size, the fundamental question with jury decision rule is the functional equivalence of juries operating with different nominal requirements. In practice, most research on jury
decision rule has focused on required agreement levels of two-thirds (.67),
three-fourths (.75), or five-sixths (.83) of the jury's members. As with jury
size, scholarly interest in decision rule peaked in the 1970s and petered out
after 1990, leaving an empirical database with only a dozen or so published
studies but large enough to draw some conclusions.

One of the best studies on the effects of decision rule was conducted
by Reid Hastie and his colleagues, and their extensive analyses were summarized in an excellent book still well worth reading today, *Inside the
Jury* (Hastie, Penrod, & Pennington, 1983). Participants in this study were
selected from a pool of people who showed up for jury duty and watched

a three-hour filmed reenactment of an actual homicide case complete with opening remarks by both attorneys and unabridged judicial instructions. They then deliberated in twelve-person mock juries using one of three decision rules (two-thirds consensus, five-sixths consensus, or unanimity), and their unlimited discussions were videotaped and content analyzed with an exhaustive coding scheme. The most important finding from this study was that jury decision rule had a notable influence on deliberation duration and indicators of deliberation quality, with juries required to reach unanimity deliberating longer and in a more ideal fashion than juries that were not required to reach complete agreement. Specifically, unanimous juries discussed key facts to a greater extent, touched on more case facts than two-thirds quorum juries, corrected mistaken assertions by members more often, elicited the participation of minority-view jurors to a greater extent, and ultimately produced a higher level of member satisfaction. In contrast, unanimous juries did not deliberate better than quorum juries in another careful study of the deliberation process in mock juries conducted by Saks (1977). In this study featuring multiple experiments with both students and ex-jurors and a thorough analysis of the content of discussion, observed differences were generally small, and neither decision rule produced consistently better levels of deliberation quality.

Although no meta-analysis has yet been published on the effects of jury decision rule, existing studies have consistently produced three results. First, unanimous juries are *more likely to hang* than non-unanimous juries (Buckhout, Weg, Reilly, & Frohboese, 1977; Davis, Kerr, Atkin, Holt, & Meek, 1975; Foss, 1981; Hastie et al., 1983; Kerr, Atkin, Stasser, Meek, Holt, & Davis, 1976; Nemeth, 1977; Padawer-Singer, Singer, & Singer, 1977; Saks, 1977; Velasco, 1995). Second, unanimous juries generally *take longer* to reach a decision (Davis et al., 1975; Davis et al., 1997; Foss, 1981; Hastie et al., 1983; Kerr et al., 1976; Nemeth, 1977; Saks, 1977). The magnitude of the time difference has varied across studies though, suggesting other variables may influence it, including the proportion of the jury required for a verdict (e.g., simple majority v. five-sixths), the absolute size of the jury, and the number of verdict options available. Oddly, real juries required to reach unanimity reportedly finished twenty minutes *faster* on average than juries not required to be unanimous in the massive "State-of-the-States" project (Mize et al., 2007). There are limitations associated with the use of retrospective reports in this study, but nonetheless the finding calls into question the existence of a reliable difference in deliberation time as a function of jury decision rule. Third, as expected, decision rule has not been found to be systematically related to jury verdicts, although unanimous juries are more likely to reach the "correct" decision when defined as the modal verdict preference in the population of study participants (e.g., Saks, 1977). Only a few studies have examined the effects of jury decision rule with civil juries, and their results do not suggest much influence on damages awards (e.g., Broeder, 1958; Kaplan & Miller, 1987).

To conclude, although the available literature base is fairly small, existing research on decision rule implies the existence of a mild dilemma. Juries required to reach unanimity *may* deliberate somewhat better than non-unanimous juries, but they may take somewhat longer to reach their decisions and are somewhat more likely to hang. As with jury size, scholarly interest in jury decision rule appears to have waned since the 1970s, but more research would be useful to determine if requiring unanimity does indeed foster better deliberation quality and, if so, whether the magnitude of the benefit is worth the cost in time.

Juror Selection

Although selection practices vary across jurisdictions and continue to evolve over time, all court systems in the United States supposedly feature the random selection of individuals from a master list of eligible persons in the jurisdiction. Those who show up for jury duty are usually screened in a process of questioning known as *voir dire*. Voir dire is a French phrase that has managed to infiltrate a legal system largely English in character, and translations of the term are amusingly diverse. One common translation is "to speak the truth." However, *voir* is the French verb for "to see" and *dire* is the verb for "to say," so the phrase means literally "to see, to say." A dollop of creative license yields the more manageable expression "to see what is said." Semantics aside, the purpose of voir dire questioning is to identify and remove members of the venire who would have a difficult time being fair and impartial jurors. Attorneys have traditionally asked most if not all of the questions, but an increasing number of jurisdictions feature questions from the judge as well as the attorneys, and judges now handle most of the questioning in the federal district courts.

Attorney Prediction Accuracy

A fundamental question of interest to many in the legal system is whether trial attorneys can correctly forecast the verdict leanings of venirepersons during voir dire. A small number of studies have examined this question and, although the results are somewhat mixed, they indicate it is a relatively difficult task.

One of the most often-cited studies supporting the efficacy of attorney predictions was done by Diamond and Zeisel in 1974 using a combination of real juries and two kinds of experimentally constructed juries. At each of ten criminal jury trials, a "shadow jury" was formed from venirepersons who were dismissed via peremptory challenge and then recruited to watch the trial and deliberate to a verdict. In addition, a second "shadow jury" was formed at each trial consisting of randomly selected members of the venire who were not seated. Although only ten trials were involved, the results were intriguing. Whereas only 50 percent of the actual juries convicted, 80 percent of the "challenged" juries convicted as did all of the randomly chosen juries. With regard to the effective use of peremptory challenges, defense attorneys were able to strike more pro-conviction jurors than pro-acquittal jurors in seven of the ten trials whereas prosecuting attorneys were successful in doing the opposite in five of the trials. On the other hand, defense attorneys struck as many friendly jurors as hostile jurors in two trials, and in one trial they actually removed more. Prosecuting attorneys were even worse, striking an equal number of sympathetic and hostile jurors in two trials and removing more pro-conviction jurors than pro-acquittal jurors in three trials.

In a follow-up study, Zeisel and Diamond (1978) compared the verdicts of juries in twelve actual criminal trials with the verdicts of twelve "reconstructed" juries composed of the first dozen people called from the venire. Combining the predeliberation verdict preferences of jurors excused via challenge and the assumption that reconstructed juries would have ultimately opted for the verdict preferred by their initial majority, Zeisel and Diamond concluded there was minimal effect of voir dire–based juror selection in seven of the trials but noteworthy impact in the other five, such that the use of peremptory challenges had a discernible effect on the probability of the final verdict (in this case, making acquittal more likely). As in their earlier study, the accuracy of peremptory challenges was again lackluster, with prosecutors on average removing as many pro-conviction as pro-acquittal jurors and defense attorneys performing only slightly better.

Research since these two classic studies by Zeisel and Diamond has generally aligned with the more pessimistic findings of the 1978 study. For example, Olczak, Kaplan, and Penrod (1991) compared the use of voir dire information and the predictive ability of attorneys to that of law students and undergraduates in a series of studies. In one experiment, attorneys displayed the same pattern of information usage as college sophomores. In the final study, participants were given the transcript from a criminal trial (murder or rape) and information about thirty-six potential jurors who had participated in a mock juror simulation. They then rated each of the potential jurors in terms of expected bias and identified those expected to be most and least favorable to their side (i.e., the defense). All participants had difficulty predicting the verdict preferences of mock jurors in this study, with attorneys no more effective than the law students, and both groups making more incorrect challenges than correct ones. Similar results were obtained in another study in which attorneys watched the videotape of an actual voir dire and tried to identify jurors who would be biased against their side (Kerr, Kramer, Carroll, & Alfini, 1991). Similar to previous studies, attorneys in this study did not perform well in terms of predicting juror bias. In another field study, Johnson and Haney (1994) examined attorney selection effectiveness in four felony jury trials in which a dispositional measure of generalized bias toward the prosecution or defense was administered. Comparing the scores of actual jurors and excused venirepersons on this bias measure, prosecuting attorneys generally struck individuals who were more pro-defense whereas defense attorneys tended to strike those who were more pro-prosecution. However, even though attorneys were generally able to identify and strike venirepersons with more extreme bias, the mean bias score for the actual juries was little different than the mean score of juries that would have existed if the first twelve venirepersons had been seated for the focal trials.

Even though this research sheds some light, there are still too few studies of attorney prediction effectiveness to draw definitive conclusions about the ability of attorneys to forecast venireperson verdict preferences at better than chance rates. The mixed results are sufficient to allow proponents and critics of peremptory challenges to perceive the effectiveness of attorney prediction as desired. This much is clear, however—attorneys cannot read jurors like open books. Nonetheless, some attorneys may be better at this task than others (Zeisel & Diamond, 1978), a possibility that deserves more attention. In the end, for a topic with such obvious practical implications, the question of attorney forecasting accuracy remains surprisingly in need of further research.

Death Qualification

Tucked under the general question of whether juror selection practices have any impact on trial outcomes is the specific issue of effects associated with *death qualification*. Death qualification is a component of juror selection in trials where the jury will determine the guilt and (if necessary) the sentence of defendants charged with a capital crime. It involves questioning venirepersons in order to identify and remove those with such strong beliefs about the death penalty that it would impair their ability to be fair and unbiased jurors.

Various legal standards have been used by the courts to exclude venireper-sons during death qualification, one of the earliest being if a venireperson possessed "conscientious scruples" against the death penalty based on moral beliefs. In *Witherspoon v. Illinois* (1968), the U.S. Supreme Court raised the threshold for exclusion to "unequivocal opposition" to the death penalty, or a belief so strong that a juror would never be willing to impose a death sen-tence. It later broadened the standard in *Wainwright v. Witt* (1985) to include those jurors holding such strong beliefs about the death penalty that it would "prevent or substantially impair" their ability to follow their instructions and execute their oath. The *Morgan v. Illinois* (1992) decision expanded the size of the excludable population still further by adding those who would *always* (or "automatically") impose the death penalty for guilt.

Death qualification is intended to produce a jury that would duly con-sider imposing the death penalty if the defendant were found guilty of a capi-tal crime. For practical reasons, most if not all states allowing the death pen-alty use the same jury to decide both the defendant's guilt and the resulting sentence in the event of conviction. The primary concern with death quali-fication is jurors' ability to separate the guilt and penalty decisions and, in particular, prevent beliefs about the appropriate punishment from preemp-tively influencing the decision about guilt. The dilemma is one of logistical expediency versus freedom from potential bias, resulting in the empirical question: Does death qualification make juries more likely to convict capi-tal defendants relative to juries that are not death-qualified? In their 1968 *Witherspoon* decision, the Court declared the paltry existing scientific data to be "too tentative and fragmentary" to answer the question of bias associ-ated with death qualification. Scholars took the message to heart, and the study of death qualification has now yielded sufficient data to allow for three meta-analyses on the subject.

Much of the work on death qualification falls under the broader heading of research on death penalty attitudes, with death qualification represent-ing a threshold point along a continuum of favorability. In a meta-analysis examining death penalty attitudes, Nietzel, McCarthy, and Kerr (1999) cal-culated a mean correlation of .11 between death penalty attitudes and mea-sures of defendant guilt from nineteen effect sizes. This suggests a modest relationship wherein jurors who are more supportive of the death penalty are somewhat more likely to convict the defendant in the guilt phase of a capital trial compared with those who are less supportive. In more concrete terms, replacing a jury of death penalty advocates with one consisting of death penalty opponents was estimated to reduce the percentage of jurors favoring conviction in a capital trial from 55 percent to 44 percent. Another meta-analysis on the same topic produced similar conclusions. Allen, Mabry, and McKelton (1998) examined fourteen data sets that reported a relationship between death penalty attitudes and verdict preference in the guilt phase of capital trials, and calculated a weighted average correlation of .18—a value somewhat higher than the corresponding value of .11 obtained by Nietzel's study and indicative of a moderate effect. Allen and colleagues estimated that, other things being equal, jurors supporting the death penalty would prefer conviction 59 percent of the time whereas those who opposed it would prefer it only 41 percent of the time—a level of conviction-proneness fairly close to that calculated by Nietzel et al.

In addition to influencing who will be seated on capital juries, simply experiencing the death-qualification process appears to make *all* jurors somewhat more likely to convict (Haney, 1984). Several studies have produced findings consistent with the notion that the death-qualification process has desensitizing and signal effects, sending the message that the government thinks the defendant is guilty and cognitively preparing jurors to convict (Cox & Tanford, 1989; Haney, 1984; Nietzel, Dillehay, & Himelein, 1987). The meta-analyses by Allen et al. (1998) and Nietzel et al. (1999) further suggest that the "process effect" associated with undergoing death qualification has more impact than the "selection effect" associated with the death penalty attitudes of those seated on capital juries.

A third meta-analysis of the death qualification literature arguably represents the best of the bunch in using only those studies that formally assessed death qualification, and estimating its impact on *jury* verdicts (Filkins, Smith, & Tindale, 1998). Filkins and his colleagues used a different meta-analytic procedure (based on d instead of r) and analyzed twelve effects from seven studies where the death-qualification process resulted in an explicit classification of participants (i.e., includable v. excludable) who then made a judgment regarding guilt. Similar to the other meta-analyses, they calculated a small but reliable effect of death-qualification on conviction proneness using this more homogeneous set of studies ($d = .13$). They also conducted several additional meta-analyses and found women ($d = .20$) and racial minorities ($d = .30$) to be more likely to be excluded during death qualification. Finally, they estimated the impact of death qualification on *jury* verdicts by running several computer simulations and applying a "two-thirds majority otherwise acquit" social decision scheme. Surprisingly, these analyses suggested the conviction rate in capital trials would decrease by only 1–3 percent if non-death-qualified juries were used. This estimate represents a mild affront to the findings of the only *jury-level* study of death qualification yet conducted. Using eligible jurors from two Ohio and New York communities, a twenty-five to thirty-minute group voir dire procedure, and a one-hour audiotaped felony murder trial, Horowitz and Seguin (1986) observed a 19 percent higher conviction rate for seventeen death-qualified juries (82%) compared with twenty-seven juries that were not death-qualified (63%)—a much stronger effect than that estimated by Filkins and his colleagues.

Since this work in the late 1990s, additional research on death penalty attitudes buttresses the conclusion that juries composed of death-qualified jurors are more likely to convict. Simon, Snow, and Read (2004) assessed death penalty attitudes of mock jurors using a fifteen-item measure developed by O'Neil, Patry, and Penrod (2004) and varied case type (a theft which either did or did not include a beating death). Categorizing participant scores on the death penalty measure, strong supporters of the death penalty convicted 44 percent of the time, moderate supporters convicted 35 percent of the time, and individuals opposed to the death penalty convicted 22 percent of the time. Butler (2007) further found that jurors who were most supportive of the death penalty tended to be more receptive to negative pretrial publicity against a well-known, real-life defendant and also more likely to feel he deserved the death penalty.

To sum up, the biasing effect of death qualification in the guilt phase of capital trials is now well established. Death-qualified jurors tend to be more conviction-prone as a result of their personal attitudes as well as simply being exposed to the process itself, resulting in death-qualified juries being somewhat more likely to convict than non-death-qualified juries. Death qualification also results in less diverse juries, systematically screening out women, non-Whites, and Roman Catholics (Summers, Hayward, & Miller, 2010). What remains to be established is how strong this biasing effect is on the verdicts of *juries*.

Scientific Jury Selection

Scientific Jury Selection (SJS) refers to the use of social science research techniques to identify desirable and undesirable jurors (Lieberman, 2011; Lieberman & Sales, 2007). The ultimate goal of using SJS is to maximize the likelihood of a favorable jury decision. SJS was first employed in a series of politicized trials in the 1970s (e.g., Angela Davis, Attica, the Camden 28, the Gainesville Eight, the Harrisburg Seven, and the Mitchell-Stans conspiracy trial), and has maintained a high profile via its use in numerous well-publicized trials since then (e.g., Rodney King, O. J. Simpson, the Menendez brothers, William Kennedy Smith, Michael Jackson, Kobe Bryant, and Scott Peterson). From its beginning as a side job for academics, trial consulting has grown into a big business, and SJS is often a major component of those efforts (Lieberman, 2011; Moran, 2008). Over time, SJS has come to be used more often in civil cases and less frequently in criminal cases, and its focus has shifted somewhat from predicting juror verdict preferences and deliberation behavior to developing case themes and trial-related strategy (Moran, 2008).

SJS can involve several methodologies but, in its classic form, features a survey of jury-eligible residents in a community. Respondents are asked about their demographic characteristics, background experiences, and attitudes, along with a set of questions about the case at hand (e.g., "How likely do you think it is that the defendant really did murder his wife?"). Statistical relationships are then determined between the various types of predictor variables (demographic, background, attitudinal) and an overall feeling about the case. SJS techniques were used originally to develop demographic profiles of the ideal juror from a defense standpoint in order to guide the use of peremptory challenges during voir dire. In the first application of SJS, Schulman and his colleagues surveyed 840 respondents in Harrisburg, Pennsylvania, to identify characteristics that correlated with verdict leanings at trial (Schulman, Shaver, Colman, Emrich, & Christie, 1973). Occasionally, trial consultants use the observation of interacting groups as well to see how different types of individuals respond to potential themes that a side could develop.

Do SJS methods work? The ideal empirical evaluation of SJS would involve comparing the verdicts of a large sample of juries selected using SJS with a large sample of juries selected via traditional voir dire. The juries would make real decisions, the cases would be matched for type across the two samples, and the same attorneys would select the matched juries—but this is obviously unrealistic. In practice, a variety of less-ideal study designs have been used to assess the effectiveness of SJS. At times the predeliberation verdict preferences of real jurors in SJS trials have been compared with the verdict preferences of jurors excused via peremptory challenge to see if SJS results in more favorable outcomes. Another option is to tally the "winning percentage" from a sample of trials in which SJS methods were used to see if it exceeds that of a comparison sample where SJS was not used, but this methodology is problematic in that defining a "win" in any given case can be tricky. For instance, the application of SJS could be considered successful if it resulted in gaining a change of venue, getting the prosecution to drop some charges or accept a plea bargain, or obtaining a conviction on a lesser included charge rather than the most serious. In other words, it isn't always obvious what constitutes success when SJS methods are employed.

Despite these obstacles, several efforts have been made to assess the effectiveness of SJS, and their findings imply a mild beneficial effect. In an early experimental study, Horowitz (1980) trained law students to use SJS or conventional methods for selecting jurors. Participants assigned to the SJS condition were provided with statistical information compiled from a pretrial survey as well as profiles of jurors for a variety of cases. Horowitz found the accuracy of SJS varied across case type, being more effective than conventional methods for some case types but less effective for others. Frederick (1984) examined the value of several different ways of rating venirepersons in two real trials, one criminal and one civil. In the criminal trial where SJS methods were used by the defense, actual jurors were found to be more sympathetic to the defense than those who were struck. In the civil trial where survey data were combined with the results of a mock trial, most mock juror predeliberation verdict preferences were predicted correctly by the statistical model (85% of the jurors classified as pro-defense; 71% classified as pro-plaintiff). Nietzel, Dillehay, and Himelein (1987) reported on the results of eighteen capital trials in which the authors conducted SJS on behalf of the defense. Death sentences were returned in 33 percent of the cases on which they worked whereas death was the jury's sentence in 65 percent of the matching trials they identified in which they did not serve as consultants. Finally, Moran (2008) reported that eight traditional published studies of the statistical utility of SJS revealed an average improvement of 17 percent with regard to predicting juror verdict preferences, whereas another compilation including an additional eleven studies was even more optimistic, suggesting potential accuracy gains of up to 26 percent.

One of the best evaluations of SJS effectiveness yet was conducted by Seltzer (2006) in what essentially represents a meta-analysis of cases in which he served as a trial consultant and used SJS methods. Data for this study were compiled from twenty-seven community telephone surveys (with sample sizes ranging from 153 to 1,000) and nine focus group studies conducted for a wide variety of cases across twelve states. For each trial, various demographic and personality variables were used to forecast values on an overall index of the respondent's feeling about the case. The predictor set varied somewhat across trials but generally included respondent sex, race, age, marital status, education level, employment status, location, religious attendance, and media habits. Across the twenty-seven studies, the percentage of variation accounted for in the overall case index by the demographic and personality variables varied widely, ranging from 4 percent to 50 percent with a median value of 18 percent. Differences also emerged across case type, with the most variation explained in cases involving pornography and the least in cases involving business or corporations. In three cases, data were available from telephone surveys as well as focus groups, allowing prediction models to be used to forecast the actual verdict preferences of other mock jurors exposed to attorney statements, testimony, exhibits, and judicial instructions. Using predicted scores generated by a statistical model to choose jurors, SJS methods produced an 8 percent improvement in the hit rate over the base-rate preference for acquittal in the first study (one juror), a 33 percent gain in the second study (four jurors), and either a 3 percent loss (one juror) or a 14 percent gain (two jurors) in the third study depending on the regression equation used. Of course, as Seltzer noted, attorneys in the real world do not get to pick their twelve preferred jurors. Results were also summarized for an earlier study that featured post-trial interviews with 190 jurors from a diverse set of thirty-one criminal trials (Seltzer, Venuti, & Lopes, 1991). A variety of demographic variables were used to "predict" predeliberation verdict preferences on a three-point guilt-certainty scale, and they were collectively able to account for 13 percent of the variation in verdict preferences. Two of the better predictors in this study were whether jurors had ever been a crime victim and their occupation.

The difficulty of evaluating SJS effectiveness in actual trials makes it interesting to consider the results of a computer simulation study by Tindale and Nagao (1986). Assuming the use of SJS methods by the defense could reduce the percentage of jurors favoring guilt by either 10 percent (the "worst-case" scenario) or 30 percent (the "best-case" scenario) and that juries would opt for the verdict preferred by two-thirds or more of their members, their analysis suggested SJS would have minimal impact on the proportion of convictions when the evidence was very weak or very strong, but could yield up to a 12 percent difference in close trials.

So what can be concluded about the impact of this applied arm of jury decision making research? Unfortunately, there is still insufficient high-quality research to make a definitive assessment. Only a dozen or so studies have been published and each has notable limitations of some type. Most importantly, no *experimental* research has involved the verdicts of real juries. Existing work nevertheless suggests that a not-inconsequential amount of variation in venirepersons' predeliberation verdict preferences can be explained (or forecasted) using a combination of demographic, personality, and attitudinal variables—about 10–15 percent on average. Some will see this as the glass being 15 percent full whereas others will view it as 85 percent empty. To complicate conclusions even further, the effectiveness of SJS methods in predicting jurors' predeliberation verdicts may vary across case type as well. Pushing the data as far as they will allow, traditional SJS seems likely to provide a modest improvement in the selection of favorable jurors over the base-rate odds associated with "unaided" attorney prediction, and this benefit could be decisive in *some* cases—particularly those involving moderately strong evidence (Lieberman & Sales, 2007; Seltzer, 2006).

Jury Instructions

Judicial instructions are a core element of all jury trials. Every jury is instructed by the judge as to the relevant law after the evidence is heard— sometimes beforehand too—and judges often issue various instructions to the jury during the course of the trial as well. Because of their fundamental importance, easy manipulation, and legal salience, there is a large empirical literature on jury instructions. Studies have thus far concentrated on three questions: (1) How well do jurors understand their instructions? (2) Can comprehension be improved by modifying standard instructions? (3) How much impact do jury instructions have on juror and jury behavior?

The bulk of existing research has addressed the question of how well jurors understand their instructions. In these studies, mock jurors typically receive instructions in written (or occasionally videotaped) form and are then subsequently tested for comprehension using multiple-choice, true-false, or open-ended paraphrase items. Some researchers have even cut right to the chase, providing instructions to participants and then testing them without any intervening (and potentially distracting) trial stimulus materials (e.g., Buchanan, Pryor, Taylor, & Strawn, 1978; Charrow & Charrow, 1979; Elwork, Sales, & Alfini, 1977; Haney & Lynch, 1997; Luginbuhl, 1992; Strawn & Buchanan, 1976; Steele & Thornburg, 1988-1989). Typically, though, researchers have tested mock jurors' instructional comprehension *after* their participation in a simulated trial (e.g., Ellsworth, 1989; Greene, 1988; Greene & Johns, 2001; Hastie, Penrod, & Pennington, 1983; Hastie, Schkade, & Payne, 1998, 1999; Ogloff, 1991; Ogloff, 1998; Severance & Loftus, 1982). Several studies have even involved assessing the comprehension of actual jurors via post-trial questionnaires (e.g., Heuer & Penrod, 1989; Reifman, Gusick, & Ellsworth, 1992; Saxton, 1998) or interviews (e.g., Bowers, 1995; Young, Cameron, & Tinsley, 2001).

Unfortunately, it is now quite clear that many jurors have difficulty understanding the instructions they receive and display poor levels of comprehension (see Ogloff & Rose, 2005, and Lieberman, 2009, for excellent reviews). This is one of the strongest and most robust findings in the empirical literature on juries, with study after study yielding the same troubling conclusion across a variety of methodologies. Although observed rates vary across studies (particularly by the format of the test), mean comprehension scores for those receiving standard instructions generally fall between 50 percent and 70 percent (i.e., in the range of D or F grades in academic settings). Participants in studies using an open-ended recall format also tend to score lower than those given multiple-choice or true-false items—generally in the abysmal range (e.g., Hastie et al., 1999; Steele & Thornburg, 1988–89). Field studies with actual jurors show the same pattern of sub-par understanding and reveal another disconcerting finding—jurors typically report understanding the judge's instructions with no problems (e.g., Cutler & Hughes, 2001; Devine et al., 2007; Saxton, 1998; Young et al., 2001). Worst of all, comprehension may be lowest in precisely those trials where it needs to be highest—those involving the death penalty. Jurors appear to have particular problems understanding the concepts of weighing, aggravation, and—most especially—mitigation (e.g., Blankenship, Luginbuhl, Cullen, & Redick, 1997; Frank & Applegate, 1998; Haney & Lynch, 1997; Lynch & Haney, 2000; Lynch & Haney, 2009). These same discouraging findings also surfaced in the extraordinary Capital Jury Project dataset (Bentele & Bowers, 2001; Bowers, 1995). Taken together, the results from this large body of research are troubling to anyone who wants to believe jurors have an accurate and nuanced understanding of relevant law. In short, jurors don't understand their instructions as well as they think they do, as well as judges would like to think they do, or as well as we in society might hope they do.

Many good studies in this domain could be singled out as exemplars, but two will suffice. The first, a well-done field experiment by Saxton (1998), involved the administration of comprehension exams to actual jurors in a sample of thirty-two criminal trials and seventeen civil trials. On average, criminal jurors correctly answered 74 percent of their questions while civil jurors managed a 58 percent accuracy rate. A subset of seven questions appeared on most tests for both civil and criminal jurors, and was administered to a group of jury-eligible participants who did not serve on a jury trial. Actual jurors averaged 70 percent on these items whereas the comparison group of non-jurors averaged 53 percent, indicating a mild beneficial effect on comprehension (+17%) associated with actually receiving the instructions.

The second study, conducted by Richard Wiener and an army of associates, examined the comprehensibility of death-penalty legal instructions via an extremely rigorous and realistic experimental design that involved eighty deliberating mock juries (Wiener et al., 2004). Participants in the main study consisted of a representative sample of 665 community residents who watched a professionally produced two-and-a-half-hour videotaped reenactment of a real murder trial. The primary purpose of the study was to examine the effect of several versions of judicial instructions on the comprehension of four types of relevant law (declarative v. procedural; constitutional v. state) both before and after deliberation. Across all conditions, mean comprehension was 61 percent across all thirty-six items on the predeliberation assessment and 62 percent after deliberation. Corrected for guessing, the mean percentage accuracy score for all participants was 28 percent prior to deliberation and 30 percent afterwards—above chance but certainly nothing laudable. Comprehension scores were alarmingly low in the area of procedural state law (12%), and aggregate (jury-level) comprehension of procedural state law was the best—and only significant—predictor of jury sentence, with juries scoring higher being more likely to return a "life" sentence. Put differently, juries made up of jurors with a perfect score for comprehension of state procedural law were estimated to be *sixty-nine times* more likely to return a life sentence than juries composed of members with a chance level of accuracy.

Scholars have also addressed the question of whether jury instructions can be revised to make them more comprehensible. Modifications have included removing legal jargon, simplifying complex sentence structures, and clarifying logic, and such changes appear to result in a noticeable improvement. Studies of simplified or enhanced instructions with mock jurors have generally yielded comprehension scores 10–30 percent higher than those associated with standard instructions (Charrow & Charrow, 1979; Diamond & Levi, 1996; Elwork, Sales, & Alfini, 1977; Elwork, Alfini, & Sales; 1982; Frank & Applegate, 1998; Luginbuhl, 1992; Severance & Loftus, 1984; Wiener et al., 2004). For example, in Wiener's aforementioned study of comprehension in death penalty trials, jurors who received simplified instructions produced overall comprehension scores that were 15 percent higher on average than jurors who received the actual instructions—the same level of improvement observed for simplified instructions in another realistic study involving capital decision making (Diamond & Levi, 1996). Although the trend is promising, increases in comprehension have varied across studies, and even moderate gains still leave considerable room for improvement.

Another question that can be asked in this domain is how much impact jury instructions have on juror or jury behavior. The results of the first meta-analysis of jury instruction effects conducted by Nietzel, McCarthy, and Kerr (1999) were not especially promising. They searched for all studies that compared any judicial instruction condition with a no-instruction condition on one or more measures of juror decision making and found one hundred fifty relevant effect sizes in forty-eight published studies. The median correlation ($r = .07$) across all studies indicated only a very weak general effect of jury instructions. On the whole, this implies that jurors' behavior is not greatly affected by the instructions they receive. In addition, there were modest (but somewhat stronger) effects associated with enhanced instructions over standard instructions (r = .10) and no instructions at all (r = .15). Although this meta-analysis suggests only a slight impact of judicial instructions, the excessive diversity of included studies makes the findings very difficult to interpret. In particular, studies were included that manipulated instructions on an assortment of topics (e.g., pretrial publicity, nullification, disregarding inadmissible evidence, eyewitness testimony, and legal definitions) and measured a host of different outcomes (e.g., verdicts, sentences, attitudes, comprehension, and recall).

A more recent meta-analysis helped to clarify the picture by limiting the scope of inquiry to studies about guilt in a criminal context and one particular kind of instruction—limiting instructions issued in the wake of contested evidence. Steblay, Hosch, Culhane, and McWethy (2006) analyzed all available studies of judicial instructions in which participants were told to either disregard inadmissible evidence (IE) or use it only for some narrow purpose (e.g., assessing the credibility of a defendant's testimony). Specifically, they assessed the impact of IE after: (1) an immediate judicial instruction to disregard it, (2) a delayed judicial instruction to disregard it (e.g., at the end of the trial), and (3) a "pre-emptive" judicial instruction to disregard it issued before a trial. In general, the authors expected IE would have an effect, and that judicial instruction to disregard it would weaken but not eliminate IE effects. Whereas Nietzel et al. (1999) found thirty-seven effect sizes related to this type of instruction, Steblay et al. rounded up a substantially larger number—one hundred seventy-five effect sizes across forty-eight studies. However, due to a paucity of research on pro-defense IE and civil trial contexts, the main analyses were conducted only on studies involving pro-prosecution IE in a criminal trial setting.

Several notable findings emerged from the Steblay et al. (2006) meta-analyses. First, across fifty-six effects, an immediate judicial admonition to disregard IE had only a very small effect in reducing the conviction rate compared to when there was no admonishment (r = -.04). Specifically, there were 6 percent fewer convictions on average following a judicial admonition to ignore the IE across forty-three effects that involved a dichotomous verdict. The results varied greatly across studies, though, and follow-up analyses revealed that, in a subset of three tests where participants were exposed to IE and either did or did not receive a judicial instruction to ignore it, those who received the limiting instruction actually convicted at a moderately *higher* rate than those not admonished (r = .29). Second, with regard to timing, pretrial instructions to disregard negative publicity had essentially no impact on verdicts in four available tests, but post-trial instructions to limit the use of evidence did have some effect, particularly when the judge provided an explanation, reducing the conviction rate by 16 percent. Thus, this research suggests that judicial instructions to ignore IE may be more effective at the end of a trial to avoid calling excess attention to the controversial evidence.

Overall, it is clear that many jurors do not understand their instructions at an adequate level—although they seem to think they do. Even worse, those who understand the instructions least well tend to be most severe in their decisions (both guilt and sentencing). Limiting instructions to ignore inadmissible evidence have a small beneficial effect, but do not eliminate the impact of the IE and in some cases serve to call more attention to it and actually make things worse.

Joinder

Joinder refers to the practice of consolidating multiple charges or trials for the sake of efficiency and is fairly common in the United States for obvious reasons—it saves time and taxpayer money (Bordens & Horowitz, 1985). It usually involves one jury hearing multiple charges against the same defendant, or one jury deciding charges against multiple defendants when all charges stem from the same incident. The general concern with joinder is that it will prejudice jurors against the defendant as the result of: (1) confusion over what evidence corresponds to what charge, (2) accumulation of the evidence across charges, or (3) inference of a criminal disposition on the part of the defendant based on the overall pattern. In essence, all of these mechanisms reflect a concern that jurors cannot keep things separate in their minds. Despite this, motions to sever charges are generally declined by trial judges, and their decisions are rarely overturned by appellate judges (Bordens & Horowitz, 1985). This sets the stage for a straightforward empirical question—does joinder indeed produce a conviction bias against the defendant?

Thus far, approximately eight published studies have addressed the impact of joinder in the context of mock criminal trials using essentially the same experimental design. It basically goes like this: A single charge against one defendant is presented to some mock jurors who serve as the control group. Participants in other experimental conditions hear the same evidence regarding the focal charge *plus* evidence corresponding to one or more additional unrelated charges. The evidence relevant to the focal charge remains the same across conditions, so if jurors can keep things separate and there is no bias against the defendant due to joinder, the conviction rate on the focal charge should remain the same across study conditions regardless of the other charges and their corresponding evidence.

In fact, the conviction rate does not remain the same—it goes up substantially. When mock jurors are presented with additional charges and corresponding evidence, the number of guilty verdicts on the focal charge invariably increases. Kerr and Sawyers (1979) and Horowitz, Bordens, and Feldman (1980) were the first studies to show the anti-defendant bias produced by joinder, with conviction rates (or guilt ratings) higher on a focal charge in a joined trial relative to the corresponding conviction rate for the same charge in a severed trial. Subsequent research replicated this finding and found it to hold across participant types, levels of analysis (i.e., individual v. group), stimulus presentation format, and outcome measures (Bordens & Horowitz, 1983; Bordens & Horowitz, 1986; Greene & Loftus, 1985; Tanford & Penrod, 1982; Tanford & Penrod, 1984; Tanford, Penrod, & Collins, 1985).

One of the best studies of joinder was conducted by Tanford and Penrod (1984), who employed videotaped trial reenactments for their stimulus cases, used adults who had been summoned for jury duty as participants, and had them deliberate in one hundred six-person mock juries. The focal charge (burglary) was judged in isolation, or along with two other charges that varied in terms of their similarity to the focal charge. The similarity (that is, homogeneity) of the evidence presented across charges was also manipulated, as was the presence of a judicial instruction intended to suppress joinder-related bias. The probability of conviction on the burglary charge was higher across the set of joined trial conditions (20%) than the control condition (10%), regardless of the similarity of the charges, the similarity of the evidence presented, or the presence of a limiting instruction from the judge. The observed effects were integrated into a model that was tested using an early application of path analysis, and the results suggested that inference of a criminal disposition was the primary mediator of joinder effects as opposed to confusion about the evidence.

So how large is the joinder effect? Tanford et al. (1985) presented an early quantitative synthesis of the joinder research using ten available effect sizes and found the mean correlation between joinder and the likelihood of conviction on focal charges to be .25, a moderately strong effect. More than a decade later, Nietzel et al. (1999) reexamined joinder studies using similar meta-analytic procedures and data from two additional studies (Bordens & Horowitz, 1986; Tanford et al., 1985). Given the considerable overlap in studies, their computed mean correlation of .25 for the effect of joinder on individual-level juror verdicts was not surprising. With regard to the potential biasing mechanisms, mean correlations were also calculated between verdicts and memory intrusion errors (ten studies) and defendant character ratings (eleven studies) and found to be of similar magnitude ($r = .25$ for memory errors and $r = .27$ for defendant character ratings). In short, joinder has a moderately strong effect on the verdict preferences of simulated jurors and this effect appears to hold across trial contexts.

Given the consistent bias associated with joinder, one question that has received some attention has been the mechanism(s) by which joinder influences verdict preferences. Initial results pointed toward different mediating culprits, with research by Bordens and Horowitz (1983) suggesting that joinder effects arise from confusion about the evidence (i.e., which evidence goes with which charge), but a study by Tanford and Penrod (1982) indicating that joinder influences verdicts by fostering a negative dispositional inference about the defendant's character. Studies by both research teams highlighted a logical resolution—multiple mechanisms may exist. Joinder appears to alter perception of the evidence *and* foster negative judgments of the defendant's character (Greene & Loftus, 1985; Horowitz & Bordens, 1986; Tanford & Penrod, 1984; Tanford, Penrod, & Collins, 1985), although the causal ordering of the two mediating processes has not been conclusively established. Of note, multiple studies found joinder to be associated with elevated memory errors on recognition tests of the evidence related to the focal charge, but only one study revealed the number of these errors to be positively related to guilty verdicts (Bordens & Horowitz, 1983). Thus, all things considered, confusion about the evidence is probably not the primary operating mechanism for the joinder effect.

Unfortunately, limiting instructions appear to have little impact on the bias associated with joinder (Greene & Loftus, 1985; Tanford & Penrod, 1982; Tanford & Penrod, 1984). One study noted some reduction (Tanford et al., 1985), although the same instructions failed to produce an effect in an earlier study by the same researchers (Tanford & Penrod, 1984). This discrepancy may be due to the use of different participant types in the two studies. Nonetheless, these results generally coincide with the findings on the effectiveness of limiting instructions in general—they don't seem to work very well.

To summarize, although the literature is relatively small, joinder has consistently produced a moderate pro-prosecution bias in the form of elevated conviction rates on focal charges relative to the conviction rates for those same charges when decided in separate trials. Joinder effects likely result in large part from negative inferences about the defendant's criminal character, and it is possible that memory errors regarding the evidence and altered perceptions of the strength of evidence presented by the two sides play a role as well. Bias against the defendant due to joinder also appears to be somewhat stronger when the joined charges are similar (Tanford et al., 1985), and relatively unaffected by judges' instructions.

Bifurcation

Bifurcation refers to a courtroom procedure where the presentation of evidence at trial is separated into two or more phases, with continuation to a later stage contingent on a particular legal finding at the preceding stage. It has been advocated as a remedy for "spillover" effects where evidence relevant to some legal issue inappropriately influences jurors' decisions about another—and there is ample indication that such spillover can occur (Bornstein, 1998; Feigenson, Park, & Salovey, 1997; Greene, Johns, & Bowman, 1999). Bifurcation is employed mostly in civil trials, although it is used occasionally in death penalty trials as well. In civil trials, there are several ways that a trial can be bifurcated, including separating the presentation of evidence on: (1) causation and liability, (2) liability and damages, or (3) compensatory and punitive damages.

The most frequently studied type of bifurcation is the separation of evidence related to liability and damages, and the consistent finding is that doing so reduces the likelihood of pro-plaintiff liability verdicts. The effect was first noted in a field study of 186 civil jury trials held in federal district court in the 1960s (Zeisel & Callahan, 1963). For trials resolved by a jury verdict, plaintiffs won 58 percent of those conducted in "unitary" (i.e., aggregated) fashion but only 21 percent of those that were bifurcated. Two subsequent experiments with deliberating mock juries yielded similar results with regard to a reduction in the likelihood of pro-plaintiff verdicts. Horowitz and Bordens (1990) observed 17 percent fewer judgments of causation and 26 percent fewer judgments of liability among their 128 mock juries when the presentation of evidence was bifurcated in one of several ways, as opposed to when all evidence was presented together in a unitary trial. Smith and Greene (2005) obtained similar results using a negligence case involving an automobile accident, with bifurcated juries returning 31 percent fewer judgments of causation than unitary juries. A decrease in pro-plaintiff verdict preferences prior to deliberation was also noted in a third study involving mock juries (Landsman, Diamond, Dimitropoulos, & Saks, 1998), but no reliable difference emerged among jury verdicts, perhaps because the weak case evidence resulted in most juries finding for the defendant.

Less can be said about the impact of bifurcation on the two types of damage awards. Studies have yielded inconsistent findings with regard to an effect on the *size* of compensatory damages and little indication of influence on the awarding of punitive damages (Adams & Bourgeois, 2006; Greene, Woody, & Winter, 2000; Horowitz & Bordens, 1990; Landsman et al., 1998; Smith & Greene, 2005; Wissler, Rector, & Saks, 2001). At present, it is unclear if there is any effect of bifurcation on damage awards in civil trials; if there is, it is probably small and may depend on other case characteristics (e.g., the defendant's conduct or wealth, or the extent of injury to victims).

What research has been done on bifurcation suggests it affects liability decisions because it accomplishes in a procedural fashion what jurors cannot do naturally—keep separate the evidence on legally unrelated issues.

Juror Aids

Historically, the courts have not been keen on identifying ways to help jurors do their jobs well. The long-standing assumption has been that a competent adult sitting in the jury box doesn't need any special assistance to be an acceptable juror. Attitudes began to change in the 1980s with growing indication of a discrepancy between the expectations of the legal system and what jurors actually can do, and a variety of "reform" mechanisms have since been proposed to help improve the performance of jurors and juries. The earliest procedural remedies identified were allowing jurors to take notes during a trial and ask questions, followed by pre-instructing jurors before they hear the evidence, revising/simplifying jury instructions, providing written copies of the instructions, supplying jurors with "notebooks" that summarize the evidence, and (more recently) allowing jurors to discuss cases among themselves prior to deliberation. Empirical results have accrued slowly, with especially good data coming via two field experiments conducted by Larry Heuer and Steven Penrod. Their first "Wisconsin" study involved sixty-seven jury trials (thirty-four civil, thirty-three criminal) held in Wisconsin state courts (Heuer & Penrod, 1988; 1989), and a second "National" study featured data from one hundred sixty jury trials (seventy-five civil, eighty-five criminal) held throughout the United States (Heuer & Penrod, 1994a; 1994b). In both studies, participating judges were persuaded to allow the random assignment of juries to study conditions, an exceptionally rare occurrence that allowed for strong conclusions about the effects of the independent variables. Several other field studies have been done (Flango, 1980; Sand & Reiss, 1985) as well as a number of rigorous experimental studies with mock jurors by Irwin Horowitz and his colleagues, so we now have enough data to draw some conclusions.

Note-Taking

Allowing jurors to take notes at trial seems like an obvious way to improve juror comprehension and recall—almost a no-brainer. Students throughout the world are encouraged to take notes in classrooms to facilitate comprehension and recall, so why shouldn't jurors be allowed to do the same? Surprisingly, there has been resistance to this practice on the part of legal professionals, primarily because of concerns that note-taking jurors might miss important information while writing, record things incorrectly, slow down deliberation, or be unduly influential during discussion. Even more surprising, early field research produced little indication that jurors who take notes will better understand their instructions or recall the evidence (Heuer & Penrod, 1988; 1994b). What these studies *did* show was that most jurors will take notes when given the opportunity, and these notes are perceived to be helpful (Flango, 1980; Heuer & Penrod, 1988; 1994b; Sand & Reiss, 1985). These studies also show that jurors who take notes generate a reasonable volume that is proportional to the duration and complexity of the trial (Heuer & Penrod, 1988; 1994b). For example, 67 percent of jurors took notes when permitted in the Wisconsin study and 87 percent did so in the National study (Penrod & Heuer, 1998), and judges reported "moderate" or "extensive" note-taking by jurors in twenty-three of thirty-two trials in another field study (Sand & Reiss, 1985). In terms of quantity, jurors took an average of 5.4 pages in the Wisconsin study, whereas in the National study, criminal jurors took 7.1 pages on average and civil jurors took an average of 14.4 pages. Overall, however, early field research did not produce the expected benefit of note-taking with regard to comprehension (Penrod & Heuer, 1997; 1998).

In contrast, well-controlled experiments with mock civil jurors suggest note-taking does in fact aid juror comprehension and recall. Much of this research has been done by Irwin Horowitz and Lynne ForsterLee using a toxic tort case involving four plaintiffs who suffered different levels of injury (ForsterLee & Horowitz, 1997; ForsterLee, Horowitz, & Bourgeois, 1994; ForsterLee, Kent, & Horowitz, 2005; Horowitz & Bordens, 2002; Horowitz & ForsterLee, 2001), but there have been a few other studies as well (e.g., Fitzgerald, 2000; Hans, Kaye, Dann, Farley, & Albertson, 2011; Rosenhan, Eisner, & Robinson, 1994). The experimental research has consistently shown moderate gains associated with note-taking. In particular, jurors permitted to take notes generally recalled more probative evidence, made fewer evidence recognition errors, provided more coherent free-recall narratives, showed less variability in their overall awards, and made more appropriate distinctions in their damage awards to the plaintiffs. The one study that examined juror note-taking in a complex criminal homicide case involving DNA evidence did not find a general comprehension benefit associated with it (Hans et al., 2011), but did show some gain when note-taking was paired with other decision aids (e.g., an evidence notebook). In short, juror note-taking appears to have a positive effect on comprehension in complex civil trials, but further study is needed to determine if it has a beneficial effect across a broad range of case types, particularly in the criminal domain.

Question-Asking

Like note-taking, permitting jurors to ask questions of the witnesses through the attorneys seems fairly innocuous. What harm could arise from allowing the jurors to clarify their confusion and misunderstanding? As with note-taking, however, the idea of allowing jurors to ask questions has generated concerns within the legal community (e.g., that doing so will slow down the proceedings or expose weaknesses in either side's evidence). As a result, researchers studying the effects of this practice have focused on the number and nature of the questions jurors ask when allowed to do so, as well as the reactions of judges and attorneys.

Regarding quantity, early research suggests that juries allowed to ask questions during trials will pose some, but not an excessive number—generally four–five on average, with one–two being the most common. For example, in the thirty-three trials in which it was permitted, criminal juries asked on average 2.3 questions that were approved by the attorneys in the Wisconsin study (Heuer & Penrod, 1988), whereas 4.4 approved questions were asked on average by criminal juries and 5.1 by civil juries in seventy-one trials in the later National study (Heuer & Penrod, 1994b). This amounted to about one question for every two hours of trial time (Penrod & Heuer, 1997). In both of these studies, about two-thirds of juror questions were directed at witnesses for the prosecution/plaintiff. Comparable results were obtained in a field study of twenty-six jury trials held in the federal district courts of the 2nd Circuit, with judges reporting that 69 percent of juries allowed to ask questions did so, and fourteen of sixteen trials producing one to "several" jury questions (Sand and Reiss, 1985). In a slightly different context, sifting through the court records of 405 jury trials held in the state of Washington, Severance and Loftus (1982) found that 24 percent of the juries submitted at least one question to the judge during deliberation (1.4 on average), and most of these questions concerned the legal definitions for "intent" and "reasonable doubt." However, in an excellent field experiment involving civil juries in Arizona, Diamond and her colleagues observed considerably more question-asking by jurors, with an average of about fourteen questions asked (and nine actually answered) during the typical trial, but thirty-four asked (and twenty-nine answered) in the average complex trial (Diamond et al.,

2003). Similar to Severance and Loftus's study, their juries posed on average only one question during deliberation.

In terms of the reaction by judges and attorneys, most were either positive or neutral. Attorneys objected to only a small proportion of the questions jurors posed (around 20%) in these studies, with judges and prosecutors favorably disposed toward the procedure for the most part whereas defense attorneys showed more variability. Alas, there are no data on the impact of question-asking on juror comprehension or trial outcomes, so the most that can be said at this point is that allowing jurors to ask questions does not appear to interfere with courtroom efficiency or systematically disadvantage either side.

Other Aids

Several other practices intended to ease the cognitive burden on jurors have received some attention from researchers as well. These practices include pre-instructing jurors (Fitzgerald, 2000; ForsterLee, Horowitz, & Bourgeois, 1993; ForsterLee & Horowitz, 1997; Smith, 1991b), allowing jurors access to the trial transcript (Horowitz & ForsterLee, 2001), and providing written summaries or "notebooks" of the evidence (Dann et al., 2006; ForsterLee et al., 2005). This preliminary work reveals modest positive effects on evidence recall that are sometimes contingent on other variables, and no systematic effect on verdicts.

One of the newest and most intriguing reforms is allowing juries to discuss the evidence as a group before the trial ends. This practice is not widespread at present, but two rare field experiments have been conducted to evaluate the effects of allowing jurors to talk about civil cases prior to deliberation (Diamond et al., 2003; Hannaford, Hans, & Munsterman, 2000). These initial studies, one of which involved videotaping the deliberations of fifty actual civil juries, revealed that jurors (1) usually (but not always) talked among themselves before deliberation when allowed, (2) usually (but not always) discussed the case with all of their members present, (3) liked being able to discuss the case before the end of trial, and (4) reported predeliberation discussions to be helpful. In addition, juries that discussed their case before all the evidence was in tended to deliberate a little faster and take their first vote a little earlier, but did not systematically prejudge the case or decide for either side more often. Further research is clearly needed on predeliberation discussion, particularly in criminal trial settings, but the data in hand suggest the practice does not meet the highest hopes of its advocates or the worst fears of its critics (Diamond et al., 2003).

Best Practices for Jury Trials

Legal scholars and social scientists have long been interested in the effect of various trial practices on jury decision making. For some practices, there are now sufficient studies to allow for meta-analyses addressing the most basic question: Do variations in trial practices affect juror comprehension and/or jury verdicts? Dispensing with nuance, the answer is yes. The overall picture that emerges from this research is one of guarded optimism in that we have made substantial progress identifying practices that have a deleterious effect on juries, as well as a variety of ways to help jurors do their jobs easier and better. Consolidating the implications of the research on trial practices, the existing data suggest juries should be (1) composed of twelve members, (2) required to deliberate to a unanimous decision, (3) given simplified/revised instructions before and after the trial, and (4) allowed to take notes. Allowing jurors to ask questions and discuss the case prior to deliberation *may* help as well and do not seem to result in substantial inefficiency or a bias toward any particular outcome.

Conversely, in terms of what to avoid, juries should not be death-qualified prior to the sentencing phase of a capital trial, and the practice of joining trials should be used with caution when it cannot be avoided. Alternatives also need to be found for the use of limiting instructions because they simply do not work in most situations and may even call undue attention to controversial evidence. Despite considerable progress with regard to understanding the effect of trial practices, further study is needed to determine when trial-related practices are most and least likely to have their effects, and how they impact the quality of deliberation. In other words, the goal for future research should be to ascertain more precisely the conditions when juries *perform* best.

4

Effects of Trial Context

A jury's focal task is to reach decisions about guilt, liability, damages, and occasionally sentence. In most trials, the evidence presented at trial is likely to be a major (if not the primary) determinant of those decisions, but other variables will sometimes have an effect as well. Some of these are *contextual* variables associated with the trial but not part of the admissible evidence, including the type of charge (or claim) against the defendant, case-related information presented in the media before or during the trial, definitions of key legal terms, the verdict options available to the jury, and the values that jurors have with regard to the applicable law. In general, the courts have less control over contextual variables than trial practices, but judges and/or attorneys often have discretion concerning *some* elements of the trial context. This chapter focuses on selected aspects of the trial context that have received empirical attention from researchers.

Community Values and Jury Nullification

Courts do not have the luxury of opening a fresh pack of jurors. Real jurors come from communities where their attitudes, beliefs, and values have been shaped extensively by many life experiences before they ever set foot in a courtroom. *Nullification* is a phenomenon that is grounded in community values and occurs when jurors knowingly disregard the law in reaching a decision in favor of a criminal defendant (Horowitz, 2008). In other words, nullification involves a jury acquitting a defendant who is seen as legally guilty based on the evidence but who acted in a morally upright or virtuous manner. Examples of nullification might include acquitting defendants arrested for protesting an immoral war, physically disabling a would-be murderer, or assisting the suicide of a terminally ill patient. Before the American Revolution, most juries in the colonies had the power to determine the facts of the case as well as the relevant law. Over time, juries lost their power to determine the law except in a few states, and are now generally left with the sole task of determining the facts of a case and applying the law given to them by the judge. The potential for nullification arises from a loophole—juries are not required to provide a rationale for their decisions, so they continue to have the implicit power to determine the law.

The limited experimental research on nullification thus far has focused on what juries do when explicitly reminded of their ability to nullify. The first published study on the topic was conducted by Irwin Horowitz in 1985, who recruited ex-jurors in Ohio in order to examine the impact of different nullification instructions in three types of criminal cases. Forty-five six-person juries were randomly assigned to one of three instructional conditions (standard jury instructions, "Maryland" jury instructions, or radical nullification instructions) and received one of three case types involving a homicide (murder, drunk driving, and euthanasia). The standard instructions made no mention of the jury's ability to nullify, whereas the "Maryland" instructions provided a subtle reminder of the possibility and the radical instructions actively encouraged juries to consider nullifying. After a brief voir dire, participants listened to the audiotape of a simulated trial involving professional actors and deliberated for up to an hour. The frequency of nullification depended on both the instructions given and the type of case. Juries receiving the radical nullification instructions acquitted *more* often in the euthanasia case compared with the other two instructional conditions, but *less* often in the drunk-driving case (with no difference in the murder case). Further, juries that received the radical instructions in the drunk-driving case spent less time discussing the evidence and more time on their personal views and experiences.

Like any good sequel, Horowitz (1988) did things bigger and better. Again using jury-eligible participants from Ohio, four variables were manipulated in conjunction with a large sample of mock juries (144). As before, the nature of the instructions given to the juries and case type were manipulated, although only two instruction conditions (standard and radical-nullification) were used, and the murder case from the 1985 study was replaced with an illegal weapons possession case. The attorneys' role was examined as well by having the defense attorney make (or not make) reference to the judge's nullification instruction in opening remarks, and having the prosecuting attorney remind (or not remind) the jury of the law's requirement to follow their oath regardless of their personal sentiments. As expected, juries that received the nullification instruction from the judge tended to acquit more often, as did juries that heard the defense attorney's argument for nullifying. As in the earlier study, though, several contingencies emerged. The defense attorney's argument for nullification succeeded in lowering guilt scores in the illegal weapons possession case but actually produced an increase in guilt scores and convictions in the drunk-driving case—in other words, a backlash. The prosecutor's reminder had something of a leveling effect, reducing the number of convictions in the drunk-driving case and increasing the number of convictions in the euthanasia case.

Initial research established that juries would not nullify on a whim simply when reminded of their implicit power to do so and that case type and instruction content play a role as well. Subsequent investigation has underscored the influence of jury instructions and identified several other contingency factors that may affect nullification frequency. These include the degree of sympathy evoked by the victim (Horowitz, Kerr, Park, & Gockel, 2006), the compassion evident in the defendant's actions (Pfeifer, Brigham, & Robinson, 1996), and juror case-related attitudes and personality characteristics (Meissner, Brigham, & Pfeifer, 2003; Wiener, Habert, Shkodriani, & Staebler, 1991).

One trait that may influence how receptive jurors are to the idea of nullification is dogmatism. In a small experimental study involving a euthanasia case, Kerwin and Shaffer (1991) assembled mock juries made up entirely of members who were low or high on dogmatism. Juries generally acquitted more often when reminded of their nullification capability, but the likelihood depended heavily on the composition of the jury. In keeping with their preference for order and structure, high-dogmatic juries were more responsive to the presence or absence of the nullification instruction and followed the judge's lead when reminded, whereas the nullification rate of low-dogmatic juries was largely unaffected by the presence of the instruction.

Other research suggests that the incidence of nullification may be even more complex. In a series of mock juror studies involving a case in which a doctor was on trial for the death of a patient who acquired AIDS from a contaminated blood transfusion at the hospital during crisis conditions, Niedermeier, Horowitz, and Kerr (1999) observed a robust effect of reminding jurors of their potential to nullify but also some indication of interaction with characteristics of the defendant. In three of four experiments, jurors who received the nullification reminder acquitted the defendant more often than those receiving the standard instruction. However, in the experiment that varied the defendant's medical background, a higher-status defendant was treated more leniently when he *did not* show remorse whereas a lower-status defendant was shown more leniency when he *did*. In other experiments that varied the accused's characteristics, the physician defendant was convicted less often when male than female, and White as opposed to Hispanic. Collectively, these studies suggest that nullification is influenced not only by the judge's instructions, but also case type, defendant's behavior, and even the personality characteristics of the jury.

The question of how often nullification occurs in real juries has been addressed by some excellent field research. In the late 1990s, a team of scholars associated with the National Center for State Courts (NCSC) set out to examine the frequency and causes of hung juries (Hannaford-Agor & Hans, 2003). Data were gathered via post-trial questionnaires from judges, attorneys, and jurors who participated in 372 felony jury trials in four metropolitan areas (the Bronx, Los Angeles, Phoenix, and Washington, DC). Only a small fraction of cases—2 out of 372, or about .5 percent—were consistent with the occurrence of nullification in its classical form (i.e., strong prosecution evidence, low juror perceptions of legal fairness, and acquittal on all or most charges). Replacing the jurors' ratings of evidentiary strength with the judge's rating of evidentiary strength yielded only a slightly larger number of trials that were potentially consistent with nullification (seven, or about 2%), but in all of these cases the jurors rated the evidence as relatively ambiguous, suggesting they were not deliberately disregarding the law but rather interpreting the evidence differently than the judge. Thus, the NCSC study suggests nullification is not a common phenomenon in the real world.

To sum up, research to date certainly is not consistent with fears that reminding jurors of their power to nullify will open a Pandora's Box of extralegal bias. Rather, nullification reminders appear to increase the chance of acquittal when the defendant clearly has altruistic motives, but prompting juries to nullify *could* also produce a backlash against the defendant when there is strong evidence of reprehensible behavior. Individual difference variables may play a role as well, with certain types of jurors (e.g., highly dogmatic) more likely to nullify, and certain types of defendants (e.g., highstatus) more likely to be acquitted.

Pretrial Publicity

Around the clock, information about crime floods the media airwaves. Case reports, mug shots, crime scene photos, interviews with victims and bystanders—all of this and more is available via network and cable news, talk shows, daily newspapers, Internet websites, cell phone apps, and the list goes on. The dilemma surrounding pretrial publicity (PTP) involves two basic principles—society's right to a free press as established by the First Amendment versus the defendant's right to a fair trial as guaranteed by the Fifth and Sixth Amendments. The courts have long been aware of the potential for bias associated with exposure to PTP (e.g., *Sheppard v. Maxwell*, 1966), and several legal remedies are used in an effort to preempt or counter its effects (i.e., voir dire, continuance, jury instructions, and change of venue). Researchers in turn have made PTP a focus of study over the last half-century (see Studebaker & Penrod, 2005, and Spano, Groscup, & Penrod, 2011, for excellent reviews). In the classic experimental paradigm, some mock jurors are exposed to negative PTP about a criminal defendant in the form of bogus newspaper reports whereas others are supplied with neutral factual information or no information at all; then conviction rates are compared across study conditions. Field research on PTP has involved content analyses of TV news and newspapers as well as community surveys assessing respondent knowledge about real high-profile cases to ascertain if case knowledge is related to evaluations of the defendant and verdict leanings.

A basic question about PTP is which side it tends to favor, and the answer is: not the defendant's. In particular, several field studies have examined the content of PTP media reports and found them to be overwhelmingly negative toward those accused of crimes. For example, Imrich, Mullin, and Linz (1995) content-analyzed crime reports appearing in fourteen large U.S. newspapers over an eight-week period and found that 27 percent suspects were described in a negative, prejudicial manner. Negative remarks most often consisted of derogatory character assertions and proffered opinions of the defendant's guilt. Based upon a content analysis of two hundred local TV news programs randomly sampled from those airing in the Los Angeles area over a two-year time span, Dixon and Linz (2002) found that one or more types of prejudicial information (as defined by the ABA) was mentioned for 19 percent of the defendants identified in those programs. Prejudicial statements were also more likely to occur in cases involving Black or Latino defendants, as well as White victims. In short, prejudicial PTP is not uncommon and may tend to cater to the stereotypical fears of the White community.

What is exceptionally clear from the research is that exposure to PTP causes jurors to evaluate defendants more negatively and, in particular, to be more likely to convict. A meta-analysis by Steblay, Besirevic, Fulero, and Jimenez-Lorente (1999) found twenty-three studies (eighteen published) reporting at least one test of the relationship between PTP exposure and juror verdict judgments. These studies yielded forty-four effects with a relatively large average sample size (131). In an effort to include as many studies as possible, conservative estimates were used for three studies that did not include precise effect sizes, although this tends to underestimate the size of any effect. The primary finding in the meta-analysis by Steblay and her colleagues is that juror exposure to negative PTP was associated with an increased rate of conviction relative to those not exposed. The mean correlation across the forty-four effects was small-moderate in size ($r = .16$), but the large number of effects allows for a high degree of confidence that the influence of PTP is real. Further, the distribution of effects was more variable than would be expected from chance alone, suggesting the impact of PTP may be contingent on one or more other variables. Accordingly, subgroup analyses showed that PTP effects were stronger for (1) survey designs (as opposed to simulation studies with mock jurors), (2) pretrial verdict assessments (as opposed to post-trial), (3) community residents (as opposed to students), (4) crimes involving murder, sex abuse, or drugs, (5) multiple types of negative PTP as opposed to one type, (6) PTP that was real as opposed to fictitious, and (7) intervals of a week or more between PTP exposure and verdict assessment.

Numerous additional studies have replicated the robust effect of negative pretrial publicity in criminal cases since the 1999 meta-analysis by Steblay and her colleagues (Arbuthnot, Myers, & Leach, 2002; Honess, Charman, & Levi, 2003; Hope, Memon, & McGeorge, 2004; Jacquin & Hodges, 2007; Kerr, Niedermeier, & Kaplan, 1999; Kovera, 2002; Ruva & McEvoy, 2008; Ruva, McEvoy, & Bryant, 2007; Shaw & Skolnick, 2004; Studebaker et al., 2002). For example, Arbuthnot et al. (2002) created a ten-item measure of case knowledge about a much-publicized Ohio murder trial for a study that involved a random telephone survey of community residents. Case knowledge was strongly correlated with estimates of likelihood that the defendant committed the crime and was the best predictor among a set that included demographic variables, attitudes toward the justice system, and awareness of PTP. Respondents whose probability-of-commission estimate exceeded their personal threshold for required certainty also had significantly higher PTP knowledge scores. Similarly, Jacquin and Hodges (2007) had participants read either no report or one of several newspaper reports (sympathetic, neutral/factual, or unsympathetic) about a defendant in a high-profile murder trial, and measured their pretrial case knowledge. In contrast to Arbuthnot et al. (2002), case-related *knowledge* was not related to preferred verdict, but participants *exposed* to the unsympathetic news report tended to convict more often than those who read sympathetic or neutral reports (although not more than those who received no report). These anomalous findings may have resulted from a very negative public perception of the real-life defendant (Andrea Yates) and a very high conviction rate across all study conditions.

Another basic question about PTP is how extensively it occurs. The available data suggest relatively few legal cases receive any media attention, but a small portion of those that do receive a very considerable amount. One approach to this question has involved monitoring media sources during the pretrial periods of high-profile cases featuring notorious defendants such as the Unabomber or Timothy McVeigh. These studies show that PTP can clearly reach saturation levels in *some* high-profile cases (Penrod, Groscup, & O'Neil, 2002, as discussed in Studebaker & Penrod, 2005; Studebaker, Robbennolt, Pathak-Sharma, & Penrod, 2000). Alternatively, a few studies have examined PTP in ordinary, run-of-the-mill cases. In an early effort, Eimermann and Simon (1970) monitored crime-related reports in two local newspapers over a two-month period and found that published reports were more likely to occur for more serious crimes, and prejudicial statements about defendants were more frequent in reports associated with more serious crimes. A similar study by Tankard, Middleton, and Rimmer (1979) provided base-rate frequency data on PTP in ordinary trials—67 percent of the news stories they found about focal cases contained at least one statement deemed prejudicial to defendants according to ABA guidelines. Finally, in one of the best studies of PTP frequency associated with serious violent crimes, Bruschke and Loges (1999) reviewed pretrial newspaper reports related to 134 first-degree murder cases over a two-year period and their search revealed that 46 percent of the cases elicited no news reports, 19 percent produced one–five reports, 18 percent yielded six–ten reports, and 16 percent generated eleven or more reports.

Some research has also investigated the conditions when PTP will be most influential. Kerr, Niedermeier, and Kaplan (1999) argued the impact of PTP should depend on the strength of the evidence and predicted the deliberation process would exacerbate juror-level PTP bias when the evidence was ambiguous, but reduce bias when the evidence was lopsided (in this case, weak). They tested their prediction using eighty mock juries composed of four individuals. As expected, prior to deliberation, participants exposed to a newspaper article containing prejudicial information about the defendant preferred conviction more than those who received a news article with exonerating information. However, as predicted, the effect of deliberation depended on the strength of the evidence, *accentuating* the bias among individual jurors when the evidence was moderate in strength but *reducing* it considerably when the evidence was weak. This resulted in a 21 percent higher conviction rate for juries exposed to the negative PTP in the moderate-evidence condition compared with those juries that were not exposed, but only a 3 percent higher conviction rate for the PTP-exposed juries than the non-exposed juries when the evidence was weak.

In another intriguing study, Kovera (2002) examined the possibility that juror attitudes would interact with exposure to PTP to influence verdicts in a rape case. Based on their responses to an attitude measure about rape, participants were classified as pro-defendant, neutral, or pro-victim, and then viewed a news story about rape that was either pro-defendant or pro-victim in slant, or a feature story on an unrelated topic. Exposure to the news story about rape had a weak and paradoxical effect. Pro-defendant participants who saw the rape news story tended to convict *more* often than pro-defendant participants who watched the unrelated story, whereas pro-victim participants who saw the rape news story tended to convict *less* than their counterparts who did not view the news story about rape. This unexpected result highlights the potential for the effect of PTP exposure to depend in part on jurors' attitudes.

Efforts are also underway to identify the causal mechanisms associated with PTP. Honess et al. (2003) had fifty students watch an extensive videotaped reenactment of a high-profile fraud trial after measuring their recall of factual PTP and affective/evaluative PTP in an interview. Those who recalled greater amounts of affective/evaluative PTP tended to be more confident that the defendant was guilty, whereas factual PTP recall was only weakly (and nonsignificantly) related to verdicts. In addition, the effect of affective/evaluative PTP appeared to be strongly mediated by elevated levels of pro-prosecution reasoning about the evidence. Hope, Memon, and McGeorge (2004) investigated whether PTP exposure might cause recipients to distort evidence presented at trial. As expected, exposure to a newspaper article with negative PTP led mock jurors to favor conviction more often than those not exposed (17%), and this effect was mediated by predecisional distortion. In essence, exposure to negative PTP appeared to make participants more likely to discount testimony that favored the defendant, translating into a higher likelihood of preferring conviction.

Two studies by Christine Ruva and her colleagues shed light on yet another potential mechanism for PTP effects—confusion about the source of the information (Ruva, McEvoy, & Bryant, 2007; Ruva & McEvoy, 2008). Mock jurors in these two studies were exposed to a series of negative PTP newspaper articles about a real murder, watched an edited videotape of the actual trial, and later were presented with a list of informational items asserted in either the PTP newspaper articles, the testimony given at trial, or both. Negative PTP had its expected prejudicial effect in both studies, increasing guilty verdict preferences by about 30 percent prior to deliberation, whereas positive (pro-defendant) PTP reduced guilty verdicts by 12 percent in the only study where it was examined. However, what was most interesting is that participants exposed to the negative PTP in both studies were more likely to confuse the source of the information—in particular, believing critical information from the PTP was provided by witnesses during the trial—and perceive the defendant as less credible. Source memory errors were found to be worse when there was a delay of even two days between watching the trial and taking the source memory test. Follow-up analyses revealed the impact of negative PTP to be mediated by both source monitoring errors and perceptions of defendant credibility in the first study, but only the latter in the second study. More research is needed to illuminate the potentially critical role of source memory errors in PTP.

Despite the strong and consistent effects observed for PTP, there are two notable limitations of the empirical literature. The first is a lack of research examining the verdicts of real juries as opposed to juror verdict preferences. Only one study to my knowledge has examined the relationship between PTP and a large number of jury verdicts. In this study, my colleagues and I collected data on a sample of 179 criminal trials held in Indiana and found an increased likelihood of conviction ($r = .22$) in trials for which judges reported being aware of extensive PTP (Devine, Buddenbaum, Houp, Studebaker, & Stolle, 2009). The PTP-verdict relationship was somewhat stronger for the most serious charge against the defendant (as opposed to secondary charges), and when the prosecution's evidence was rated by the judges and/or attorneys as being between "moderate" and "strong." A second limitation of the PTP literature is that there are still only a few studies on civil juries (Kline & Jess, 1966; Otto, Penrod, & Dexter, 1994; Bornstein, Whisenhunt, Nemeth, & Dunaway, 2002), although the negative effects of PTP have been found consistently in these studies. For instance, Bornstein et al. (2002) examined PTP in a tort case wherein exposure to a toxic chemical agent allegedly caused ovarian cancer in the plaintiff. Pro-victim PTP increased the percentage of liability verdicts relative to the control condition and pro-defendant PTP marginally reduced them, but PTP did not influence juror damage awards. In a larger follow-up study, the impact of a judicial admonition to ignore PTP was examined along with two levels of PTP (no information or pro-victim PTP). Again, pro-victim PTP increased the percentage of liability verdicts and this time it also influenced damage awards. Thus, at present, it appears that PTP affects jurors in civil trials as well as criminal.

To sum up, exposure to PTP with negative information about the defendant makes jurors—and juries—more negative toward defendants and more likely to return an adverse judgment (e.g., conviction). This effect is small-moderate in size but reliable, being observed in study after study, and does not seem to be much affected by limiting instructions or other procedural remedies save for a change of venue (i.e., swapping exposed jurors for unexposed). It appears to occur by way of negative judgments about the defendant and perhaps confusion over whether PTP information was part of the trial evidence. That said, the impact of PTP may depend somewhat on the strength of the evidence presented at trial, likely having more influence when the evidence is somewhat ambiguous. All of this is very consistent with the Story model and the general notion that jurors will use information that is relevant and available in constructing their stories regardless of its source.

In-Court Inadmissible Evidence

Jurors can be exposed to inadmissible evidence (IE) prior to trial in the form of PTP but also during a trial. Unlike PTP, judges know exactly what extra-legal information jurors are exposed to when it occurs in the midst of a trial. In-court IE can come in many forms, including inadvertent statements by witnesses (e.g., hearsay), presentation of evidence obtained via questionable or outright illegal means (e.g., coerced confessions), and calculated "slips" by the attorneys (e.g., revealing that the defendant has a prior criminal record). As with PTP, research on IE has focused on its impact on jurors both in the presence and absence of instructions from the judge to disregard it.

Fortunately, the extensive literature on IE has been quantitatively summarized in an excellent series of meta-analyses by Nancy Steblay and her colleagues involving 175 effects obtained from forty-eight studies (Steblay, Hosch, Culhane, & McWethy, 2006). As a prelude to examining the effectiveness of limiting instructions, they sought to ascertain the influence of IE as well as evidence contested by one side but subsequently ruled admissible. Several major findings emerged from these analyses. First, as expected, exposure to "questionable" focal evidence that was not challenged increased the conviction rate by 8 percent on average in fifteen tests ($r = .13$). This reflects the impact of critical evidence of the type that could be ruled inadmissible and shows that such evidence does indeed affect jurors. Second, and perhaps more importantly, twenty-nine tests were available comparing participants not exposed to IE and those exposed to IE that was ruled inadmissible with an immediate instruction to ignore it. Despite the admonishment, IE exposure produced a 9 percent higher conviction rate in the twenty-five tests that calculated them ($r = .14$ overall). The findings were less straightforward with regard to the impact of IE when coupled with a judicial charging instruction given at the end of a trial, but IE continued to have some impact there as well. Finally, and rather shockingly, the analyses revealed that a serious risk is taken by the defense when questionable evidence is challenged. Twenty-one tests were found comparing the conviction rates of mock jurors who received questionable critical evidence with no special attention called to it and those exposed to the same questionable evidence when it was challenged by the defense *and* subsequently ruled admissible by the judge. Mock jurors exposed to the challenge as well as the judge's ruling of admissibility returned 28 percent *more* convictions ($r = -.29$). In these instances, objection from the defense may simply serve to call jurors' attention to contested evidence and make them more likely to use it, not less.

A more concrete sense of IE effects can be obtained from the conviction rates in fifteen studies which included all three of the following conditions: a no contested evidence/no admonition control condition (35%), an IE + admonition condition (45%), and a challenged-evidence-ruled-admissible condition (69%). This analysis also allowed the effects of different types of IE to be estimated, with hearsay ($r = .04$) and mention of a prior conviction ($r = .07$) showing weak effects; illegal wiretaps ($r = .11$) and illegal searches ($r = .14$) displaying modest effects; mention of a prior criminal record ($r = .19$) or a confession ($r = .23$) generating moderate effects; and multiple types of IE producing a strong effect ($r = .43$).

One question that can be asked about IE is why it has an effect at all given that judges instruct jurors to disregard it. One theory is that jurors react badly to being told what to do and so do the opposite (Brehm & Brehm, 1981). A second theory is that the judge's ruling calls attention to the forbidden material and, ironically, makes it more salient to jurors (Wegner, 1994). A clever study involving critical hearsay testimony that was either unusual or mundane in nature was able to test these potential explanations (Pickel, Karam, & Warner, 2009). In two experiments, jurors had a harder time discounting critical evidence when it was unusual and ruled inadmissible (i.e., highly memorable), suggesting IE has its effect due to enhanced accessibility in jurors' memory.

All in all, the research on IE is consistent with the extensive research on PTP and very much in accord with the Story model. When jurors learn of information that seems to be relevant, it influences their thinking by providing another piece of the puzzle. Once a puzzle piece has snapped into place, it is difficult for jurors to remove it just because the judge says so. In cases where the defendant is unsympathetic or clearly culpable of *something*, jurors may not want to set aside this information even if they could (which is questionable). Nonetheless, more research is needed to establish the impact of pro-defense IE and the effect of IE in civil trials.

Charges, Verdict Options, and Sentences
Charge Seriousness, Lesser Included Charges, and Penalty Severity

There is an interesting parallel between legal decision making and statistical hypothesis testing (Kerr, 1978). The "null hypothesis" facing a criminal jury is that the defendant is innocent, and the "alternative hypothesis" is that he or she is guilty. Two types of error are then possible: Type 1 errors occur when an innocent defendant is convicted; Type 2 errors occur when an actual perpetrator is acquitted. The *severity-leniency hypothesis* asserts that jurors (and juries) are less willing to risk convicting an innocent person as the negative consequences associated with conviction become greater, leading them to require more evidence of guilt before they are willing to convict on more serious charges. In other words, there is assumed to be a trade-off between charge severity and the likelihood of conviction— the more severe the crime (and its corresponding penalty), the lower the probability of conviction.

A number of experimental studies have examined the severity-leniency hypothesis in a manner of sorts by manipulating the charges available to jurors on which they could convict. The watershed study of this type was done by Vidmar (1972), who presented mock jurors with a homicide case summary and had them choose a verdict from one of seven different option sets representing all possible combinations of the following charges: first-degree murder, second-degree murder, and manslaughter. In other words, some mock jurors chose between first-degree murder and acquittal; others chose between first-degree murder, second-degree murder, and acquittal; and so on. The primary result was basically consistent with the severity-leniency hypothesis: Fewer convictions occurred when the least-serious charge (i.e., manslaughter) was not in the choice set. Similar results were obtained using homicide cases in other studies involving four options related to the charge (Kaplan & Simon, 1972) or two options (Hamilton, 1978), with conviction rates highest for the set that included the least-serious charge. Chantal Koch and I also found that the option to convict on a lesser charge resulted in more guilty verdicts but only when the term "beyond reasonable doubt" was not elaborated upon, as opposed to defined as "firmly convinced" of the defendant's guilt (Koch & Devine, 1999). Although less applicable to juries given that they rarely decide sentences, a few studies have also manipulated the severity of the penalty for conviction and revealed only a weak trend for fewer convictions when penalties were more severe (e.g., Davis, Kerr, Stasser, Meek, & Holt, 1977), or interactions involving penalty severity and other variables related to the nature of the crime or the decision context (e.g., Hester & Smith, 1973; Kaplan & Krupa, 1986).

Alas, these studies all share an important limitation in that charge seriousness and penalty severity were not manipulated independently. Observed effects may have been due to assumptions that participants made about likely punishment, as opposed to the moral seriousness of the charge. This problem was avoided in two studies where charge seriousness and penalty severity were manipulated independently (McComas & Noll, 1974; Kerr, 1978). Both produced an effect for charge seriousness, with guilt ratings (and/or conviction rates) lower for defendants charged with first-degree murder as opposed to second-degree murder, and lower for second-degree murder than for manslaughter. The results differed for penalty severity, though, with McComas and Noll finding no effect when continuous guilt ratings were used, whereas Kerr grouped the four penalty levels into two categories (mild and severe) and observed fewer guilty verdicts when the penalty was severe.

There is yet another obstruction in the road to a conclusion, however, in that more serious charges *require* more evidence for conviction. If the evidence is held constant, the greater evidentiary requirements for more serious charges should naturally result in a lower conviction rate on these charges. Freedman, Krismer, MacDonald, and Cunningham (1994) conducted a series of eight experiments in order to systematically test this by teasing apart the effects of charge seriousness, penalty severity, and evidentiary requirements. Their first study successfully replicated the typical pattern of effects seen in the literature when evidentiary requirements were not controlled (i.e., an effect of charge seriousness but no effect of penalty severity). For the remaining seven experiments, they used two different cases in which the charged crime had clearly been committed, leaving only the decision of whether it had been committed by the defendant. In these studies, as expected, there was no indication of a penalty severity effect and the effect of charge seriousness also disappeared. Thus, this research suggests fairly convincingly that when evidentiary requirements are controlled, neither charge seriousness nor penalty severity affects mock juror verdicts.

In addition to these experimental studies conducted with simulated jurors, some field research has addressed issues related to charge with actual criminal juries. Mock jurors need not worry about the consequences of an errant acquittal, but real jurors might *lower* their subjective threshold for conviction when faced with the possibility of sending a violent perpetrator back into the community. Two early field studies nevertheless produced some support for the severity-leniency effect. Myers (1979) analyzed archival data from 201 jury trials held in Indianapolis and found a measure of crime severity (i.e., the prison sentence in years associated with conviction on the primary charge) to be essentially uncorrelated with the jury's verdict, although a moderate negative relationship emerged when six other case variables were accounted for. A similar pattern was observed in another archival study of 206 criminal trials in Utah where charge seriousness was measured using a five-point scale ranging from Class B misdemeanor to first-degree felony (Werner, Strube, Cole, & Kagehiro, 1985). Similar to the Myers study, the seriousness of the primary charge was only weakly correlated with jury verdict to begin with, but a moderate negative relationship resulted when other case characteristics were statistically controlled. Indeed, in the most inclusive analysis, the seriousness of the primary charge was one of only three variables that explained a significant portion of unique variance in the primary verdict.

In contrast, several more recent field studies suggest real jurors may *lower* their subjective requirements and be more likely to convict when faced with the prospect of errantly returning a violent perpetrator to the community. In two studies that I conducted using post-trial survey data on Indiana criminal juries, the results were not consistent with the severity-leniency hypothesis. In the first study involving seventy-nine jury trials, conviction was somewhat *more* likely when the primary charge was more serious ($r = .27$), but this relationship disappeared when other predictors were controlled for in a larger analysis (Devine, Olafson, Jarvis, Bott, Clayton, & Wolfe, 2004). In the second study with a larger sample of 179 criminal juries, we again found the level of the primary charge to be *positively* related to conviction, and this relationship was slightly stronger when the prosecution's evidence was rated by the judge and/or attorneys to be moderate in strength (Devine et al., 2009). Similar findings emerged from a study conducted by Flowers (2008) using archival data from 293 criminal jury trials held in and around Baltimore. In this study, the seriousness of the primary charge was positively related to three indices of guilt: (1) the odds of conviction on *any* charge, (2) conviction on the *primary* charge, and (3) conviction on a *lesser* charge in the event of acquittal on the primary charge. These relationships held up even when a variety of other case characteristics were controlled. Thus, existing field studies are mixed regarding a severity-leniency effect.

Overall, the research on charge seriousness is rather equivocal and firm conclusions do not seem warranted at this point. The best experimental study by Freedman and his colleagues (1994) seems to show that neither charge seriousness nor penalty severity have reliable effects when the evidence is controlled, but all of the experimental research in this domain is relatively low in external validity and largely confined to trials involving homicide. The five nonexperimental field research studies obviously come with no realism concerns, but they are not capable of disentangling the effects of charge seriousness and penalty severity and have produced some conflicting results. Regrettably, no work has been done on the issue of claim seriousness in civil trial settings. At this point, the safest conclusion seems to be that the seriousness of the charge facing the defendant *may* affect real juries, but more and better research is definitely needed to isolate any effects and determine if they are contingent on other variables.

Alternative Verdict Options: Beyond Guilty or Not Guilty

In many if not most criminal jury trials in the United States, the jury has two options to choose from—not guilty (NG) or guilty (G). On occasion, however, nontraditional alternative verdict options are made available, especially when trials involve a defendant with known or suspected mental illness. Two of these nontraditional verdict options are Not Guilty by Reason of Insanity (NGRI) and Guilty but Mentally Ill (GBMI). Although widely misunderstood by the general public, NGRI verdicts usually result in defendants serving some amount of time in a secure psychiatric institution—occasionally more than if they had been convicted. The GBMI option was designed to reduce the perceived incidence of inappropriate NGRI verdicts by allowing defendants to be held responsible for their actions while acknowledging their impaired mental status. Both NGRI and GBMI are controversial and have received empirical attention from researchers regarding whether and how they draw jurors away from the traditional verdict options.

To begin with, studies with mock jurors consistently show that NGRI and GBMI verdict options are attractive when available (e.g., Finkel & Duff, 1989; Poulson, 1990; Roberts & Golding, 1991; Roberts, Golding, & Fincham, 1987). In general, the presence of nontraditional verdict options has a large impact on verdict distributions, reducing the frequency of both types of traditional verdicts (i.e., G and NG). Of particular note, Savitsky and Lindblom (1986) manipulated the strength of evidence against a defendant with psychiatric

symptoms and provided six-person mock juries with either the two traditional verdict options (G, NG), three options (G, NG, NGRI), or four options
(the other three plus GBMI). The nontraditional verdict options proved
very attractive to mock jurors in general, but their impact depended on the
strength of the evidence. When the evidence against the defendant was very
weak, all juries acquitted in the traditional two-option condition, but 100
percent returned NGRI verdicts in the three-option condition, whereas 75
percent of the juries opted for the GBMI verdict in the four-option condition. In contrast, when the evidence of guilt was very strong, 100 percent of
juries chose the traditional guilty verdict in the two-option condition, but 80
percent did so when NGRI was available in the three-option condition, and
none did in the four-option condition—where all juries chose GBMI. Thus,
assuming some degree of accompanying incarceration, the NGRI verdict
option was a disadvantage to the defendant when the evidence was weak,
whereas the GBMI verdict was an attractive alternative to traditional guilt
(and thus perhaps advantageous) when the evidence of culpability was moderately strong.

Another nontraditional verdict is the "Not Proven" (NP) option, which
is legally equivalent to the traditional NG verdict in terms of securing the
defendant's release. Used in Scotland and a few other jurisdictions, the NP
verdict is intended for cases in which the jury believes the defendant might
be culpable, but the prosecution did not meet the legal standard needed to
convict. Although it has negative moral connotations, NP is the same as an
acquittal for all practical purposes. Similar to the work on NGRI and GBMI
verdicts, the very limited empirical research thus far on the NP option has
focused on whether it draws jurors away from convictions or acquittals, and
the existing data suggest that it tends to attract those who would otherwise
acquit. Smithson, Deady, and Gracik (2007) examined the impact of the NP
option using a clever design with two trial scenarios, one criminal and the
other civil. They had participants make two decisions for each case—first
when the two traditional verdict options were available (i.e., guilty v. not
guilty, liable v. not liable), and then when NP was included as a third option.
The availability of the NP option in both cases lured more mock jurors away
from pro-defense verdicts. Two additional experiments partially replicated
and extended the findings of the first study using two criminal homicide
cases, adding the possibility of convicting on one (or more) lesser included
charges (LIC) related to manslaughter. Both the NP and LIC options had
large effects on the verdict distributions, with the NP option tending to draw
jurors away from NG verdicts and the LIC (manslaughter) option drawing
jurors away from conviction on murder.

One possibility is that the impact of nontraditional verdict options depends on the tilt of the evidence against the defendant. Hope, Greene, Memon, Gavisk, and Houston (2008) investigated the attractiveness of the NP option in two experiments when strength of evidence was varied and found the NP option to have more impact on verdicts when the strength of evidence was moderate. In the first study, as in the Smithson et al. study, the proportion of NG verdicts was significantly reduced when the NP option was available, although the mean rating of probability-of-guilt for jurors who opted for NP was about the same as those who opted for not guilty. A second study employed a different case type, three levels of evidence strength (weak, moderate, strong), and interacting mock juries. The general drawing power of NP over outright acquittal was replicated at all levels of evidence strength for both individuals and juries. However, the only time the NP option made much difference on guilty verdicts was when the evidence strength was moderate—the conviction rate for jurors was 33 percent with two verdict options but only 5 percent when NP was available.

The few studies of alternative verdict options suggest large effects on the distribution of traditional jury verdicts, but whether alternative verdicts lure juries away from guilty or not guilty verdicts very likely depends on other factors such as the strength of the evidence (i.e., pro-defense or pro-prosecution). In particular, when the evidence is only moderately strong, NGRI and NP are probably attractive to those who might otherwise acquit, whereas LIC verdict options and GBMI are more attractive to those who would otherwise convict.

Definition of Key Legal Concepts

Language is dynamic and adaptive. New words continually enter the lexicon while old words drop out or take on new meanings. This fluidity can be problematic when it comes to the legal system, which features a variety of important terms that are assumed to be understood and interpreted by jurors in the same way. Researchers have devoted relatively little attention to the study of how legal terms are interpreted and how their understanding can be influenced by the legal definition provided to jurors. The two legal concepts that have received the most attention are *insanity* and *reasonable doubt*.

Insanity

The concept of insanity has a long history in English law, with its origins in the Roman concept of mens rea (or "guilty mind"). In the last two centuries its legal definition has evolved as the result of several key court cases. The first influential definition in the modern era emerged in the aftermath of an 1843 trial in England involving Daniel McNaghten, with insanity basically viewed as the inability to appreciate the wrongful nature of actions or the consequences of those actions. The *McNaghten* definition migrated to the United States and was adopted by many jurisdictions. Some jurisdictions added an "irresistible impulse" clause that expanded insanity to include persons who could distinguish right from wrong but not conform their behavior accordingly. Another well-known definition was offered by a federal appellate court judge in the 1950s in the *Durham* case (*Durham v. United States*, 1954), which basically held that defendants were not criminally responsible if their actions were the product of mental disease or defect. Continuing controversy and dissatisfaction within the legal community led to formulation of yet another definition in 1962 by the American Law Institute (ALI). This definition featured both a "cognitive" prong associated with appreciating the wrongfulness of behavior as well as a "volitional" prong reminiscent of the irresistible impulse test that dealt with defendants being able to conform their behavior. The ALI definition sanctioned in *U.S. v. Brawner* (1972) was subsequently adopted by many jurisdictions and appears to be the most commonly used definition in the United States today.

None of this wordsmithing appears to make much difference to jurors. A handful of empirical studies have examined the effect of varying the definition of insanity given to jurors, and none of them point toward the legal definition having a noteworthy effect on juror decisions. The first study to systematically vary the legal definition of insanity was part of the Chicago Jury Project in the late 1950s. Rita Simon and her colleagues presented actual venirepersons from two different jurisdictions with the summary of either a housebreaking case or an incest case (Simon, 1967). A third of the mock juries received the McNaughton definition, a third received the Durham definition, and a third received no definition. The results were underwhelming. In the housebreaking case, the conviction rate did not vary much as a function of the definition provided; in the incest case, the conviction rate was somewhat lower for juries given the Durham definition. Subsequent research using similar experimental designs has yielded much the same thing—little impact of the wording associated with "insanity" (Finkel, 1989; 1991; Finkel & Handel, 1988; Finkel, Shaw, Bercaw, & Koch, 1985; Ogloff, 1991).

If the legal definition has only marginal influence on juror decisions in cases involving insanity, then what else explains those decisions? For one, juror attitudes toward the insanity defense apparently play a substantial role. Several measures of attitudes related to insanity have been developed, with the Insanity Defense Attitudes–Revised (IDA-R) instrument being the most promising (Skeem, Eno Louden, & Evans, 2004). Numerous studies have found insanity-related attitudes to be fairly good predictors of mock juror verdicts in insanity cases (Bailis, Darly, Waxman, & Robinson, 1995; Cutler, Moran, & Narby, 1992; Daftary-Kapur, Groscup, O'Connor, Coffaro, & Galietta, 2011; Ellsworth, Bukaty, Cowan, & Thompson, 1984; Homant & Kennedy, 1987; Poulson, Brondino, Brown, & Braithwaite, 1998; Rendell, Huss, & Jensen, 2010; Roberts & Golding, 1991; Roberts et al., 1987; Skeem et al., 2004). For example, across four different case scenarios, Eno Louden and Skeem (2007) found the total score on the IDA-R to correlate strongly with juror verdicts (r values ranging from -.49 to -.61). Some research even suggests juror attitudes toward insanity are more predictive of juror verdicts than the case facts (e.g., Roberts & Golding, 1991). This line of inquiry is of particular interest given the widespread disdain for the insanity defense in the general public, with many laypersons subscribing to a variety of "myths" about the insanity defense and viewing it as simply a ploy for guilty defendants to avoid criminal responsibility (Perlin, 1994; Silver, Cirincione, & Steadman, 1994).

The scant impact of insanity definition, along with the robust relationship between insanity-related attitudes and verdicts, has led researchers to examine how jurors conceptualize the concept of insanity. In a watershed study, Norman Finkel and Sharon Handel (1989) examined jurors' personal construal of the term insanity and found they possess cognitive prototypes of "insane" individuals shaped via their life experiences (e.g., exposure to the media). These prototypes are complex and nuanced, and do not neatly coincide with legal definitions (explaining in part their lack of influence). To better understand insanity-related prototypes, Finkel and Groscup (1997) had participants generate insanity case stories that were typical and atypical, then content-analyzed them. Some features were found to be common across stories and obvious connections were noted with salient media portrayals, but no consistent differences distinguished the stories as a function of their "typicality." Skeem and Golding (2001) took the idea of prototypes one step further by asking former venirepersons to generate a vivid mental image of a typical individual who was not responsible for criminal actions due to mental illness, then describe this "insane" individual's characteristics. The resulting characteristics were sorted into categories and ultimately reduced to three prototypes via multivariate analyses—*severe mental disability* (extreme and chronic impairment; "beastlike"), *moral insanity* (i.e., psychosis and extreme psychopathy), and *mental-state centered* (unable to tell right from wrong at the time of the crime). Insanity prototypes were in turn somewhat related to verdicts in a case involving insanity, with those participants adhering to the mental-state centered prototype being more likely to return a NGRI verdict. On the other hand, Eno Louden and Skeem (2007) compared the relative influence of insanity attitudes and insanity prototypes on case judgments and found prototype category to add little to the explanation of which verdict a juror would favor.

In addition to individual differences in attitudes and prototypes related to insanity, the available verdict options influence juror verdicts as well. As noted already, verdict distributions are drastically affected by the presence/absence of the NGRI and/or GBMI options. A variable that may interact with the availability of nontraditional verdict options is knowledge of the consequences associated with NGRI or GBMI. Two studies have manipulated the provision of outcome information and found juror decisions to be influenced by knowledge of what will befall the defendant if a nontraditional verdict is selected (Whittemore & Ogloff, 1995; Wheatman & Shaffer, 2001). In the Wheatman and Shaffer (2001) study, deliberation produced a tendency for greater leniency among jurors who were informed that NGRI defendants would be held in a state mental health facility pending court approval of release, with only 60 percent of the mock juries that received the outcome information convicting compared with 100 percent of those that did not receive such information.

Standard of Proof

In every jury trial, jurors are instructed regarding the burden of proof that must be met before a verdict can be decided. The ubiquitous standard needed to justify conviction in criminal trials is "beyond reasonable doubt," whereas in civil trials the jury is typically instructed to decide their verdict based on the "preponderance of the evidence." Definitions associated with these concepts represent some of the most critical phrases in the entire legal system.

A rather fundamental question related to the legal standard of proof is how jurors interpret its definition with regard to the level of certainty required to decide against the defendant. To this end, several studies have obtained estimates of the subjective probability needed to justify convictions in criminal trials. In general, jurors report threshold probabilities that many legal scholars consider unacceptably low (e.g., Simon & Mahan, 1971; McCauliff, 1982; Hastie et al., 1983; Dane, 1985; Horowitz & Kirkpatrick, 1996). Specifically, although judges and legal experts have argued that "beyond a reasonable doubt" should correspond to a subjective level of certainty around 90 percent, a number of studies involving different case types and participant types have found that jurors are willing to convict at levels of perceived probability considerably lower than this threshold.

With regard to wording, the phrase "beyond reasonable doubt" is defined differently across court systems. Efforts to explicitly define reasonable doubt are constrained by judges' concerns that saying too much, or telling jurors the wrong thing, may lead to reversal by an appellate court. Some jurisdictions do not elaborate on the phrase, leaving its interpretation completely up to jurors. Over time, various legal definitions for "beyond reasonable doubt" have been used, and some have been the target of scrutiny by the Supreme Court (e.g., *Cage v. Louisiana*, 1990; *Sandoval v. California*, 1994; *Victor v. Nebraska*, 1994). Some definitions have been upheld whereas others have been ruled unconstitutional (Horowitz, 1997). In particular, wording that equates reasonable doubt with "grave uncertainty" or "substantial doubt" has been viewed by the Court as setting the bar too high and violating the defendant's rights. In contrast, defining "beyond reasonable doubt" in terms of possessing an "abiding conviction" or "doubt that would cause a reasonable person to hesitate to act" has been deemed acceptable. Probably the most influential wording that has passed muster with the Court was offered by the Federal Judicial Center in 1987. This definition essentially says that proof beyond a reasonable doubt is proof that leaves a juror "firmly convinced" of the defendant's guilt.

The impact on jurors of varying the definition of "beyond reasonable doubt" has been the subject of a handful of studies. This type of research has generally involved exposing study participants to different verbal definitions of reasonable doubt (or sometimes no definition at all) and then comparing the conviction rates that result. These studies show that different definitions do produce different conviction rates. For instance, in one of the first studies on the topic, Kerr et al. (1976) examined the impact of three different variations of reasonable doubt. In the "lax" condition, reasonable doubt was defined as a serious and well-founded misgiving that was substantial, fair, based on reason, and able to be articulated. In the "strict" condition, the prosecution's burden was identified as convincing jurors to a moral certainty such that they were sure and certain of guilt. If the facts of the case were seen as compatible with any theory other than guilt, reasonable doubt was said to exist and should result in acquittal. A third "undefined" condition used the term "reasonable doubt" but did not elaborate on its nature. After watching a fifty-minute simulated rape trial and deliberating in six-person juries, 11 percent of the lax-condition juries convicted, 27 percent of the undefined-condition juries convicted, and 42 percent of the strict-condition juries convicted.

The impact of wording was also evident in an experimental study conducted by Horowitz and Kirkpatrick (1996), who examined five different verbal definitions of reasonable doubt (including the Federal Judicial Center's "firmly convinced" standard) while varying the strength of evidence (i.e., weak or strong) presented in a murder trial. Mock jurors listened to an audiotape, viewed slides of actors playing the roles, and then deliberated in juries of six persons. The conviction rate for juries was basically unaffected by the definition of reasonable doubt when the evidence was strong. However, when the evidence was weak, the "firmly convinced" definition produced significantly fewer convictions than the other definitions, including the "undefined" condition (0% v. an average of 47% across the other four conditions). Just as importantly, the firmly convinced wording produced the highest reported level of certainty required to justify a guilty verdict prior to deliberation (81%), with all other definitions yielding much lower values (i.e., 50–62%).

Given the promising findings associated with the "firmly convinced" definition of reasonable doubt, Chantal Koch and I (Koch & Devine, 1999) conducted an experiment to compare the "firmly convinced" and "undefined" definitions from the Horowitz and Kirkpatrick (1996) study. We observed no overall difference in the conviction rate for mock juries as a function of how reasonable doubt was defined, but did find that the effect of the wording associated with reasonable doubt depended on the possibility of convicting on a lesser charge (i.e., manslaughter v. murder). When reasonable doubt was defined in terms of being firmly convinced, it didn't make much difference in the conviction rate whether the manslaughter option was available (although "firmly convinced" juries tended to opt for guilt on murder at a higher rate). However, when reasonable doubt was not elaborated, juries convicted eight times more often when they had the option of finding the defendant guilty of manslaughter than when they could only convict on murder (i.e., 64% v. 8%). Overall, we did not observe the "firmly convinced" instruction to produce a lower conviction rate than undefined reasonable doubt as did Horowitz and Kirkpatrick (1996).

In addition to assessing the impact of different ways of verbally defining the concept, some research has found that providing a quantified confidence threshold for "beyond reasonable doubt" may affect jury verdicts. For example, Kagehiro and Stanton (1985) examined the impact of three legal definitions (i.e., "preponderance of the evidence," "clear and convincing evidence," and "reasonable doubt"), along with three required confidence levels quantified in terms of subjective probabilities (i.e., 51%, 71%, 91%). "Clear and convincing evidence" was defined as having a firm belief or conviction regarding guilt, whereas "reasonable doubt" was said to be present when jurors did not feel an abiding conviction, to a moral certainty, in the plaintiff's case. In two studies, the verbal definitions alone did not influence juror verdicts whereas the quantified definitions did, with fewer verdicts for the plaintiff when the level of required subjective confidence was higher. This finding is intriguing, and highlights the need for more research to determine if juror decision making can be improved by providing a standard of proof quantified in terms of subjective confidence.

Why Care about Trial Context?

Trial context variables have a certain innocuous quality to them—why should minor wording issues, what a juror reads in the newspaper months before trial, or an extra verdict option make much difference in the face of the evidence? Nonetheless, large amounts of research now show convincingly that several contextual variables have moderate and consistent effects on juror verdicts—most notably, pretrial publicity, in-court inadmissible evidence (ICIE), nontraditional verdict options, and the wording used to define the standard of proof. Less attention has been paid to why these variables have their effects, but it is likely that trial contextual variables serve to prime or activate existing cognitive structures in the minds of jurors. Pretrial publicity, ICIE, and the charge/claim probably influence juror cognition by activating stored schematic information that is subsequently used to construct mental representations of a trial in addition to evidentiary material. More serious charges may conjure images of violent perpetrators and highlight the risk of sending a dangerous felon back out into the community. Nontraditional verdicts and lesser included charges may prompt the generation or examination of alternative stories that would otherwise receive little or no consideration, and allow for compromises when jurors have difficulty agreeing on a story that fits the evidence. In contrast, based on a lifetime of experience interpreting the behavior of others, jurors probably feel that they have a fairly well-established sense of what it means to be "crazy" (i.e., insane), which could explain why definitions of insanity have little effect. Future research on trial contextual variables should aim to establish the magnitude of their effects, identify the conditions when those effects will be strongest, and find ways to prevent or remediate their influence.

5

Trial Participant Characteristics

Juries are supposed to make decisions based on the evidence—not irrelevant characteristics of the people involved. A long-standing concern of legal scholars and interested observers is that juries do in fact base their decisions, at least at times, on *who* is involved and what they are like. Social scientists have devoted a great deal of empirical attention to this possibility, but isolating the effect of specific participant characteristics is unfortunately not easy to do. Many participants are involved in every jury trial, and they each possess a variety of characteristics that *could* affect jury decisions. Specifically, the attributes of at least seven different types of participants might influence juror or jury decision processes at trial: (1) defendant, (2) victim, (3) plaintiff, (4) juror, (5) judge, (6) prosecuting/plaintiff attorney, and (7) defense attorney. Characteristics of the individuals in these roles that have been studied include their race, gender, age, socioeconomic status (SES), religious affiliation, sexual orientation, physical attractiveness, and a host of personality traits. Some additional characteristics are also relevant to certain roles, such as the defendant's criminal background, courtroom behavior, and demeanor; a juror's previous experience as a juror or crime victim; the nature and severity of the injuries suffered by the victim(s); and the nature of the parties involved in civil trials (e.g., individuals, groups of individuals, or organizations). To complicate matters even further, every jury will consist of multiple jurors, and there are sometimes multiple victims, plaintiffs, and even defendants for them to consider.

The way jurors perceive and categorize trial participants, particularly the defendant, is likely to affect the stories they formulate with the evidence. Jurors will categorize trial participants in terms of their existing person-related categories (i.e., stereotypes) and tend to assume that people possess the characteristics associated with those categories. Categories activated early in the process (e.g., upon first seeing the defendant) should heavily affect what evidence is attended to and how it is interpreted. Jurors thus have access to two sources of information that can be used to construct a narrative story explaining the facts of the case: information acquired at trial through exposure to the evidence, and stored information activated via the social cognitive processes of categorization and attribution.

There are two major types of studies in the voluminous empirical literature on participant characteristics: laboratory experiments involving mock jurors and simulated trials, and archival data analyses of actual jury decisions. Existing studies are not distributed evenly across the set of characteristics either, with considerably more attention devoted to demographic characteristics such as race and gender. Studies are spread unevenly over participant types too, with the vast majority examining characteristics of defendants and (especially) jurors as opposed to victims, judges, or attorneys. Fortunately, enough studies exist on most characteristics to allow for meta-analytic examinations. In particular, Narby, Cutler, and Moran (1993) meta-analyzed the relationship between juror authoritarianism and verdicts; Schutte and Hosch (1997) assessed the relationship between juror gender and verdicts in rape and child sexual abuse cases; and several meta-analyses have been conducted on race (Sweeney & Haney, 1992; Mitchell, Haw, Pfeifer, & Meissner, 2005). One of the broadest meta-analytic examinations was undertaken by Ronald Mazzella and Alan Feingold (1994), who quantitatively summarized the empirical research on physical attractiveness, race, gender, and SES for both victims and defendants (i.e., eight meta-analyses). These meta-analyses provide a good starting point for any summary of the empirical literature and will be emphasized accordingly.

Defendant Characteristics

Some characteristics may have reliable associations across trial contexts because they consistently lead jurors to view defendants in a positive or negative light and therefore serve as the basis for story construction. Sufficient research has been conducted to draw conclusions about several of these characteristics.

Physical Attractiveness

We tend to have positive attitudes toward people and objects that we find physically attractive, and treat that which is beautiful as good (Dion, Berscheid, & Walster, 1972). In legal settings, jurors have been hypothesized to be more favorable toward defendants perceived to be attractive—an *attraction-leniency bias*. Efran (1974) conducted the first published study on physical attractiveness in a legal decision-making context, followed by a stream of others in the next two decades and then a steady trickle after the mid-1990s. Most of these studies have been experimental in nature and involved mock student jurors making decisions as individuals about guilt or sentencing in criminal trials after being exposed to photographs of unattractive or attractive defendants.

Does the physical attractiveness of defendants influence jurors? Mazzella and Feingold (1994) conducted the first and thus far only meta-analysis on the subject using experimental studies in which the physical attractiveness of the defendant was manipulated visually (e.g., via photographs) and judgments of guilt or punishment were obtained. Surprisingly, only seven studies were found that reported an effect of defendant attractiveness on guilt, but twenty-five studies were available for the analysis of sentence. In keeping with the attraction-leniency hypothesis, defendant physical attractiveness had small favorable effects on mock juror judgments of guilt ($d = .19$) and punishment ($d = .12$), although there was considerable variation in the effects for both analyses such that any relationship may depend on other variables. Although the Mazzella and Feingold meta-analysis has generally been interpreted as showing a beneficial effect of defendant attractiveness on criminal juror decisions, it suffers from several limitations that sharply curtail its value. First, and most importantly, only seven studies were available for the most relevant analysis (i.e., attractiveness and guilt judgments). Second, and relatedly, the analyses only included experimental studies where attractiveness was manipulated and thus none of them featured judgments by real jurors. Third, 20 percent of the effects for the analysis involving sentence were treated as zero due to the absence of precise statistical values in the original reports. Fourth, a high proportion of the included studies involved cheating or swindling—case types not commonly heard by juries. Thus, although the Mazzella and Feingold (1994) meta-analysis does point toward a weak attraction-leniency bias for defendant physical attractiveness, it is far from definitive.

Given this, it is useful to consider field studies that were not included in the Mazzella and Feingold meta-analysis as well as research done since then to get a better sense of the effects of defendant attractiveness. Unfortunately, existing field studies do not show a consistent pattern of results and most come with methodological caveats. For example, Stewart (1980; 1985) conducted two studies in which courtroom observers rated the attractiveness of defendants. In both studies, defendants rated as more attractive were more likely to be acquitted, but it is not clear whether all of the cases were decided by juries. Another field study of thirty-eight sexual assault trials yielded only a very modest positive association between juror ratings of defendant attractiveness and a predeliberation verdict preference to acquit (Reskin & Visher, 1986; Visher, 1987), and a similarly weak correlation was reported for juror ratings of defendant attractiveness and "the verdict" in another study (Sannito & Arnolds, 1982). Both of these studies utilized retrospective reports and, in the latter study, it was unclear whether the outcome referred to juror's predeliberation preference or the jury's verdict. Finally, in a fourth field study, my colleagues and I observed fairly weak relationships between mean juror ratings of the defendant's physical attractiveness and their jury's verdicts for the three most serious charges against the defendant—a pattern that held even when the strength of the prosecution's evidence was controlled (Devine et al., 2009).

Results have been similarly mixed in post-1994 experimental studies, with defendant attractiveness tending to produce no effect (Beckham, Spray, & Pietz, 2007) or weak effects that varied according to other variables, such as whether mock jurors deliberated (Patry, 2008), juror processing style (Gunnell & Ceci, 2010), the attractiveness of the victim and the strength of the evidence (Erian, Lin, Patel, Neal, & Geiselman, 1998), and even whether the defendant was smiling (Abel & Watters, 2005). The effect of physical attractiveness has been studied a few times in civil trials, but here again no clear pattern emerges from the findings. This result may be because, in most civil trials, there are *at least* two target individuals to consider—the plaintiff and the defendant. In keeping with this, the effects of defendant attractiveness have been found to depend on other variables such as the processing mode used by jurors (Lieberman, 2002), as well as the attractiveness of the plaintiff and gender of the juror (Wuensch & Moore, 2004). The limited research in civil trial settings thus does not suggest a straightforward effect of defendant attractiveness.

In sum, research on physical attractiveness has been driven by the hypothesis that jurors will act more favorably toward defendants whom they perceive to be attractive. Taken together, the mixed findings suggest a modest leniency bias in favor of physically attractive defendants that probably depends on other variables and appears to be somewhat stronger for judgments of punishment as opposed to guilt. In particular, the physical attractiveness of other trial participants—victims and plaintiffs, most notably—may play a role in some cases, along with the strength of the evidence. Further, some of the inconsistency in research findings is likely due to the fact that physical attractiveness is not an objective quality—it is clearly a perceptual variable with a strong subjective component and will accordingly vary to some extent across jurors. Experimental research has nonetheless taken an objectivist approach thus far—assuming that defendants either are or are not attractive to all jurors—and one explanation for the tepid findings is that study participants have not always appraised the defendant's attractiveness the same as the researchers. Future research on physical attractiveness should examine multiple case types, use deliberating groups, manipulate (or measure) the attractiveness of all focal participants as well as strength of evidence, and account for within-jury differences in the perception of physical attractiveness.

Remorse

There are many aspects of defendant demeanor at trial that could influence jurors, but only one has received concerted attention in the literature—the display of remorse. Niedermeier, Horowitz, and Kerr (2001) argued for the existence of a widespread assumption that remorse is expected when a transgression has occurred, and jurors may react negatively in its absence. Consistent with this view, a large and diverse set of studies has focused on the expression of remorse via defendant facial expressions and shown that remorseful defendants generally *are* treated more leniently (e.g., Bornstein, Rung, & Miller, 2002; Forgas, O'Connor, & Morris, 1983; Gold & Weiner, 2000; MacLin, Downs, MacLin, & Caspers, 2009; Robinson, Smith-Lovin, & Tsoudis, 1994; Rumsey, 1976). Most of these studies featured experimental designs and the use of mock jurors, but an analysis of field data involving nearly 1,200 capital jurors corroborates this finding with real jurors as well (Antonio, 2006). In this latter study, perceptions of the defendant being sorry and sincere were related to predeliberation and first-vote preferences for life without parole, even when legally relevant aggravating factors were statistically controlled.

Although the data clearly support a leniency effect associated with the display of remorse, most studies on the topic have focused on defendant punishment in circumstances where guilt had already been determined or was strongly indicated (e.g., the sentencing phase of capital trials). In situations where guilt has not been established, remorse may be treated by jurors as an indication of culpability and thus have a detrimental effect on defendant outcomes. Consistent with a backlash effect on judgments of guilt, two studies found remorseful defendants to be convicted more often than defendants who did not show remorse (Jehle, Miller, & Kemmelmeier, 2009; Niedermeier et al., 2001). The display of remorse may thus be a double-edged sword for defendants—more likely to result in conviction but also more likely to yield leniency when jurors have a choice about what charge to convict on, or what punishment to hand down.

Prior Criminal Record

Various aspects of a defendant's background might be of interest to jurors as they go about constructing stories out of the evidence, but one characteristic probably stands above the rest—the defendant's past criminal behavior. It is easy to see how jurors might perceive a pattern when it comes to such behavior—if a defendant broke the law before, why would he or she not do so again if it were expedient? The U.S. Supreme Court has acknowledged the possibility that jurors will use information about previous crimes to infer a criminal disposition, and so jurors are usually prevented from learning anything about the defendant's criminal history. The primary exception is when defendants testify, in which case their background is considered relevant to their credibility as a witness and thus may be revealed to jurors. Judges typically issue a limiting instruction telling jurors to use the prior record information only for the purpose of assessing credibility, but whether they in fact abide by this admonition and refrain from making inferences about the defendant's current guilt is an empirical question. A defendant's prior record might also be inferred from what is said (or not said) at trial, or communicated inappropriately through some form of inadmissible evidence.

Regardless of how it happens, jurors who find out that a defendant was convicted of a past crime tend to convict more often in the present case. In one of the first published studies on the topic, Doob and Kirshenbaum (1973) informed half of their mock jurors that the defendant had seven prior convictions for burglary whereas the other half heard nothing about a criminal record. Those who learned of the defendant's lengthy rap sheet returned a considerably higher proportion of guilty verdicts. In a follow-up study, Hans and Doob (1976) found the biasing effect of criminal history to hold for juries, too. They observed little effect of defendant prior record before deliberation (i.e., only a 5% difference in guilty verdict preferences), but a striking difference at the jury level, with a 40 percent conviction rate for juries learning of the defendant's prior conviction as opposed to 0 percent for juries that heard nothing about a previous record.

One aspect of the defendant's criminal history that has received special attention is the degree of similarity between previous offenses and the present charge. The hypothesis here is that jurors will be more likely to convict as similarity increases, presumably because they will infer a proclivity for the defendant to commit a certain kind of crime. Jurors have indeed been found to be more guilt-prone when they learn of previous convictions for charges similar or identical to the present charge, whereas convictions for dissimilar previous offenses have tended to yield weak or negligible effects (e.g., Allison & Brimacombe, 2010; Greene & Dodge, 1995; Lloyd-Bostock, 2000; Sealy & Cornish, 1973; Wissler & Saks, 1985).

For example, Wissler and Saks (1985) found that, despite a limiting instruction in all conditions, defendants with no prior record were convicted less often (43%) than defendants who had a prior conviction of any sort (63%), and defendants with a prior conviction for the present offense were found guilty at a higher rate than defendants previously convicted of a dissimilar offense or perjury (75% v. 53% v. 60%, respectively). Another experimental study by Sally Lloyd-Bostock (2000) manipulated juror knowledge of the existence, similarity, and recency of a previous conviction with regard to a present charge and also produced signs of an effect for prior conviction similarity. Twenty-four versions of a 30-minute videotaped trial were created (eight study conditions x three types of present cases) and shown to 214 jury-eligible community members who deliberated in twelve-person juries. A similar, recent prior conviction produced the highest guilt-likelihood ratings both before and after deliberation, and a slightly elevated (roughly 6% greater) predeliberation preference for conviction relative to the two conditions in which there was no mention of a previous conviction. The latter trend, however, was not statistically significant and basically disappeared after deliberation. One explanation for the fairly weak effect of prior conviction similarity on verdicts is that 66 percent of jurors in the no record condition reported inferring on their own that the defendant had a criminal record.

Not every study has returned an effect for prior convictions, though, and it is unclear whether their anomalous results are due to idiosyncratic aspects of the cases used or other contingency variables that affect the strength of the relationship. In one study, the prior conviction was said to have occurred when the defendant was a juvenile, and jurors were pointedly told that a light sentence had been given at the time (Clary & Shaffer, 1980). In another study, the prior conviction was for perjury and the case involved a claim of negligence in the wake of a farm accident (Tanford & Cox, 1988). A third study produced a typical pattern of results (i.e., higher guilt ratings for a similar previous conviction; no elevation associated with a dissimilar prior conviction), but the differences were not large enough to be significant (Jones & Harrison, 2009). Finally, in the Lloyd-Bostock (2000) study, a dissimilar prior conviction actually resulted in a *lower* estimate of probability-of-commission and fewer guilty verdicts relative to the two conditions where the defendant did not have a previous criminal history.

In addition to the bulk of the experimental research, data from the field also indicate that criminal defendants with prior convictions are more likely to be found guilty. Using information from prosecutorial case files and court records, Myers (1979) analyzed the association between defendant prior convictions and jury verdicts in a sample of 201 jury trials conducted in Indianapolis. In a subset of 134 trials with full case information available, the number of previous convictions involving the defendant was positively correlated with guilty verdicts ($r = .18$), and this variable had a stronger relationship than any other predictor variable in the multivariate analyses. In contrast, a study based on interviews with 331 jurors involved in forcible sexual assault trials yielded no association between juror's predeliberation assessment of the defendant's guilt and actual mention of the defendant's prior criminal record at trial as recorded by courtroom observers (Visher, 1987; Visher & Reskin, 1986). However, several extraneous variables could explain the findings from these field studies, including diverse case types, different levels of analysis, differences in how prior convictions were coded, and whether jurors actually knew of the defendant's record. With regard to the latter, it was not stated in the Myers study whether jurors were made aware of the number of previous convictions for the defendant, whereas in the study by Reskin and Visher, not having a prior record was combined with no mention of it for purposes of the analysis.

One of the best examinations to date of influence associated with the defendant's criminal history comes from the National Center for State

Court's study of 311 non-capital felony jury trials held in four different metropolitan jurisdictions (Givelber & Farrell, 2008). A notable strength of this study was that the researchers were able to determine if the defendant's criminal history was made known to the jury. In the majority of trials (57%), the defendant had a criminal past but the jury did not learn of it; in about a quarter of the cases (23%), the defendant had a criminal record but the jury did find out about it. The results corroborate the experimental findings with mock jurors in that the defendant's prior record was clearly associated with jury verdicts. When the defendant had no prior record, juries convicted in 57 percent of the trials; however, when the defendant had a criminal record and the jury learned of it, the conviction rate rose to 81 percent. Interestingly, in those trials where the defendant had a prior record but the jury was not informed of it, the conviction rate was still 79 percent—almost as high as when the jury was told of the defendant's record. The tendency for juries to convict when they knew of the defendant's prior record persisted even when a variety of other control variables were included in a series of multivariate models. In fact, prior conviction status was the best predictor of jury verdict in the most inclusive statistical model, with juries being four times more likely to acquit defendants who did not have a previous criminal conviction compared with defendants who did. So, in addition to supporting an effect of defendant criminal record in actual jury trials, this study also suggests that jurors may infer the existence of a criminal record even when not directly informed of it.

In contrast, two studies have investigated whether a previous *acquittal* in a criminal trial would be sufficient to trigger a bias against defendants, and this does not appear to be so. In Clary and Shaffer's (1980) study, jurors were not more conviction-prone when informed that the defendant had been acquitted of a similar charge in a previous trial. Manipulating three levels of prior criminal history (no record, prior acquittal, prior conviction) in the context of a bank robbery trial, Greene and Dodge (1995) observed a higher conviction rate for a defendant who had been previously convicted of breaking and entering, compared with a defendant who was acquitted of that charge or a defendant with no criminal history whatsoever. Moreover, mock jurors who learned of the previous acquittal were no more likely to convict than those who were not given any information about a prior record. Being previously acquitted of a crime may therefore not be sufficient to trigger a bias against defendants.

Overall, juries are indeed more conviction-prone if they learn that the defendant has been previously convicted of a crime similar to the present one. This effect appears to be medium in size and very reliable, with good convergence across lab and field studies. The findings are also consistent with the idea that jurors will infer a criminal disposition when they learn that a defendant has committed crimes in the past. The courts are therefore quite right to limit knowledge of the defendant's prior record when it is deemed irrelevant to the current case, as limiting instructions are generally ineffective in preventing the use of such information. At present, the data are insufficient to tell if there are prejudicial effects associated with other types of previous legal system involvement, including having been arrested for a similar crime, acquitted of a similar charge, or convicted of a dissimilar offense.

Socioeconomic Status

Class-related distinctions are a robust and enduring aspect of human society. Although definitions differ somewhat, *socioeconomic status* basically refers to how successful a person has been in society and corresponds fairly closely to the notion of affluence. It has been operationally defined using a diverse array of characteristics including education level, occupation, income, and accumulated wealth (Lieberman & Sales, 2007). There are two primary reasons why defendant SES may influence criminal jury verdicts. First, high-SES defendants might be seen as leading successful lives and having little reason to engage in nefarious behavior that could jeopardize their standing. Alternatively, high-SES defendants might be perceived as having desirable traits and qualities (e.g., intelligent, hard-working, socially adept, honest) that cause jurors to make favorable assumptions about their character and treat them more leniently as a result. In contrast, in civil trials, the *deep pockets hypothesis* holds that jurors will find civil defendants liable for more damages when they are perceived as wealthy (Chin & Peterson, 1985).

Mazzella and Feingold examined the literature on defendant SES in criminal trials in their 1994 meta-analysis. They found only fifteen usable studies that assessed the impact of defendant SES on either judgments of guilt (ten effects) or punishment (thirteen effects), but when they crunched the numbers they did indeed find a tendency for criminal jurors to go easier on high-SES defendants. Such individuals were less likely to be found guilty (d = .15) and given lighter sentences when convicted (d = .15). These modest effects varied somewhat across case type, raising the possibility that the effect of defendant SES depends on the charge. Although consistent with expectations, the Mazzella and Feingold meta-analysis left something to be desired in that relatively few studies were available for analysis, the inclusion criteria for usable studies were not specified (but appear to have been fairly lenient), and there was substantial variation across studies in terms of how SES was manipulated. As such, this meta-analysis is certainly not the final word on the subject.

Subsequent research on defendant SES has produced small effects consistent with the modest values calculated by Mazzella and Feingold. For example, one of the best experimental studies on this topic yielded only a negligible (and nonsignificant) effect of defendant SES on dichotomous judgments of guilt in a vandalism case (Conley, Turnier, & Rose, 2000). Actual veni-repersons from two trial courts in North Carolina watched a realistic trial videotape and then deliberated in juries of six to twelve persons. In addition to the defendant's race (White v. Black), defendant SES (upper class v. lower class) was manipulated by employing two different actors and varying their clothing, housing, family situation, and occupation. In the end, however, defendant SES had little effect on predeliberation or postdeliberation juror verdicts, although a trend was evident whereby low-SES defendants of both races were convicted 3–6 percent more often than high-SES defendants both before and after deliberation.

More recently, the findings of several studies converge on the notion that the effect of defendant SES may depend on other participant characteristics such as race. In a series of experiments with mock jurors, Espinoza and Willis-Esqueda (2008; Willis Esqueda, Espinoza, & Culhane, 2008) manipulated defendant SES (low v. high) along with several other variables. These included the race/ethnicity of the defendant (Mexican American v. White), the race/ethnicity of the defendant's attorney, and the type of case (auto theft v. embezzlement). Defendant SES had no consistent effect on dichotomous guilt verdicts but low-SES Mexican Americans were found guilty more often—and received longer sentences—than low-SES White defendants and high-SES defendants across the two case types. In keeping with an ingroup bias, these effects were not found in the one study using only Mexican American mock jurors.

Research by Pfeifer and Bernstein (2003) also supports a contingency between defendant SES and defendant race. Defendants were convicted more often in two experiments when portrayed as low-SES rather than high-SES, regardless of their race. However, when no information was explicitly provided about the defendant's SES, mock jurors were more likely to assume the Black defendant was low-SES and the White defendant was high-SES. Consistent with this, Black defendants also garnered higher mean guilt scores than White defendants in both studies when no SES information was provided (although the difference only occurred in the second study when participants did not receive specific jury instructions— an unrealistic situation). Collectively, these studies suggest the effect of defendant SES may depend on other variables such as the defendant's race.

There has been very little examination of defendant SES in actual criminal jury trials thus far, but one exception is a study by Adler (1973). Archival data were used to investigate the relationship between defendant SES and jury verdicts using one hundred jury trials (fifty convictions, fifty acquittals). Defendants in the two groups were matched on their age, sex, race, and the specific charge against them, and the National Opinion Research Center's (NORC) occupational prestige scale was used to measure the SES of both defendants and jurors. Although the mean NORC score for defendants found guilty was about the same as those who were acquitted, conviction was more likely as the difference increased between the jurors' mean NORC score and the defendant's NORC score.

Turning to a manifestation of defendant SES—wealth—and its potential role in civil trials, there is little support for the well-known *deep pockets hypothesis* (Greene & Bornstein, 2003). Several archival analyses were the first to reveal an apparent discrepancy in jury awards as a function of whether the defendant in a civil suit was an individual or a corporation (e.g., Chin & Peterson, 1985; Ostrom, Rottman, & Goerdt, 1996), and some early experimental studies found that corporate defendants were assessed greater damages than individual defendants for the same claims (Hans & Ermann, 1989; Wasserman & Robinson, 1980). However, subsequent experimental research distinguished defendant wealth from defendant identity (i.e., individual v. corporation), and this work strongly indicates there is no effect of defendant wealth on damage awards in civil trials (Bornstein, 1994; Greene et al., 2000; Landsman et al., 1998; MacCoun, 1996).

In essence, defendant SES may have a weak general effect on juror verdict preferences in criminal trials that depends somewhat on other variables such as the defendant's race. Defendant wealth in civil trials appears to have no systematic influence on liability decisions or the size of damage awards. The existing empirical database nevertheless has its limits, including an over-reliance on simulation studies and a lack of consensus regarding how SES should be measured. Indeed, one potential explanation for the modest effects of SES observed in some studies is simply a failure to manipulate it well. Despite this, there is sufficient convergence to conclude that jurors will act more favorably toward high-SES defendants in some trial circumstances.

Juror Characteristics
Authoritarianism/Dogmatism

Authoritarianism refers to the degree to which individuals value clear rules, social order, conventional norms, and strong leadership (Adorno, Frenkel-Brunswik, Levinson, & Sanford, 1950). Individuals with high levels of authoritarianism believe strongly in conservative values, support the exercise of power to enforce them, and favor harsh punishment for those who deviate from societal norms. Their thinking also tends to be rigid and inflexible. At trial, jurors with high levels of authoritarianism may have a tendency to perceive criminal defendants as societal deviants who are likely culpable and deserving of harsh sentences. *Dogmatism* is similar to authoritarianism but without the right-wing/conservative political elements (Shaffer & Wheatman, 2000; Rokeach, 1960). Highly dogmatic individuals are seen as rigid in perspective, closed-minded, and morally conventional. These overlapping traits have very similar implications for jury decision making and are treated here together.

Juror authoritarianism was very popular with researchers in the 1970s and 1980s, and more than two dozen studies have now been conducted using several different measures. The first general measure of authoritarianism was created by Adorno et al. in 1950 (i.e., the California F scale—*F* denoting "Fascism"). Focusing on legal settings, Boehm (1968) constructed the Legal Attitudes Questionnaire (LAQ), the first measure of authoritarianism customized for jurors. The LAQ captures respondent attitudes toward constitutional liberties and the rights of accused persons, but has been criticized for its complex structure and questionable psychometric quality. This led to a significant revision of the instrument in 1993 in the form of the Revised Legal Attitudes Questionnaire (RLAQ; Kravitz, Cutler, & Brock, 1993), which has been the most commonly used measure over the last two decades.

Douglas Narby, Brian Cutler, and Gary Moran (1993) conducted a meta-analysis of twenty studies (thirty-two effects) that measured authoritarianism and culpability in criminal settings. Overall, their main analysis revealed a modest positive association between juror authoritarianism and measures of guilt ($r = .16$), with the relationship estimated to be somewhat stronger for measures of legal authoritarianism ($r = .19$) than traditional authoritarianism ($r = .11$). In other words, jurors who scored highly on authoritarianism were more likely to favor convicting criminal defendants or rate them as more culpable. Across the studies, the effects were very consistent and no negative correlations were observed, suggesting the relationship is fairly robust.

Observed effects were however somewhat stronger in studies that were more realistic (i.e., those using live or videotaped trial materials and actual venirepersons or jurors). One caveat associated with the Narby et al. (1993) meta-analysis is the inclusion of ten effects based on an instrument designed to measure general attitudes about the legal system (i.e., the Juror Bias Scale) as opposed to authoritarianism per se. The mean correlation for the nine studies using true legal authoritarianism measures can be calculated from the data reported in their Table 1, and this value ($r = .24$) is actually somewhat stronger than the overall association reported ($r = .16$). Legal authoritarianism may thus be a better predictor of juror verdicts than previously recognized.

Since the 1993 meta-analysis, a few more studies have been conducted on juror authoritarianism, and they add support to the conclusion that legal authoritarianism is associated with juror decisions in criminal cases in general (Butler, 2010; De la Fuente Solana, Garcia, & Tamayo, 1998; Landwehr et al., 2002) and capital crimes in particular. For example, Barnett, Brodsky, and Davis (2004) examined the effect of authoritarianism on capital sentencing decisions using a series of written vignettes which altered the potential mitigating circumstances present in the case. A measure of traditional authoritarianism (i.e., Right-Wing Authoritarianism) correlated positively with the total number of death-penalty decisions meted out across ten vignettes ($r = .17$), whereas Rokeach's measure of dogmatism correlated even more strongly ($r = .28$). In another study, Butler and Moran (2007) supplied an edited and condensed version of an actual case to venirepersons reporting for jury duty in a Florida jurisdiction. Participants were asked to indicate the extent to which fourteen aggravating factors and twelve mitigating factors were present in the evidence and recommend an appropriate sentence. Legal authoritarianism was positively related to the number of aggravating factors endorsed and negatively related to the number of mitigating factors endorsed, and those scoring highly on legal authoritarianism were more likely to choose the death penalty over life in prison.

Another notable feature of the research on authoritarianism (and its dogmatism cousin) is support for impact at the jury level. Bray and Noble (1978) measured mock jurors using a version of the California F scale and classified each one as low, moderate, or high on authoritarianism. Forty-four, six-person juries were then composed of individuals who were either all low or all high on authoritarianism. As expected, high authoritarians were 20 percent more likely to feel the two co-defendants were guilty prior to deliberation, and high-authoritarian juries were 35 percent more likely to convict than low-authoritarian juries and also gave more severe sentences. High-authoritarian jurors also changed their preferred verdict more often than low authoritarians, a finding replicated in another mock jury study involving three separate experiments with both students and venirepersons (Lamberth, Krieger, & Shay, 1982). Three additional studies conducted by David Shaffer and his colleagues show similar evidence of dogmatism's relevance at the jury level. In the first study, the proportion of highly dogmatic jurors was nearly twice as large in the twelve juries that convicted as the six juries that acquitted (Shaffer & Case, 1982). In the second, the only two juries that acquitted in the entire study contained a majority of low-dogmatic members, and there was at least one low-dogmatic juror in the minority of the nine juries that hung, whereas no hung jury had a minority composed of a sole high-dogmatic juror (Shaffer, Plummer, & Hammock, 1986). In the third study, juries with a majority of high-dogmatic members were much more responsive to the presence of a nullification instruction than juries with a majority of low-dogmatic jurors. High-dogmatic juries ended up convicting more often than low-dogmatic juries when the instruction was present but acquitting more often in its absence (Kerwin & Shaffer, 1991).

There has been less interest in the potential effect of juror authoritarianism in civil trials, and only a few studies have been done. Although insufficient to draw any conclusions, their results do not point toward the existence of a reliable effect in this domain. Two studies involving a claim of rape produced no straightforward effects of authoritarianism but rather complex, unpredicted interactions with other variables (Foley & Pigott, 1997a; Schutte, 1994). A third study by Vinson, Costanzo, and Berger (2008) examined relationships between authoritarianism and judgments of liability and punitive damages in three different civil cases, and found that authoritarianism did not significantly predict either trial outcome. This work is especially notable for employing a highly representative sample of community residents, but an older measure of authoritarianism with poor internal consistency may have obscured the relationship.

Pulling this all together, highly authoritarian jurors are somewhat conviction-prone in criminal trials relative to jurors with lower levels of the trait, and this tendency appears to hold at the jury level as well. The impact on jury decisions seems likely to be more pronounced in situations where there are large proportions of jurors who are extreme on this characteristic, and community mores are made salient by the defendant's actions or the judge's instructions. Conversely, authoritarianism seems less relevant in civil trials except perhaps those involving an established source of societal authority (e.g., a governmental agency or a prestigious corporation), but there is insufficient research at present to draw a definitive conclusion.

General attitudes and beliefs about the legal system

Jurors possess diverse backgrounds and life experiences, which in turn are associated with different attitudes and beliefs regarding the trustworthiness of the police, the motives of defendants, the accuracy of witnesses, and the relevance of experts. These attitudes and their underlying cognitive structures may serve as a filter at trial, focusing jurors' attention on some aspects of the evidence while diverting it from others. The study of general attitudes and beliefs about the legal system began in the 1970s as part of the general search to identify personal characteristics that could forecast juror verdicts.

In one of the earliest studies that anticipated many others, Davis, Spitzer, Nagao, and Stasser (1978) measured the beliefs of their student mock jurors regarding the general likelihood that defendants accused of rape were actually guilty. The resulting belief distribution was trichotomized, and each participant classified as pro-prosecution, moderate, or pro-defense. Mock jurors then watched a videotaped mock rape trial and were formed into 120 homogeneous six-person juries on the basis of their belief categorization. As expected, the attitudinal composition of the juries was associated with differences in the conviction rate, with juries composed entirely of individuals with higher baseline estimates of guilt probability more likely to convict. Specifically, pro-prosecution juries convicted about as often as the moderate juries (49% v. 48%, respectively), but the conviction rate for these juries together was almost double that of the juries composed solely of pro-defense jurors (28%).

In 1983 Kassin and Wrightsman offered the Juror Bias Scale (JBS), a measure designed to capture an individual's tendency to systematically favor the prosecution or defense in criminal trials. The twenty-two items on the JBS purportedly measure two separate but related constructs. The probability of commission (PC) sub-scale captures a juror's beliefs about how likely criminal defendants are to have committed a crime. The reasonable doubt (RD) sub-scale assesses the level of subjective certainty needed to (personally) justify convicting a defendant. In other words, the RD sub-scale gets at the extent to which individuals see the burden of proof as falling on the prosecution. The initial published report described a set of three studies that evaluated the predictive validity of the JBS and compared it to that of several other individual-difference constructs (Kassin & Wrightsman, 1983). Consistent with expectations, pro-prosecution jurors reported a lower level of perceived certainty needed to justify conviction and, across three samples of college students and several case types, those who were more pro-prosecution tended to report greater confidence that the defendant was guilty.

The JBS has been the most frequently used measure of general legal attitudes in the empirical literature on juror decision making since 1983, and numerous published studies have found scores on the JBS to predict juror verdict preferences (e.g., Chapdelaine & Griffin, 1997; Cutler, Moran, & Narby, 1992; De la Fuente, De la Fuente, & Garcia, 2003; Dexter, Cutler, & Moran, 1992; Tang & Nunez, 2003; Warling & Peterson-Badali, 2003). Indeed, only two studies have failed to find a significant association between JBS scores and verdict measures, although prosecution-biased jurors did report a lower threshold of certainty for conviction in one study (Kassin & Garfield, 1991), and the other yielded a positive association between JBS scores and juror verdict preferences that was not large enough to be statistically significant (Weir & Wrightsman, 1990). Overall, based on the ten studies identified in the Narby et al. (1993) meta-analysis, the JBS displays a low-moderate association with individual-level judgments of culpability ($r = .17$).

Despite this evidence of predictive validity, there are concerns about the JBS as a measure of legal attitudes. Specifically, the JBS may be deficient in failing to capture the full domain of legal attitudes, and it is not clear that the JBS captures two distinct dimensions. Failure to replicate the expected two-dimensional factor structure led Myers and Lecci to develop a revised version of the JBS and then an entirely new instrument (Myers & Lecci, 1998; Lecci & Myers, 2002; 2008). Their twenty-nine-item Pretrial Juror Attitude Questionnaire (PJAQ) is designed to measure six separate dimensions—conviction proneness, system confidence, cynicism toward the defense, social justice, racial bias, and innate criminality. These PJAQ scale scores correlated well with juror verdict preferences in several studies and explained some variation in guilt judgments over and above scale scores from the JBS and a measure of legal authoritarianism (Lecci & Myers, 2002; 2008). Similarly, Martin and Cohn (2004) argued for the need of a more inclusive measure of legal attitudes and developed the Attitudes Toward the Criminal Legal System (ATCLS). This thirty-eight-item measure assesses perceptions of integrity, competence, and fairness for seven different aspects of the legal system. Five experiments were conducted that demonstrated the reliability and construct validity of the ATCLS, and suggested that authoritarianism and belief in a just world are determinants of legal attitudes.

In short, a consistent relationship has been observed in the literature between legal attitudes and juror verdict preferences. What is less clear is what exactly is captured by the primary existing measure (i.e., the JBS)—authoritarianism, trust in the legal system, cynicism, belief in a just world, or some mix of these things. Concerns about the JBS have led researchers to develop new and more inclusive measures of attitudes about the legal system. A taxonomy of legal system attitudes would be especially beneficial for further research in this domain, along with efforts to compare old and new measures of legal attitudes in terms of their coverage of the domain, reliability, and predictive validity.

Need for Cognition

In the late 1970s and early 1980s, Petty and Cacioppo offered a broad theory of attitude formation and change known as the Elaboration Likelihood Model (ELM; Petty & Cacioppo, 1986) that proposed two potential approaches (or "routes") for processing persuasive communication attempts—systematic and peripheral. *Systematic processing* involves evaluating the coherence and plausibility of arguments based on logic and rationality. Information processing using this approach is relatively slow and effortful. Conversely, *peripheral processing* relies heavily on the use of mental shortcuts and rules-of-thumb to evaluate arguments. As such, it is quicker and easier than systematic processing and the default approach used by people most of the time. Which approach is adopted by an individual in any particular situation is theorized to be determined partly by the decision context (such as the decision's importance and its reversibility) and partly by the decision maker's enduring dispositional tendencies. With regard to the latter, Cacioppo and Petty (1982) argued that people differ in the extent to which they enjoy cognitive activity and are willing to engage in it. In other words, other things being equal, people with a strong *need for cognition* (NC) will be more likely to use systematic processing than individuals with low NC. Research supports the utility of the NC construct in a variety of decision-making contexts (Cacioppo, Petty, Feinstein, & Jarvis, 1996).

In the courtroom, the ELM implies that jurors may adopt different approaches to evaluating the evidence, with some jurors basing their decisions on systematic processing while other jurors employ quicker and easier peripheral processing. Specifically, NC should have implications for how much jurors will process trial evidence, although not necessarily their belief about the appropriate verdict, with high-NC jurors likely to ponder and scrutinize the evidence more than low-NC jurors. In particular, high-NC jurors may be more likely to see weaknesses or gaps in the evidence, be better able to grasp underdeveloped connections, and understand the ramifications of certain pieces of evidence.

Accordingly, a first wave of research on juror NC tested the notion that high-NC jurors analyze the evidence more thoroughly than low-NC jurors and are more sensitive to logical flaws in either side's case (DeWitt,

Richardson, & Warner, 1997; Graziano, Panter, & Tanaka, 1990; Kassin, Reddy, & Tulloch, 1990). A second wave of research examined the role of juror NC in processing expert testimony, which tends to be complex and requires effort to follow (Bornstein, 2004; McAuliff & Kovera, 2008; Leippe, Eisenstadt, Rauch, & Seib, 2004). Two studies in particular suggest that high-NC jurors are indeed better able to appreciate variation in the quality of scientific research presented by expert witnesses than low-NC jurors. In a civil trial featuring allegations of lead poisoning, Bornstein (2004) separately manipulated the presence of anecdotal evidence and experimental evidence in the testimony of the defense expert. In contrast to low-NC jurors, high-NC participants were unaffected by the presence/absence of the low-validity anecdotal evidence. In another civil case, McAuliff and Kovera (2008) predicted high-NC jurors would be more sensitive to flaws in the evidence presented by a plaintiff's expert witness in a gender discrimination case. Three variables pertinent to the quality of the expert's research were manipulated within a trial summary: ecological validity of the research setting (external validity), publication status (general peer acceptance), and inclusion of a control group (internal validity). Although the ecological validity and publication status of the research had no general effects, high-NC jurors who read about the research featuring a control group were nearly four times more likely to find in favor of the plaintiff than jurors in other conditions.

One intriguing research question yet to be fully explored is the idea that high-NC jurors are more influential in deliberation. Only two studies by Shestowsky and her colleagues have studied juror NC with research designs that involved participant interaction, and their results are somewhat surprising. Using dyads primed to prefer different verdicts in a negligence case, results of the first study were entirely in accord with expectations—participants with higher NC scores than their partner were more successful at changing their partner's view of the correct verdict (Shestowsky, Wegener, & Fabrigar, 1998). In a second study involving four-person mock juries, high-NC jurors were more active, assertive, and persuasive than low-NC as rated by themselves, jury-mates, and independent observers (Shestowsky & Horowitz, 2004). High-NC jurors also objectively spoke more than low-NC jurors but, surprisingly, were *not* judged to offer better arguments to support their views and were less likely to change their verdict preference than low NC jurors. Finally, high-NC jurors showed less sensitivity than low NC-jurors to the quality of arguments they encountered. This study suggests that high-NC jurors may serve the role of active persuader during deliberation while low-NC jurors play the part of quiet contemplator.

To summarize, no one is arguing that juror NC should be systematically related to juror decisions, and no such pattern has been observed. However, NC should affect a juror's willingness to scrutinize and analyze trial evidence, and may also play a role in terms of who influences who during deliberation. High-NC jurors may be more sensitive to the strength of the evidence in general and the quality of expert testimony in particular. Observed effects have been fairly small and most existing work has been conducted in settings with relatively low external validity, but at least there is a good, well-established measure of NC available for use (Cacioppo, Petty, and Kao, 1984). Additional studies of juror NC are needed that involve deliberating groups and characteristics of the evidence such as its strength and complexity.

Attributional Tendencies

One thing jurors often must do, directly or indirectly, is decide what happened—and why. Social psychologists have identified several traits relevant to how people perceive the causes and consequences of behavior, and the two that have received the most attention from jury researchers are *locus of control* (LOC) and *belief in a just world* (BJW). Conceived by Julian Rotter (1966) as part of his social learning theory of personality, LOC refers to a general tendency for people to attribute behavior to either internal (dispositional) or external (situational) causes. People with an internal LOC tend to see the behavior of others as planned, intentional, and purposeful, whereas those with an external LOC tend to view behavior as heavily driven by nonvolitional sources such as fate, luck, or the actions of others. Conversely, BJW refers to a systematic tendency to view the world as a fair place where people get what they deserve and deserve what they get. According to Lerner (1970; 1980), BJW allows us to avoid the unsettling conclusion that bad things happen to good people (and vice versa). In essence, both LOC and BJW represent aspects of a belief system that helps people to see life as fair, orderly, and predictable, as opposed to arbitrary and inexplicable.

In the context of jury trials, LOC and BJW may influence how jurors process trial-related evidence and construct stories. Specifically, jurors with an internal LOC might be more likely to view defendants as responsible for their own behavior (and thus more culpable) than jurors with an external LOC. Similarly, jurors with strong BJW might be more inclined to feel that events played out as they should and the parties involved got what was coming to them. Along those lines, studies in a variety of contexts have shown that high levels of BJW are associated with "blaming the victim," or viewing victims as responsible for their own suffering. However, studies of LOC and

BJW in juror decision making have produced weak and scattered effects that are difficult to reconcile (e.g., Beckham et al., 2007; Butler & Moran, 2007; Foley & Pigott, 1997a; Foley & Pigott, 2000; Follingstad, Polek, Hause, Deaton, Bulger, & Conway, 1989; Osborne, Rappaport, & Meyer, 1986; Phares & Wilson, 1972; Pope & Meyer, 1999; Sosis, 1974; Vinson et al., 2008; Weir & Wrightsman, 1990). On the whole, this research does not lend credence to the idea that BJW and LOC play a major role in shaping juror decisions.

Unfortunately, it is difficult to draw any conclusions about the role of LOC or BJW from the empirical literature for several reasons. First, LOC and BJW have typically been measured with instruments that have questionable psychometric qualities (i.e., Nowicki & Duke, 1983; Rotter, 1966; Rubin & Peplau, 1975). Second, they have been analyzed using statistical practices that result in the systematic underestimating of relationships (e.g., dichotomizing continuous measures). Third, there is theoretical ambiguity regarding *who* will be the focus of jurors' attributional tendencies. Many trials, especially civil, involve multiple actors, and jurors could take the perspective of any one of them (e.g., defendant or the victim). Jurors might not all focus on the same actors either. Fourth, LOC and BJW are conceptually similar and may overlap with each other (Furnham & Procter, 1989; Martin & Cohn, 2004). Specifically, high BJW may well be an offshoot of an internal LOC.

Gender

Gender is very salient in society, and many people (including writers, stand-up comedians, judges, attorneys, and jurors) have strong views about how men and women differ. Based on stereotypes that portray women as generally more empathetic, caring, and compassionate than men, some have argued that female jurors will be more sympathetic toward the defense in criminal trials and more generous toward plaintiffs in civil trials. Others have argued that male and female jurors tend to be more sympathetic to same-sex defendants. Fortunately, there is no shortage of relevant data, as the gender of participants is far and away the most commonly measured predictor variable in the domain of jury decision making. Whether treated as a focal variable or recorded merely for reporting purposes, literally hundreds of jury studies have measured participant gender. Unfortunately, these data have not always been analyzed when collected and results not always reported when the data were analyzed. Formal hypotheses or even explicit expectations regarding participant gender are actually rather rare.

So what does the huge empirical literature show with regard to juror gender? For starters, it definitely does not support the proposition that women will tend to be overly sympathetic to criminal defendants and civil plaintiffs (Baldwin & McConville, 1979; Devine et al., 2009; Fulero & Penrod, 1990; Hastie et al., 1983; 1998). It also does not suggest that jurors will systematically favor defendants of the same gender, although a few studies have observed this pattern to hold for jurors (e.g., Stephan, 1974) or juries (e.g., Nagel & Weitzman, 1972). What is much more notable is the *rarity* of interactions involving juror gender and defendant gender that would signify the existence of a same-gender leniency effect. One factor that would complicate any such leniency effect would be the existence of participants at trial other than the defendant—most notably, victims and/or plaintiffs. It is unclear in these situations who jurors would identify with more, or whether there might even be higher-order interactions. Thus, the existence of competing roles (e.g., victim) and a lack of supporting data combine to raise doubt that a reliable same-gender leniency effect exists with regard to defendants.

In contrast, it is now overwhelmingly clear that there *is* an effect of juror gender on preferred verdicts, but it varies by the type of case. Specifically, dozens of studies have shown that female jurors are more likely than male jurors to favor conviction in trials that involve crimes of a sexual nature with child or female victims. Focusing only on cases involving rape or child sexual abuse, Schutte and Hosch (1997) conducted a meta-analysis of the relationship between juror gender and juror verdicts, and found gender to be moderately correlated with individual verdicts across seventeen studies in child sexual abuse cases ($r = .21$) and modestly correlated in nineteen studies involving rape ($r = .13$). In both analyses, female jurors were more likely to convict than males, and remarkably no study produced the opposite result. The typical difference is small-moderate in magnitude but extremely consistent, with female jurors usually being 5–15 percent more likely to favor conviction than male jurors in these types of cases. Presumably, the heightened preference for conviction is due to female jurors being more likely to identify and empathize with the victim, perhaps in part because women are more likely to be the victim of sexual crimes and continue to be more likely than men to be primary caregivers for young children. That said, the Schutte and Hosch meta-analysis was confined to only two case types, focal analyses involved a fairly small number of studies for both case types, and almost all of the research used student mock jurors.

Juror gender has not been examined nearly as often in other types of cases with the possible exception of sexual harassment claims in civil trials, where a meta-analysis has shown that women tend to view a wider variety of behaviors as constituting sexual harassment than men (Rotundo, Nguyen,

& Sackett, 2001). However, enough studies have been done to conclude that male jurors are more likely to prefer a sentence of death in capital trials. Men have consistently been found to have attitudes that are more supportive of the death penalty, which in turn are moderately related to verdicts in capital cases (e.g., O'Neil, Patry, & Penrod, 2004). Women are also more likely to be excluded during death qualification in capital cases (Butler, 2007; Lynch, 2009), a finding that suggests they would be less likely to vote for death in a capital trial if seated on the jury. Finally, and most directly, male jurors have been found to vote for death in specific cases more often than female jurors (e.g., Beckham et al., 2007; Lynch & Haney, 2000; 2009; Miller & Hayward, 2008). In one of the best of these studies, 60 percent of male jurors preferred a sentence of death prior to deliberation as opposed to 51 percent of female jurors (Lynch & Haney, 2009).

Overall, female jurors are more likely to prefer conviction in criminal cases involving rape or child sexual abuse and more likely to side with plaintiffs in cases involving sexual harassment, whereas male jurors are more likely to prefer death sentences in capital trials. Future research that systematically examines the impact of juror gender in deliberating groups using a variety of case types (e.g., robbery, theft, battery, auto accidents) would be beneficial.

Juror and Defendant Race

No characteristic of trial participants has received more attention from legal scholars and jury researchers than race. In general, defendants perceived to be similar to jurors have been expected to be treated more leniently—i.e., a *similarity-leniency effect*. However, one circumstance where perceived similarity might not produce a leniency effect is when an ingroup defendant has clearly done something wrong (Marques, 1990; Kerr, Hymes, Anderson, & Weathers, 1995). In cases where the evidence of wrongdoing is overwhelming, perceived similarity might actually work *against* the defendant. Jurors may naturally want to think highly of an ingroup defendant, but to do so would be inconsistent with the positive qualities associated with the ingroup if the defendant has obviously done something despicable. Therefore, to maintain a positive attitude toward one's ingroup, jurors may psychologically distance themselves from a "wayward" member and adopt an inordinately harsh and punitive attitude toward the individual—in effect, ceasing to view them as an ingroup member. This potential race-related backlash in the face of strong evidence has been referred to as the *black sheep effect* (Marques, 1990; Marques, Yzerbyt, & Leyens, 1988).

A large empirical literature now exists on participant race in the context of legal decision making, consisting primarily of two types of studies:
archival analyses of the sentencing decisions of actual juries in death-penalty
trials, and experimental studies using mock jurors in which the race of the
defendant was manipulated and juror race was measured. Most studies in
this domain have focused on the race of jurors and/or defendants, although
some have also measured or manipulated the race of victims and a few studies manipulated the race of one or more of the attorneys. The first wave of
research on race in the 1970s and early 1980s failed to produce indication
of a strong association between race and verdicts. This work included several well-known experimental studies that found no appreciable correlation
between the race of mock jurors and their individual verdict preferences
(e.g., Hastie et al., 1983; Penrod, 1990), several field studies yielding low correlations between the race of actual jurors and their reported predeliberation
verdict preferences obtained via post-trial questionnaire (Mills & Bohannon,
1980; Moran & Comfort, 1982; 1986; Reskin & Visher, 1986), and some archival research showing that jury verdicts were not associated with defendant
race or jury racial composition (Baldwin & McConville, 1979; 1980; Deosaran, 1981). Based on the underwhelming findings from this first wave of
studies, a frequent conclusion of scholarly reviewers has been that race is not
reliably associated with juror or jury decisions.

Meta-Analyses

Since the 1980s, research on race in trial settings has continued to accumu-
late, allowing for three meta-analyses that examine the effect of juror and/or
defendant race in experimental studies (Mazzella & Feingold, 1994; Mitchell,
Haw, Pfeifer, & Meissner, 2005; Sweeney & Haney, 1992). The three meta-
analyses differ in terms of their research questions, inclusion criteria, and
outcome measures, but collectively they suggest juror decisions are influenced somewhat by race.

Sweeney and Haney (1992) conducted the first and narrowest meta-analytic examination of racial bias in the experimental literature. They were
interested in learning if White mock jurors would display an outgroup bias
against Black defendants, and so limited their focus to studies in which
White mock jurors made sentencing decisions and the race of the defendant
was manipulated. An effort was made to isolate and examine effects associated solely with White mock jurors, but this was not always possible to do
and so some included studies featured samples with participants whose race
was unspecified (but presumably mostly White). Based on fourteen studies

(nineteen effect sizes) in which defendant race was manipulated (i.e., White v. Black), their overall analysis identified a small but significant bias (d = .17) against African American defendants for sentencing decisions. Unfortunately, this study is plagued by nearly every major concern that can arise in meta-analysis, including a relatively small number of effects, inclusion of data sets with unknown proportions of non-focal participants, the presence of an outlier study that dwarfed the others in terms of sample size, a high percentage of imprecise ("nonsignificant") effects that were estimated to be zero (42%), and limited scope in the primary studies (i.e., White decision makers, sentencing decisions, and mostly cases involving rape). In fact, acknowledging the confound introduced by studies in which the race of participants and/or victims was unknown, the authors concluded that their initial estimate was "misleadingly small" and recalculated it using only those studies that explicitly specified juror and victim race (presumably White in most instances). Doing so produced a stronger and arguably better estimate of the effect of White juror bias against Black defendants for sentencing decisions (d = .26).

Mazzella and Feingold (1994) conducted a second meta-analysis of the mock juror literature on race using broader criteria. Specifically, they included studies of African American as well as White participants, and studies obtaining judgments of guilt in addition to those that measured sentencing decisions. Their search yielded twenty-nine usable studies (sixty-three effect sizes) and a total sample size over twice as large as the earlier meta-analysis. They found essentially no effect of defendant race on guilt judgments (d = .01) and, in contrast to Sweeney and Haney's meta-analysis, observed only a weak effect on sentencing decisions (d = .06). Unfortunately, this study did little to improve upon Sweeney and Haney's work and took a step backward in at least one important respect by not attempting to account for the race of the jurors. In keeping with this heterogeneity, the observed effects were scattered enough to suggest the existence of moderator variables, and a follow-up analysis indicated that racial bias may vary by case type. Although intriguing, it is difficult to interpret the results of the Mazzella and Feingold meta-analysis on defendant race because of the fundamental confound involving the race of mock jurors.

The limitations and discrepant results of the two previous meta-analyses—along with another decade's worth of research—led Mitchell et al. (2005) to meta-analytically examine the issue of racial bias in jury decisions yet a third time. In contrast to the earlier meta-analyses, they adopted a theory-driven view of racial bias that took into account the race of both the juror and defendant, defining bias as the harsher treatment of a defendant who is of a different race than the juror (i.e., an outgroup member). Further, to be included, studies had to experimentally manipulate the race of the defendant *and* report separate effects for each juror race. Overall, thirty-four usable studies (forty-six effects) were found involving judgments of guilt and sixteen usable studies (twenty effects) for sentencing decisions. The primary analyses produced larger estimates of bias than earlier work ($d = .09$ for verdicts; $d = .19$ for sentencing decisions), indicating small detrimental effects against defendants when jurors were of a different race. Especially intriguing was a breakdown of effects by defendant *and* juror race, with ten studies involving African American mock jurors and White defendants producing considerably larger estimates of outgroup bias for both verdict ($d = .43$) and sentencing decisions ($d = .73$) than the thirty-six studies involving White mock jurors and African American defendants ($d = .03$ for verdicts and $d = .10$ for sentencing). In other words, these analyses suggest a slight similarity-leniency effect for White jurors but a rather strong one for African American jurors.

The results of the Mitchell et al. meta-analysis imply juror race and defendant race need to be considered jointly and that when this is done, there is more coherence in the empirical literature. However, one limitation attached to the findings of all three meta-analyses is that they are based on the judgments of non-interacting mock jurors. It is thus important to consider the findings of two other types of studies: (1) experimental research with interacting mock juries where defendant race is manipulated, and (2) field research on real juries where the race of defendants and jurors was measured.

Research on Deliberating Groups

Some experimental research has addressed the possibility of racial bias in the context of interacting juries. Most of these studies involved manipulating defendant race and measuring mock juror race, although a few studies were able to employ mock juries assembled with specific racial compositions. Strength of evidence has sometimes been manipulated as well. In general, findings from this research are consistent with a similarity-leniency effect at the jury level in showing that defendants are disadvantaged when they are a different race than the majority of jurors. For example, using an armed robbery case, Perez, Hosch, Ponder, and Trejo (1993) found that six-person, White-majority juries convicted a Hispanic defendant at a much higher rate than a White defendant, whereas Hispanic-majority juries showed a similar pattern of outgroup bias but to a lesser degree. Chadee (1996) had mock jurors from Trinidad watch the videotaped trial of a defendant of African descent accused of murdering a person of East Indian descent. Juries were composed so that two-thirds of their members were from one of the ethnic groups while the remaining one-third were members of the other group. Consistent with a similarity-leniency effect, African-descent jurors on East Indian–majority juries tended to convict *less* often than East Indian jurors when the evidence was weak, but this trend all but disappeared when the evidence was strong. Conversely, African-descent jurors on African-majority juries convicted *more* frequently than East Indian–descent jurors when the evidence was strong—a finding consistent with a black sheep effect.

One of the best studies of the effects of juror race on the deliberation process was conducted by Samuel Sommers, who manipulated the racial composition of mock juries in a simulated sexual assault trial with a Black defendant (Sommers, 2006). Half of the participants deliberated in homogeneous all-White juries whereas the other half deliberated in racially diverse juries that included four Whites and two Blacks. In keeping with the similarity-leniency effect, Black mock jurors voted to convict about half as often as White mock jurors in general, although White jurors in diverse juries were less likely to convict than White jurors in all-White juries *even before deliberation*. Unfortunately, 41 percent of the twenty-nine juries could not reach unanimity after an hour of deliberation, making it difficult to ascertain jury-level effects. Perhaps more importantly, analyses of the content of group discussions indicated that racially diverse juries deliberated *better* than homogeneous juries. Diverse juries talked longer, discussed more case facts, made fewer factual errors, left fewer factual inaccuracies uncorrected, and tended to mention "missing" evidence more often. Most of these improvements could be traced to the behavior of White participants, suggesting White jurors may modify their behavior depending on the racial composition of their jury.

In contrast to the experimental research, the few field studies able to obtain the racial composition of the jury along with the race of the defendant in non-capital cases have yielded little indication of race-related effects (Baldwin & McConville, 1980; Daudistel, Hosch, Holmes, & Graves, 1999). For instance, in one excellent study, Hannaford-Agor and her colleagues (2002) obtained data on over three hundred jury trials from four different metropolitan areas. Black jurors reported being more lenient on their first vote during deliberation when deciding the fate of minority defendants, but the overall effect was due largely to an inordinately high rate of acquittal voting by Black jurors in one jurisdiction (Washington, DC) when minority defendants were facing drug-related charges, and it tended to wash out during deliberation. Taylor and Hosch (2004) examined data from 418 non-capital jury trials held in two different counties in Texas and estimated a critical control variable, strength of evidence, from case files. This field study—the only one yet to formally test for the presence of race-related interaction effects at the jury level—yielded no support for a similarity-leniency effect, outgroup-punitiveness effect, or a black sheep effect. Consistent with this, in one of my studies involving a sample of criminal jury trials in Indiana, we observed only modest correlations between jury verdicts and several indicators of jury-level racial composition (Devine et al., 2009). With regard to similarity-leniency, the number of jurors who matched the defendant on race and/or race-gender was only weakly correlated with jury verdicts regardless of the prosecution's strength of evidence (low, moderate, or strong). In sum, these field studies suggest that jury racial composition is not strongly associated with jury verdicts in non-capital trials, but all three likely suffered from a lack of variation with regard to jury racial composition that may have obscured any real relationship. For example, in our study (Devine et al., 2009), no jury contained a non-White majority nor did any consist entirely of White jurors. This range restriction in jury racial composition would make it difficult to discern *any* race-related effects that exist.

Racial Bias in Capital Trials

A fair amount of research on participant race has been conducted in the context of capital trials where the jury must decide if the defendant is guilty and, if so, whether the death penalty is to be given. In sharp contrast to studies involving mock jurors, data from actual juries provides very strong evidence of racial bias against African American defendants (Butler, 2008; Lynch, 2009). Various archival studies conducted at different times in different states and by different researchers uniformly indicate African Americans are convicted of capital crimes at a higher rate and sentenced to death at a higher rate if convicted. Some of the best research on this topic was done by David Baldus and his colleagues, who used sophisticated multivariate statistical procedures to analyze jury decisions from several jurisdictions (e.g., Georgia, Pennsylvania, Nebraska). An impressive feature of this research is the statistical control of many confounding variables that could have been responsible for observed discrepancies (e.g., the number of persons killed, the number and nature of aggravating and mitigating factors present). Even when a boatload of confounding variables was accounted for in the analysis, African American defendants were consistently more likely to receive the death penalty than White defendants, a discrepancy magnified when an African American was charged with killing a White victim (e.g., Baldus, Pulaski, & Woodworth, 1990; Baldus, Woodworth, Zuckerman, Weiner, &

Broffit, 1998). Although the racial composition of the jury was not available for any of these studies, it is probably safe to assume that most capital juries in the United States are composed of White majorities.

Fortunately, some fantastic field research on real juries is available to corroborate the findings of the archival analyses regarding the influence of race in the sentencing phase of capital jury decision making. Using data from 1,155 juror interviews associated with 340 death-penalty trials held in fourteen states, Bowers, Steiner, and Sandys (2001) examined the relationship between jury racial composition and jury verdicts. They found two jury-level effects involving juror race in seventy-four cases involving a Black defendant and a White victim—a "White male dominance" effect and a "Black male presence" effect. The White male dominance effect referred to a marked 41 percent increase in the probability of a death sentence when there were five or more White males on the jury compared with when there were fewer (i.e., rising from 30% to 71%). The Black male presence effect corresponded to a 34 percent greater probability of a death sentence when no Black male was on the jury compared with when there was one or more Black males present (i.e., rising from 38% to 72%). The "White male dominance" and "Black male presence" effects were independent of each other but limited to cases in which Black defendants were charged with killing a White victim—jury racial composition displayed little relation to jury sentencing decisions in cases where the defendant and victim were of the same race. A subsequent analysis by Brewer (2004) of data from 865 jurors in the Capital Jury Project (CJP) database revealed a potential explanation for these findings, with Black jurors being more receptive to mitigating factors and reportedly giving them greater weight than White jurors. Although the number of Black jurors in the CJP database was relatively small, there was a tendency for jurors of the same race as the defendant and victim to be more likely than other-race jurors to prefer the death penalty—a finding consistent with the black sheep effect.

Finally, a recent experimental simulation conducted under very realistic conditions corroborates many of the findings of the archival and interview research (Lynch & Haney, 2009; 2011). This study utilized professionally developed trial materials portraying the sentencing phase of a capital trial, and a representative sample of 539 community residents who deliberated in one hundred, six-person juries. Using different actors, four versions of the 55-minute videotape were created so as to systematically vary the race of the defendant (White v. Black) and race of the victim (White v. Black). Juries displayed a "punitiveness shift" over the course of deliberation, with more juries opting unanimously for a death sentence compared with the number that had a majority of their members preferring death prior to deliberation. Non-Whites were less likely to prefer the death penalty than Whites, and the number of White male jurors on the jury was significantly associated with the likelihood of the jury opting for the death penalty. Basically, the more White males on the jury, the greater the likelihood of a death sentence. Content analysis of the deliberations suggested this was due in large part to the differential evaluation of mitigating factors, with White males giving less weight to these when the defendant was Black.

Summary: Juror and Defendant Race

In general, the research to date is consistent with a similarity-leniency effect when it comes to race and the judgments of White and Black jurors, particularly in capital cases where a Black defendant is charged with killing a White victim. This conclusion coincides with the most recent (and best) meta-analysis of the experimental literature on juror race (Mitchell et al., 2005), high-quality experimental studies of interacting mock juries (e.g., Lynch & Haney, 2009), extensive archival research (Baldus et al., 1983; 1998), and excellent interview research with capital juries (Bowers et al., 2001). That said, the magnitude or even occurrence of a similarity-leniency effect may depend somewhat on other variables. In particular, similarity-leniency appears more likely in serious cases where jurors must make value-laden decisions—i.e., the sentencing phase of death-penalty trials—and may be stronger for some groups (i.e., Black jurors). Conversely, similarity-leniency effects may be weaker (or even reversed) when the evidence against the defendant is very strong (i.e., the black sheep effect).

Reflections on Effects Related to Trial Participant Characteristics

Several conclusions emerge from the extensive empirical literature on participant characteristics. First, research to date has not been guided strongly by theory, although recent work in the area of race has been shaped by the similarity-leniency hypothesis and the black sheep effect, which represents progress. Second, a wide variety of individual difference variables have been identified and studied, but little effort has been made to determine which ones are most important and whether they interact with one another. Lack of agreement regarding how to conceptualize, measure, and analyze participant characteristics has produced a large and unruly empirical literature that led some reviewers to throw up their hands and conclude that few if any participant characteristics are meaningfully associated with juror verdict preferences. Some focal characteristics are similar in nature and may even tap the same underlying constructs (e.g., authoritarianism and dogmatism; belief in a just world and internal locus of control). Third, despite these obstacles, meta-analyses on the characteristics of trial participants and juror-level decisions have revealed small-moderate effects for several participant characteristics on juror verdict preference; this suggests that some do play a role in jurors' thinking. Fourth, participant-related effects almost certainly depend on other variables, including the nature of the charge/claim, characteristics of other participants (e.g., victim, plaintiff), and the strength of the evidence. Moving forward, our theoretical understanding of the impact of trial participant characteristics will benefit from the development of a comprehensive taxonomy of important participant characteristics, and theory-based examinations of the interactions involving participant variables, case type, and evidence strength.

6

The Evidence

How much do juries *really* base their decisions on the evidence? If there were one question that jury scholars could ask of a real-life Magic Eight Ball, it would probably be that. Fortunately, there are plenty of data available that address this issue. Although doubted by some legal critics and commentators, the strongest determinant of the jury's ultimate decision in most cases is undoubtably the strength of evidence (SOE) against the defendant. In dozens of experimental studies with mock jurors, SOE has been systematically varied by providing, withholding, or altering the evidence presented to study participants. These manipulations typically have a substantial impact on resulting decisions, often producing differences in conviction rates of 20–60 percent (Devine et al., 2001).

Numerous field studies corroborate the conclusion that SOE has a strong impact on jury decisions in showing that ratings of evidence strength are moderately to strongly correlated with jury verdicts. For instance, when presiding judges are asked to indicate their opinion of the appropriate verdict for jury trials heard in their courtrooms (e.g., Kalven & Zeisel, 1966; Diamond et al., 2003; Eisenberg et al., 2005; Heuer & Penrod, 1994b), judges and juries generally agree on the appropriate verdict in 70–80 percent of trials, suggesting juries do indeed base their decisions on the evidence (assuming that judges are doing the same). Archival research has also revealed robust associations between the presence/absence of legally relevant factors (i.e., aggravating and mitigating) and jury judgments in the sentencing phase of death penalty trials (e.g., Baldus et al., 1983; 1998). More directly, ratings of the prosecution's SOE provided by judges and/or trial attorneys have also been found to be moderately-strongly associated with criminal jury verdicts across a variety of geographically diverse jurisdictions (e.g., Devine et al., 2009; Hannaford, Hans, & Munsterman, 2000; Hannaford-Agor et al., 2002). Thus, field studies involving actual juries complement the findings of the experimental research with mock juries, and together the two streams converge on the conclusion that SOE has a large impact on jury decisions. Nonetheless, we still lack a good theory explaining what makes evidence "strong" from the jurors' perspective as well as a general-purpose measure of evidence strength to use in studying it. As a result, in any given case, it is difficult to quantify the strength of evidence prior to (or even at) trial, and difficult to predict how jurors will evaluate it. Aiming to build a foundation, this chapter reviews research addressing the question: What makes evidence "strong?"

Eyewitness Characteristics

We humans rely heavily on what our senses tell us—particularly our eyes and ears. This sensory dependence helps explain why eyewitness testimony has traditionally been viewed as one of the most powerful forms of evidence at trial. Perhaps because the impact of eyewitness testimony is so intuitive, jury researchers have not made it a focus of empirical examination. In contrast to the huge literature on eyewitness identification accuracy, relatively few studies have dealt with the effects of eyewitness testimony on jurors or juries. However, a few eyewitness characteristics—age, confidence, and consistency—have prompted enough research to merit a review of their findings.

Age

Does it matter to jurors how old an eyewitness is? The answer appears to be a qualified yes. Most research on this topic to date has involved simulated criminal trials and cases featuring robbery, homicide, or sexual abuse. Some studies have compared child eyewitnesses to adults whereas others have varied the age of child eyewitnesses. The role of the eyewitness has differed as well. In studies involving sexual abuse, the eyewitness has usually also been the victim; in studies involving other case types, the eyewitness has typically been an uninvolved bystander. The general expectation has been that adult eyewitnesses will be perceived as more credible (and more influential) than child eyewitnesses, and that older children will be viewed as more trustworthy and reliable than younger children. It may not be that simple though. Gail Goodman and her colleagues (Bottoms & Goodman, 1994; Goodman, Golding, & Haith, 1984) argued that perceptions of credibility are a function of two component dimensions: cognitive competence and trustworthiness. According to this view, witnesses perceived as highly competent and trustworthy will be viewed as most credible. Adults will generally be perceived as more cognitively competent than children, but younger children may be seen as more trustworthy in some cases because they are viewed as lacking the motivation or capability to be deceptive. In any given trial, the credibility of a younger eyewitness may depend on which dimension of credibility is more salient to jurors.

What does the research tell us? Overall, the effect of eyewitness age on juror decisions has been relatively small and varied somewhat depending on the nature of the case. In studies where the eyewitness was a bystander and the focal crime was a fleeting event (e.g., robbery), adult eyewitnesses have generally been perceived as more *credible* than child eyewitnesses, but the impact of eyewitness age on *verdicts* has often been negligible (Bottoms, Golding, Stevenson, Wiley, & Yozwiak, 2007; Najdowski & Bottoms, 2008). However, some bystander-eyewitness studies have also yielded interactions between eyewitness age and contextual variables such as police interview style (Ruva & Bryant, 2004), the presence of a cautionary warning from the judge about child witnesses (Nikonova & Ogloff, 2005), and the speaking style (e.g., powerful v. powerless) of the eyewitness (Nigro, Buckley, Hill, & Nelson, 1989). These contingencies imply that the effect of bystander eyewitness age may vary across circumstances.

The results have been more consistent in studies involving child sexual abuse where the primary eyewitness was also the victim. In these cases, the identity of the alleged perpetrator is usually not an issue and jurors might be expected to put more stock in the testimony of younger witnesses to the extent they are seen as lacking the knowledge and cognitive capacity to generate fabricated stories involving sexual behavior. There are at least a dozen published studies on this type of case and, in most, younger child victims were perceived as more credible and produced a higher conviction rate than older victims (Bottoms et al., 2007). Interestingly, an archival analysis of 466 Canadian jury trials involving historic (i.e., retrospective) child sexual abuse found the odds of conviction decreased by a small amount for each additional year of victim age at the time of the alleged abuse. However, some studies of child sexual abuse have not found a discernible effect for eyewitness age (e.g., Crowley, O'Callaghan, & Ball, 1994; Holcomb & Jacquin, 2007; McCauley & Parker, 2001), and one study yielded an interaction between eyewitness age and the manner in which the victim was questioned (Castelli, Goodman, & Ghetti, 2005). Indeed, if there is a reliable effect of victim-eyewitness age and jury verdicts, it may not be linear in nature. Duggan, Aubrey, Doherty, Isquith, Levine, and Scheiner (1989) found that the highest conviction rate in their study occurred with a nine-year-old victim and the lowest with a thirteen-year-old victim, with the conviction rate for the five-year-old victim falling between the two. Therefore, even in child sexual abuse cases, the relationship between eyewitness age and juror decisions may depend on other factors such as the exact age of the child, the specific allegations against the defendant, or the existence of corroborating evidence.

Confidence

What could be more convincing to a juror than an eyewitness who confidently identifies the defendant? In keeping with this intuition, the courts have underscored the importance of eyewitness confidence and indicated how jurors should evaluate it (e.g., *Neil v. Biggers, 1972*). Unfortunately, it is now well-known that confident eyewitnesses are not necessarily accurate eyewitnesses. Many studies have shown that the relationship between eyewitness identification confidence and accuracy is positive but far from perfect (Penrod & Cutler, 1999). Compounding this problem, jurors tend to take eyewitnesses at their word and are heavily influenced by stated confidence levels, tending to convict more often when eyewitnesses report being very confident (Bradfield & Wells, 2000; Brewer & Burke, 2002; Moore & Gump, 1995; Penrod & Cutler, 1999; Tenney, MacCoun, Spellman, & Hastie, 2007). For example, Cutler, Penrod, and Stuve (1988) manipulated ten variables related to eyewitness identification accuracy in the context of an armed robbery case presented by videotape. Eyewitness confidence was varied by having the victim claim either 80 percent or 100 percent confidence in her identification of the robber. Of the ten variables, only eyewitness confidence had a significant impact on convictions, although the effect was fairly small (just 7%). Using the same videotaped trial and stated levels of confidence, Narby and Cutler (1994) replicated the confidence effect and actually found it to be stronger (i.e., 40% difference in verdicts). Likewise, Culhane and Hosch

(2004) observed a 16 percent difference in conviction rates using two levels of confidence even less distinctive (i.e., 100% confident v. less than 100% confident).

Although a growing body of work suggests eyewitness confidence has a strong and reliable effect on jurors (Tenney et al., 2007), research has thus far been focused on the defendant's *identification* to a much greater extent than *details* of the event. One exception is a study by Brewer and Burke (2002) that manipulated general eyewitness confidence in a nonverbal fashion via an audiotaped armed robbery trial. The high-confidence eyewitness responded to all questions in a concise and assertive manner; the low-confidence eyewitness responded with hesitation or qualification to roughly a third of the questions posed. Similar to studies focusing on confidence in the defendant's identification, substantially more convictions (30%) resulted when jurors were exposed to high-confidence eyewitness testimony compared with low-confidence testimony.

One question that has received some attention is whether the influence of eyewitness confidence essentially overrides ("trumps") all others. Bradfield and Wells (2000) were one of the first to study this by manipulating eyewitness confidence along with several other variables related to the *Biggers* criteria (i.e., view, attention, descriptive correspondence, and duration of exposure), and they found an additive effect of confidence on juror decisions. In two experiments, eyewitnesses who claimed to be "positive" about their identification produced substantially higher measures of guilt confidence than those who said they were "not really sure." However, two other studies suggest the effect of stated confidence may depend on additional considerations, such as the accuracy of other statements made by the witness as well as the strength of the remaining evidence. Demonstrating that a highly confident eyewitness is wrong during cross-examination has been shown to cause a backlash with jurors as well, lowering conviction rates more so than when a non-confident witnesses is similarly revealed to be in error (Tenney et al., 2007). Jurors may also just be less sensitive to variations in eyewitness confidence when the evidence is very strong (Moore & Gump, 1995).

Overall, consistent with intuition, eyewitness confidence in the identification decision very clearly has a strong impact on juror verdict preferences, but little is known about the effect of confidence regarding other aspects of eyewitness testimony. More research is thus needed concerning eyewitness confidence about the details of the event, as well as the mode in which confidence is expressed (i.e., verbally v. nonverbally) and its quantified level.

Consistency

Like confidence, the influence of eyewitness consistency seems very intuitive. In daily life, we are typically very skeptical of people who give different versions of the same event, particularly when they alter their story in a self-serving way. At trial, if witnesses add (or delete) details, prevaricate on some matter, or say something downright contradictory, it may well undermine their credibility and call into question the veracity of *everything* they say. One might expect jury researchers to have studied eyewitness consistency with fervor, but there is actually little research on the topic. Perhaps the expected results just seem too obvious.

If so, the existing data must rate as something of a surprise. In general, although studies have shown a reliable impact of eyewitness consistency on perceived *credibility*, its effect on juror probability-of-commission judgments and *verdicts* has been elusive. In particular, two early studies produced the expected impact of testimonial consistency on eyewitness credibility, but no difference in verdicts as a function of whether the eyewitnesses made contradictory statements at trial concerning the defendant's hair color (Lindsay, Lim, Marando, & Cully, 1986), or made statements at trial that conflicted with earlier pretrial statements—even when highlighted by the opposing attorney during cross-examination (Leippe & Romanczyk, 1989).

The strongest support for an effect of eyewitness consistency on juror judgments comes from two studies conducted by Garrett Berman and his colleagues using a simulated armed robbery trial. In the first study (Berman, Narby, & Cutler, 1995), eyewitness consistency was manipulated separately for two types of details: "central" (important), and "peripheral" (tangential). The inconsistent conditions associated with each type of detail featured four assertions made at trial that contradicted pretrial statements and were pointed out by the opposing attorney during cross-examination. Evaluations of the eyewitness were lower in the face of inconsistency related to both central and peripheral details, but the conviction rate was only reduced by equivocation on central details. In a subsequent study (Berman & Cutler, 1996), the nature of inconsistent statements was varied using an elaborated version of the same trial and a mixture of students and community members. Three types of inconsistency were examined (along with a control condition featuring no inconsistencies): novel information not mentioned prior to the trial, contradictions between pretrial and on-the-stand statements, and contradictions occurring solely within the context of statements made at trial. Ratings for probability-of-commission and verdicts were both influenced by the nature of the inconsistency, with conviction rates highest when no inconsistencies occurred, lower for the novel information condition, and lowest in the two conditions that involved outright contradictions.

Three subsequent experimental studies by Neil Brewer and his colleagues muddied the water still further with regard to the effect of eyewitness consistency. All three featured two consistency conditions (i.e., inconsistent v. consistent) but varied the type of trial and the number and nature of the inconsistent statements associated with the consistency manipulation. In the first study, Brewer and Burke (2002) used an audiotaped trial based on Berman and Cutler's (1996) stimulus materials and manipulated consistency via the presence/absence of four contradictory statements. Eyewitness consistency had little effect on juror verdicts, although the accompanying manipulation of eyewitness confidence was quite strong. Semmler and Brewer (2002) used a different type of case (i.e., vehicular homicide) and boosted the strength of the consistency manipulation by including eight inconsistencies—four factual and four inferential—spread over multiple witnesses. Probability-of-commission ratings were reduced by the testimonial inconsistency of the prosecution witnesses, but verdicts again were not affected. Continuing to search for the elusive consistency effect, Brewer and Hupfeld (2004) modified the Berman and Cutler (1996) stimulus materials to feature a different crime in a different setting (assault causing grievous bodily harm) and incorporated five inconsistencies representing a mix of all three types identified by Berman and Cutler (1996). This time testimonial inconsistency had a whopping negative influence on probability-of-commission as well as verdicts, with very few convictions occurring in the presence of inconsistent eyewitness testimony.

Most recently, attention has begun to turn to how an eyewitness's testimonial consistency might interact with their identification decision. Joanna Pozzulo and Julie Dempsey (2009) conducted a mock juror study in which an eyewitness's testimonial consistency was manipulated along with their identification decision (positive, foil, or none). Both factors had some effect but they did not interact. Defendants were rated as more culpable and the eyewitness as more credible when consistent testimony was given, and culpability ratings were also higher for partially consistent testimony in comparison to inconsistent testimony. Interestingly, although the identification decision did affect culpability ratings, jurors were more influenced by the consistency of the testimony.

The research noted previously dealt with within-witness consistency, but some studies have also examined the consistency of reports across multiple eyewitnesses. In one of the first, Leippe (1985) conducted two experiments with mock jurors in which the defendant was charged with armed robbery, and the number and nature of eyewitnesses were varied. In both experiments, the presence of a non-identifying defense eyewitness drastically reduced the conviction rate. Relatedly, Lindsay et al. (1986) varied the number of eyewitnesses testifying for the prosecution and defense and found the conviction rate to be influenced in a linear fashion by both. In particular, unopposed testimony by either one or two prosecution eyewitnesses resulted in more convictions than when their testimony was opposed by another eyewitness for the defense or an alibi eyewitness (although not when the alibi witness was a relative of the defendant). This implies the consistency of the overall "story" may be more important than the number of story advocates.

Looking across these studies, several conclusions seem warranted about eyewitness consistency. First, it likely has a strong and pervasive effect on juror judgments. Consider the extreme case of a single eyewitness who waffles on every single response—how could a jury trust such testimony? Studies that failed to produce an effect may simply have featured inconsistencies that were not salient enough for jurors to notice. Second, current research is limited somewhat in being based mostly on a single set of stimulus materials initially developed by Berman and his colleagues involving an armed robbery. Little has been done to examine the effect of eyewitness consistency in trials involving other types of charges, and few data are available concerning the effect of consistency in the prosecution's case as a whole. Third, the impact of eyewitness consistency may depend on other variables such as the number and nature of inconsistencies, their salience to the jurors, and how they coincide with the remaining evidence. More research is needed to identify potential higher-order contingencies associated with eyewitness consistency.

Expert Witness Characteristics

Expert witnesses are common at trial, and people hold several different views of them. For some, the phrase "expert witness" produces the mental image of a learned, dispassionate professional imparting knowledge to the jury on some technical matter—the *benevolent educator*. There is another view of expert witnesses though—one that portrays them as professional witnesses, paid to offer a particular conclusion and to marshal any arguments to support it—the *hired gun*. Yet another view is that so-called expert witnesses rarely tell fact-finders anything they don't already know or couldn't figure out with common sense— the *superfluous pontificator*. Which of these views best coincides with reality?

Numerous studies have addressed whether expert testimony affects juror decisions and, if so, when it is most influential. Only one quantitative review of the empirical research on expert testimony has been published, however (Nietzel, McCarthy, & Kerr, 1999). It summarized the results of 149 effects from twenty-two studies comparing some type of expert testimony condition with a condition featuring no expert testimony. Their main analysis revealed a modest overall effect of expert testimony ($r = .11$), with juror decisions showing a mild tendency to be consistent with the slant (i.e., direction) of the expert's information and/or opinion. However, this main analysis included *every* study in which jurors made judgments about some outcome and—not surprisingly—revealed an excessively large amount of variation in the observed effects. This strongly indicates that there is no generalized effect of expert testimony but rather that it depends on other variables and will not be consistent across trials. The remainder of this section considers some of those other variables, focusing on research that has been conducted since 1999, as well as secondary analyses in the Nietzel et al. report.

Unopposed Testimony and Opposition (Expert v. No Expert, Expert v. Expert)

Perhaps the most fundamental question about expert testimony is whether it has *any* effect on juror decisions. If so, the next question would be whether such influence is reduced or eliminated by the testimony of an opposing expert who rebuts the first expert. In one of the analyses, Nietzel et al. (1999) examined seventy-five effects stemming from unopposed expert testimony and found, on average, a small positive effect ($r = .15$). One weakness of this literature is a general lack of field studies conducted with actual juries, but there are a few exceptions. For instance, Read, Connolly, and Welsh (2006) analyzed data from 466 Canadian jury trials involving historic (i.e., retrospective) allegations of child sexual abuse and found some surprising results. When no expert testified at trial, the conviction rate was 92 percent; when an unopposed expert testified for the defense, the conviction rate was only 75 percent. However, when an expert testified *for the Crown only*, the conviction rate was 82 percent (i.e., 10% *lower* than when no expert testified for the prosecution). This finding may have been an anomaly associated with small numbers of cases for some of the expert conditions, but it could also be due to differences in the strength of the evidence across cases. On balance, unopposed expert testimony appears to have a modest influence on juror decisions that probably depends on other variables.

More surprising, though, the Nietzel et al. meta-analysis revealed essentially the same effect of expert testimony on juror decisions ($r = .14$) when the first expert was countered by a second expert. Although based on only eighteen effects, this finding suggests the impact of testimony by an initial expert is not dampened by a subsequent dissenting expert, and is consistent with the Story model of juror decision making in that what comes first has more influence on the story ultimately created. Under some circumstances, though, opposing testimony may have a strong effect (e.g., Levett & Kovera, 2008; 2009).

A focus of the recent research on expert testimony is the ability of jurors to appraise the validity of complex scientific research presented by experts in civil trials. In general, studies have shown that jurors are not very good at this task, but some may be better at it than others—for instance, high-NC jurors (McAuliff & Kovera, 2008). All jurors seem better able to recognize more salient aspects of low internal validity (e.g., a missing control group), as opposed to subtler threats such as a confounding variable or researcher awareness of the hypotheses (McAuliff & Duckworth, 2010; McAuliff & Kovera, 2008; McAuliff, Kovera, & Nunez, 2009). Jurors also seem better able to appreciate problems associated with scientific evidence when highlighted by the testimony of an opposing expert (Levett & Kovera, 2008). Studies also show that jurors rely on heuristic cues such as publication status (McAuliff & Duckworth, 2010) or judicial admission into evidence (Schweitzer & Saks, 2009) to evaluate scientific evidence, even though these are not perfect indicators of validity.

Content Specificity and Form (General v. Specific, Clinical v. Actuarial)

Expert testimony can be divided into two categories. *General expert testimony* is intended to educate jurors with regard to underlying theory, baseline frequencies, and patterns of association. *Specific expert testimony* applies general theory and empirical findings to the case at hand. Which type has more influence on juror decisions? In their meta-analysis, Nietzel et al. (1999) estimated three effects related to the specificity of expert testimony: general testimony versus no expert testimony (r = .16), specific testimony versus no expert testimony (r = .22), and general testimony versus specific testimony (r = .13). Put differently: expert testimony tends to have more influence when applied concretely to the facts of the present case than when it consists of general research findings, and both kinds of expert testimony (specific and general) are more efficacious than no expert testimony at all.

Since the 1999 meta-analysis, a handful of additional studies has addressed the *form* of expert testimony, primarily in the context of decisions about the likelihood of future violent behavior by the defendant. This research has manipulated whether the expert's judgment was *clinical* in nature (based on unaided holistic assessment) or *actuarial* (i.e., based on an algorithmic combination of empirically verified "risk factors"). Although theoretically independent of specificity, actuarial testimony tends to be general in nature while clinical testimony is necessarily case-specific. Traditionally, mental health professionals have used the clinical approach and argued that their training, knowledge, and experience allow them to arrive at accurate decisions. Unfortunately, a large empirical literature shows clearly that predictions about future violent behavior are far from perfect although more likely to be correct when generated by actuarial means (Monahan, 1981; Monahan & Steadman, 1994).

Jurors nonetheless seem to prefer expert testimony based on the clinical approach. A well-known study on this topic was conducted by Krauss and Sales (2001), who manipulated two factors in the context of a simulated capital sentencing: the nature of the prosecution's expert testimony (clinical or actuarial) and the nature of the defense's response (i.e., a methodology-based cross-examination, a credentials-based cross-examination, an opposing expert from the same discipline, or an opposing expert from a different discipline). Mock jurors read a summary of a capital sentencing case and were asked to rate the defendant's dangerousness at three points in time. Prosecution expert testimony of both types influenced juror ratings of dangerousness, although its impact was reduced by cross-examination or an opposing expert, but clinical expert testimony had more influence than actuarial testimony. The relative efficacy of clinical testimony compared with actuarial testimony was replicated by Krauss and Lee (2003) with deliberating groups, and by Krauss, Lieberman, and Olson (2004) who added a third type of expert testimony to the mix (Guided Professional Judgment). The preference for purely clinical testimony was reduced but not eliminated in the latter study when jurors were prompted to process the evidence in a systematic (analytic) fashion as opposed to heuristically. These findings contrast with those of Guy and Edens (2003; 2006) who examined decisions about the civil commitment of a sexually violent predator. In these studies, mock jurors were similarly influenced by clinical and actuarial testimony, although the conviction rate was fairly high in both studies and may not have afforded a good test of the two approaches.

Overall, these studies indicate that jurors are influenced more by specific testimony applied to the case at hand than general testimony, and perhaps when testimony is offered in clinical rather than actuarial form. However, research on the form of expert testimony has been confined largely to two trial contexts (capital sentencing and sexually violent recidivism) and there isn't all that much of it, so any conclusion about expert specificity or form must necessarily be qualified at present.

Content Domain: Eyewitness Reliability

Expert witnesses testify about many things in actual courtrooms (Cutler & Kovera, 2011; Faigman, 2008), but the topic of eyewitness reliability has probably generated more empirical research on expert testimony than on any other topic. The cognitive processes associated with observing, encoding, recalling, and integrating information are complex and fraught with many opportunities for errors, and eyewitnesses can be influenced by a host of things that take place during as well as after the focal event (Brewer, Weber, & Semmler, 2005; Cutler & Penrod, 1995; Pansky, Koriat, & Goldsmith, 2005)— particularly aspects of the identification test procedure (Brewer & Palmer, 2010). Most alarmingly, a substantial amount of empirical research indicates that eyewitness confidence is only weakly-moderately associated with identification accuracy (Sporer, Penrod, Read, & Cutler, 1995). Although the relationship is positive and may be stronger in some circumstances than others (Brewer, 2006), it is not strong enough to justify the faith that many jurors seem to have in it. Unfortunately, the assertion of "100% confidence" by a witness is no guarantee of accuracy.

All of this gives expert witnesses a lot to talk about on the stand. When experts are allowed to testify about eyewitness reliability, they usually aim to educate jurors on a fairly well-established body of research findings concerning eyewitness error and the dangers of overreliance on eyewitness confidence (Leippe & Eisenstadt, 2009; Martire & Kemp, 2011). Two effects could follow from such efforts. First, expert testimony on the problematic nature of eyewitness testimony could make jurors more wary and less trusting of eyewitnesses in general, leading them to be less inclined to trust any eyewitness (i.e., *juror skepticism*). Conversely, expert testimony on eyewitness fallibility could cause jurors to devalue eyewitness testimony only under certain specific conditions (i.e., when potential problems with the current case coincide with elements of the expert's testimony). In other words, expert testimony could cause jurors to be selectively (and appropriately) critical of some eyewitnesses or some aspects of their testimony depending on the circumstances surrounding it. This desirable effect has been termed *juror sensitization.*

What does the research tell us about the impact of expert testimony on eyewitness accuracy? This question was addressed in the meta-analysis by Nietzel et al. (1999) using forty-one effects from ten different studies. The average effect for these studies was modest ($r = .18$), but still somewhat higher than the overall effect for all expert testimony effects combined ($r =$ .11). In other words, jurors who hear expert testimony on eyewitness reliability tend to make decisions that are consistent with that testimony (i.e., almost always pro-defense). More recently, Martire and Kemp (2011) comprehensively reviewed the research on expert testimony related to eyewitnesses. They found twenty-four studies and classified them into three categories based on their research design. There was a fair amount of support for skepticism effects across the set of studies and only limited support from a few studies for the more desirable sensitization effect. Most importantly, however, the authors called attention to the scarcity of studies (only three) that address the most important issue regarding expert testimony on eyewitnesses—can experts provide information that helps jurors to make more *accurate* judgments? To answer this question, research is needed that involves expert testimony and eyewitnesses who actually observe some event (so the perpetrator can be known). The data at present suggest that expert testimony on eyewitnesses tends to make jurors less trusting of eyewitnesses in general and, perhaps at times, more appropriately sensitive to the strengths and weaknesses of the eyewitness testimony they encounter. What we don't know yet is whether expert testimony on eyewitness error can help jurors make better decisions.

Content Domain: Battered Woman Syndrome

In 1979 Lenore Walker coined the term "battered woman syndrome" (BWS) to refer to a particular mind-set that arises in the context of domestic violence and can eventually lead an abused woman to kill her abusive partner (Walker, 1979). According to Walker's theory, BWS involves a recurring three-stage cycle of violence consisting of tension-building, violence, and contrition. As these cycles repeat over time, the battered woman feels increasingly isolated and helpless, eventually experiencing something akin to psychological paralysis where no recourse is perceived other than to kill the abusive partner. When this happens and the case goes to trial, defendants sometimes put forth a claim of justifiable homicide based on self-defense, and a mental health expert may be called by the defense to testify about BWS and provide a context for understanding the defendant's behavior.

Although the theory of BWS is controversial, a fair amount of empirical research has addressed the impact of expert testimony on BWS since the late 1980s, much of it conducted by Regina Schuller and her colleagues (see Schuller, 2003, and Schuller & Jenkins, 2007, for reviews). Research has examined not only the presence/absence and various aspects of BWS testimony but also influence associated with the specific circumstances of the killing and the trial context. More than a dozen studies have now been published, and they generally show modest beneficial effects associated with expert testimony on BWS. The earliest research revealed essentially no impact of expert testimony on individual mock jurors (Finkel, Meister, & Lightfoot, 1991; Follingstad et al., 1989) or interacting mock juries (Kasian, Spanos, Terrance, & Peebles, 1993). However, more recent work by Schuller and her colleagues suggests an effect of BWS expert testimony that varies according to other contextual variables. For example, expert testimony pertaining to battered women has resulted in greater leniency on the part of jurors when (1) the expert concluded that BWS fit the defendant (Schuller, 1992); (2) the expert's testimony was given early in the trial and by a female (Schuller & Cripps, 1998); (3) the instructions from the judge included a mention that it was appropriate to nullify the law in order to avoid an unfair verdict (Schuller & Rzepa, 2002); (4) the abuser was killed in a nonconfrontational manner; and (5) a form of nonclinical testimony was provided emphasizing the social context of the homicide (Schuller, Wells, Rzepa, & Klippenstine, 2004). Further, the effect of BWS expert testimony may vary depending on the nationality and gender of the jurors (Schuller, McKimmie, & Janz, 2004). In essence, expert testimony on the causes and consequences of battering appears to have a modest impact that depends on a number of other variables.

Expert Personal Characteristics

At trial, the degree to which jurors scrutinize expert testimony in an analytic, effortful manner could depend on many characteristics, such as the expert's age, race, experience, education level, professional credentials, or status among peers. Given that attorneys have discretion regarding who testifies for their side as an expert witness, there are obvious practical implications associated with how jurors react to these characteristics.

Intuitively, it seems that jurors might be influenced by an expert's status or prestige, but the very limited research on this topic to date suggests no straightforward effects associated with an expert's credentials. In one of the first studies on the topic, an expert testifying for the plaintiff in a product liability case was more influential with strong as opposed to weak credentials, but only when the testimony was highly complex (Cooper, Bennett, & Sukel, 1996). Impressive credentials may not always be better either. A recent study involving expert testimony on child sexual abuse found experts with better credentials to have no more impact than experts with worse credentials

(Klettke, Graesser, & Powell, 2010). A third study by Cooper and Neuhaus (2000) involving a series of three experiments revealed the possibility of a backlash against experts with strong credentials when they were highly paid and known to testify often as an expert, particularly when their testimony was complex. One caveat of these mixed results is that expert credentials have not been manipulated the same way across all studies, underscoring the need for a better understanding of what aspects of an expert's professional background make a difference to jurors (e.g., publication record, education, current employment, etc.)

Of the characteristics noted previously, expert gender is the only one to be examined with any frequency thus far. Initial research in the 1980s was guided by the belief that jurors would be more influenced by male rather than female experts, but two early studies showed the opposite (Swenson, Nash, & Roos, 1984; Schuller & Cripps, 1998) and two others found no effect for the gender of a polygraph expert (Vondergeest, Honts, & Devitt, 1993) or a medical doctor (Memon & Shuman, 1998). These mixed findings raise the possibility that any effect of expert gender depends on other variables—such as the degree to which the expert's testimony concerns matters perceived to be more masculine or feminine (Schuller, Terry, & McKimmie, 2001). In essence, male experts might be more influential when offering testimony on "masculine" issues whereas female experts might have greater impact when the testimony concerns "feminine" issues. Some support for this *gender-con-gruency* hypothesis arises from three studies involving alleged price-fixing among suppliers in an industry that was either stereotypically masculine (construction) or feminine (women's clothing) (McKimmie, Newton, Terry, & Schuller, 2004; Schuller et al., 2001; Schuller, Terry, & McKimmie, 2005). However, all three studies involved a price-fixing civil case, damage awards, relatively low psychological fidelity, and fairly small observed effects. In contrast, research that varied expert gender using six-person mock juries produced no effect on predeliberation verdict preferences or jury verdicts for an automobile accident case in which the expert was an automotive engineer (Couch & Sigler, 2002). At this point, it does not appear that the gender of an expert makes much difference, except perhaps when testifying about matters that are strongly associated with a particular gender.

Scientific Evidence

Beginning in the 1980s, researchers became interested in how jurors reach verdicts in trials that revolve around *scientific evidence*—testimony provided by an expert witness that features some combination of the following: a formal underlying mathematical model, standardized measurement/testing procedures, and a probability-based conclusion about "match." The first wave of research on scientific evidence was directed at polygraph exams and blood type, but the focus has increasingly shifted to DNA testing and other forms of biological trace evidence such as hair and fingerprints.

Polygraph Tests

In contrast to most other types of scientific evidence, social scientists and legal experts have been fiercely critical of polygraph evidence from its inception (Faigman, Kaye, Saks, & Sanders, 1997; Lykken, 1998). Initial research suggested jurors might be more receptive to it. In two early studies, mock jurors were presented with a case summary, provided individual verdicts, and then asked if additional polygraph evidence unfavorable to the defendant (Koffler, 1957), or contrary to their original judgment (Carlson, Pasano, & Jannuzzo, 1977), would have caused them to change their verdict. The results were highly intuitive—a moderate number of participants in both studies reported they would have returned a different verdict if they had received the polygraph evidence.

Subsequent research has been more methodologically sound and is uniform in revealing little influence associated with polygraph evidence. In the first true experiment on the topic, Markwart and Lynch (1979) found the presence (yes-no) and nature (favorable-unfavorable) of polygraph evidence had some impact on jurors prior to deliberation in a homicide case, but relatively little afterwards. Several other studies produced similarly bland results (Myers, Rosol, & Boelter, 2003), including two that featured interacting mock juries (Myers & Arbuthnot, 1997; Spanos, Myers, DuBreuil, & Pawlak, 1992–1993). In perhaps the best study on this topic, no differences in juror or jury verdicts emerged as a function of the presence or type of polygraph exam used by the polygraph expert (i.e., the Control Question Test, the Guilty Knowledge Test, or no polygraph evidence), and polygraph test results were rated as the least important type of evidence presented, with jurors reporting that they spent on average less than 2 percent of deliberation time discussing it (Myers & Arbuthnot, 1997). In one of the few studies to produce an effect, pro-defense polygraph evidence reduced the conviction rate, but only in the absence of a judicial caution about its reliability (Cavoukian & Heselgrave, 1980). The limited available data on polygraph evidence thus do not suggest that it has much impact on juror decisions, but there remains a need for field research examining the relationship of polygraph test results and actual jury verdicts.

Blood Type and Hair

Prior to 1997, research on scientific evidence other than the polygraph was focused on the use of blood type comparison tests to identify perpetrators. The major question underlying this work was whether probabilistic information offered by an expert would be used correctly by jurors to "update" their estimated likelihood of the defendant's guilt according to Bayes's model. Research in other areas of psychology has shown that people tend to under-utilize base-rate information regarding event frequency (Bar-Hillel, 1980; Kahneman & Tversky, 1982; Saks & Kidd, 1980–81), which is to say that they do not give it as much weight as it should have. Do jurors have the same trouble?

The first studies on blood type and hair suggested that jurors may fall prey to two potential decision fallacies when asked to make decisions based on statistical information, each one named for a misguided hypothetical attorney (Thompson & Schumann, 1987). Given a declared match between the defendant and evidence taken from the crime scene, the *prosecutor's fallacy* sets the probability of the defendant's guilt equal to 1.00 minus the proportion of persons with the focal characteristic in the population. Thus, if a test revealed a match between the defendant and a crime-scene sample for some characteristic possessed by only 1 percent of the population, victims of the prosecutor's fallacy would believe there was a 99 percent probability that the defendant was guilty. In contrast, the *defense attorney's fallacy* essentially discounts a matching test result by setting the probability of the defendant's guilt equal to 1.00 divided by the number of people expected to match the result based on the incidence rate. For example, if prevalence data suggested the existence of one hundred "matches" in the community, the defendant's estimated probability of guilt according to the defense attorney's fallacy would be 1/100, or 1 percent. These fallacies are intuitively appealing, but neither represents a valid inference because they both focus solely on the "new" probabilistic-match information and ignore all the other evidence in the case (as captured by the prior odds). Several studies have investigated whether people in legal decision-making situations fall prey to these two fallacies. Although early work indicated that anywhere from 25–70 percent of participants do (Thompson & Schumann, 1987), even after deliberation (Schumann & Thompson, 1989), later research found these proportions to be much lower (Nance & Morris, 2005; Smith, Penrod, Otto, & Park, 1996).

What emerges most clearly from the research on hair and blood type is that jurors have trouble processing statistical information and tend to be relatively insensitive to its variations. A series of experiments has shown that mock jurors do not adjust their final estimated probability of guilt as much as Bayes's model says they should (Faigman & Baglioni, 1988; Goodman, 1992; Smith et al., 1996; Thompson, 1989; Thompson & Schumann, 1987). These studies manipulated the reported frequency of different blood types (e.g., 40%, 20%, or 5%) and several used repeated-measures designs to determine the impact of probabilistic-match information at different points in time. Surprisingly, there was little or no effect of varying reported blood type frequency in the population, and comparisons of final guilt probability estimates to Bayesian benchmarks indicated underutilization of the statistical evidence as well as minimal improvement associated with instructional aids designed to help jurors correctly process information. In one of the better studies, Smith et al. (1996) manipulated seven independent variables (including five aspects of the statistical evidence as well as the level and explicit quantification of eyewitness confidence), and obtained measures of guilt likelihood at five separate times (after each of four witnesses and after instructions at the end). In general, the defendant was judged more likely to be guilty when the frequency of the matching blood enzyme in the population was lower (35% v. 80%) and when the eyewitness was more confident. Across measurements, immediately prior judgments of guilt probability were the best predictors of subsequent guilt probability, but "new" statistical evidence introduced by the expert witnesses improved prediction and continued to have an effect even after the period when it was introduced, suggesting jurors reevaluated the evidence in light of additional testimony (i.e., the defendant's alibi). Comparing ratings of guilt probability to the predictions of Bayes's model suggested that many jurors slightly underweighted the statistical evidence, but some jurors overweighted it—and exposure to instructions on using Bayes's model did not affect this result.

DNA Evidence

In the mid-1990s, national attention was drawn to a relatively unknown type of statistical evidence—Deoxyribonucleic acid, or DNA—featured in two trials involving O. J. Simpson. DNA is a protein containing the biological instructions for living organisms found in all cells of the body except red blood cells. More than 99 percent of the DNA molecule is common to all humans, but the relatively small amount that varies across persons can be very diagnostic in determining its source. The testing process involves comparing DNA from two samples at a number of sites on the DNA molecule (usually a dozen or so) to determine if the same molecular structure exists at each site. The probability of a coincidental match at any one comparison site is a function of the frequency of different molecular structures in the population; the probability that two DNA samples from different sources will coincidentally ("randomly") match at *all* of the comparison sites is essentially the product of all the probabilities of coincidental match at the individual comparison sites. Random match probability (RMP) values are exceedingly small, typically less than one in a million or even a billion, but these types of errors have received a great deal of attention from scholars. A second category of error associated with DNA evidence is laboratory error (LE), which can occur for a variety of reasons, including degradation or contamination of the DNA sample, mistakes by the analyst during the testing, or equipment miscalibration. LE rates have been estimated via the proficiency testing of crime labs that conduct DNA testing and range anywhere from one in two thousand to one in two hundred (Koehler, Chia, & Lindsey, 1995).

Initial studies of DNA in the late 1990s focused on the impact of varying explicit probabilistic information about the likelihood of an incorrect "match" (i.e., RMP or LE). Particular attention was devoted to the absolute level of RMP as well as the wording used to convey the quantitative magnitude. Logically, one might expect that varying the reported numeric likelihood of RMP and/or LE would have a strong effect on jurors, whereas varying the wording surrounding the number might be expected to have a weak effect. Conversely, research has generally found the opposite. One early finding since replicated was that varying the reported absolute levels of RMP or LE had relatively little effect on jurors (Koehler et al., 1995), whereas varying the quantitative format used to convey statistical probabilities (i.e., frequencies, likelihood ratio, odds ratio) had a marked impact (Koehler, 1996). In other words, different ways of expressing error probability affect how jurors evaluate DNA evidence—but different error probabilities themselves have relatively little impact.

Schklar and Diamond (1999) proposed two potential explanations for sub-optimal juror decision making in the context of DNA evidence: Jurors make *errors* because they have difficulty working with probabilities, and jurors have different *expectancies* regarding the likelihood of test-related error (e.g., analyst mistake or police tampering) based on their life experiences. The results of their research provided some support for both explanations. Jurors tended to have trouble aggregating statistical information in an optimal (i.e., Bayesian) fashion, and they also reported differing expectancies with regard to testing error. Jurors apparently did not think about the two types of error in the same way either, as the conviction rate was significantly higher when RMP was not provided and LE was extremely small, compared with a mathematically equivalent scenario when LE was absent and RMP was extremely small. Providing instructions on how to optimally combine values for the different types of error rates did not substantially reduce this phenomenon. With regard to expectancies, explicit mention of LE probability *increased* the number of convictions compared with no mention of LE, implying that "untutored" expectations of LE likelihood were higher than the value explicitly provided in the study (e.g., 2%).

The relative inefficacy of manipulating absolute levels of RMP and LE probability spurred the development of *exemplar cueing theory* (Koehler, 2001; Koehler & Macchi, 2004). This theory has its roots in the availability heuristic and basically asserts that the perceived probative value of DNA (and, by extension, any other statistical evidence) depends on the ease with which jurors can call to mind persons other than the defendant who would match the obtained DNA profile (i.e., "exemplars"). When it is easy for jurors to envision a coincidental match, DNA evidence should have less impact; when it is difficult to do so, DNA evidence should be very compelling. Two aspects of RMP presentation were viewed as likely to affect a juror's ability to imagine matching exemplars: the *frame* of the RMP information (i.e., a single individual v. multiple individuals who might match in a given population), and the quantitative *form* used to convey the probabilistic information (e.g., frequency, probability, or odds). The theory predicts general effects for both variables as well as an interactive effect whereby conviction rates should be considerably lower when RMP frame refers to multiple individuals *and* is conveyed in a frequency form (Koehler & Macchi, 2004). For instance, jurors should be much less likely to convict when told that five people might coincidentally match the perpetrator in a community of one million, as opposed to learning that there is a .000005 percent chance that any single community member might coincidentally match.

Exemplar cueing theory has now accrued decent support over six laboratory experiments (Koehler, 2001; Koehler & Macchi, 2004). Koehler (2001) summarized four of those experiments conducted with students, written case summaries, minimal evidence other than a DNA match, and manipulation of one or more focal aspects of DNA evidence identified by exemplar cueing theory. Some support emerged across the studies for the effect of how statistical information was framed, but other expected effects generally failed to materialize. Koehler and Macchi (2004) revised the theory by adding a new variable (size of the referent population) and predicted the effects of frame and form would be stronger when the surrounding referent population was large, thereby making it easier to envision coincidental matches. As expected, conviction rates were lowest in the conditions when the theory would predict that it was easiest to identify coincidental exemplars—when

RMP information referred to multiple persons from a large surrounding population.

Although most research on DNA evidence has addressed RMP and LE error-rate information, some attention has been directed to a more basic question—how much impact does a declared DNA match have in general and relative to other types of evidence in particular? In one of the first published studies on the topic, Golding, Stewart, Yozwiak, Djadali, and Sanchez (2000) examined the efficacy of prosecution DNA evidence in two experiments involving a child sexual assault case and obtained more convictions when DNA evidence was presented compared with the victim-testimony baseline condition, but the difference was reduced when mock jurors also heard the testimony of an alibi witness for the defendant. Simon, Snow, and Read (2004) had participants play the role of an arbitrator deciding whether an individual had committed a crime against a construction company. Along with other evidence, the case summary included DNA evidence that either incriminated the defendant (i.e., a match with a very low RMP) or exonerated him (a non-match). Those who received the incriminating DNA evidence convicted more than twice as often as those who heard the exonerating DNA evidence (i.e., 70% v. 32%), although a surprising number of individuals judged the defendant to be guilty even in the face of a non-matching DNA test result. In yet another example, a 51 percent higher conviction rate resulted from a declared DNA test match compared with a non-match (Pozzulo, Lemieux, Wilson, Crescini, & Girardi, 2009). As in the Simon et al. study, a non-matching DNA result reduced the number of convictions but did not eliminate them.

One of the best studies on DNA evidence was done by Nance and Morris (2005). This study involved a large sample of Illinois residents who showed up for jury duty, and employed a complex design featuring nine experimental groups and two comparison conditions: one that featured no forensic evidence (i.e., the control condition), and one in which the DNA expert declared a match with no accompanying mention of either RMP or LE (i.e., the "mere match" condition). Final probability-of-guilt ratings by participants were notably higher—and the number of guilty verdicts five times greater—in the mere-match condition relative to the control condition that received no DNA testimony. In turn, guilt-probability ratings were significantly higher and there were twice as many convictions in the nine experimental groups compared with the mere-match condition, suggesting the provision of error-rate information actually enhanced the perceived probative value of DNA evidence. Consistent with previous research, a frequency presentation form reduced the number of convictions in some conditions, LE presentation had no impact on probability of guilt or convictions, and "untutored" (i.e., uninformed) estimates of LE probability were higher than "tutored" estimates. In addition, as in prior studies with other kinds of scientific evidence, the DNA test results were *underweighted* in all experimental conditions, although somewhat less so in certain conditions involving a visual aid.

The results of this research are further supported by a series of experiments conducted by Joel Lieberman and his colleagues (Lieberman, Carrell, Miethe, & Krauss, 2008). In the initial study conducted via the Internet, both student and community respondents rated DNA evidence as more accurate and more persuasive than other types of evidence, including fingerprints, hairs and fibers, videotape surveillance, and suspect confession. Participants also read a brief summary of either a murder case or a rape case featuring one of five types of evidence (DNA, fingerprints, hair fibers, eyewitness testimony, or victim testimony) that either incriminated or exonerated the defendant (i.e., matched or failed to match). When DNA evidence was compared to the other four evidence types collectively, incriminating DNA evidence produced a higher (100%) conviction rate in both cases than did other types of incriminating evidence, whereas exonerating DNA evidence produced the lowest conviction rate in the rape case and one of the lowest in the murder case. A second study essentially replicated the potency of DNA evidence with a more extensive case summary that included a damaging cross-examination as well as reasonable doubt instructions. A third study focused solely on DNA evidence, and manipulated the reliability of the testing laboratory and the focus of the cross-examination (on the expert's qualifications or the probative value of the evidence). Despite a gratuitously strong manipulation that featured the forensic equivalent of the Keystone Cops running the unreliable lab, nearly all respondents viewed the test results from both labs as highly accurate and reliable. A four-item dispositional measure of trust in DNA was the only significant predictor of guilt probability ratings as well as juror verdicts.

One published study of DNA evidence involving real juries corroborates the strong effect of DNA evidence observed under experimental conditions. Briody (2004) analyzed 150 homicide cases that occurred in Queensland, Australia, half of which involved DNA evidence. The cases without DNA evidence were selected from homicides that occurred within the same time period and jurisdiction. Various independent variables relating to the offense, defendant, victims, and evidence were coded from computerized police records and used to predict three outcomes: whether the case reached court, whether it resulted in a guilty plea, and whether it resulted in a guilty verdict by a jury. DNA evidence, coded as present or absent, was a significant predictor of whether a case reached court, but not whether a guilty plea was made. Of the 150 cases, ninety-two were eventually tried by jury and nine of twenty-two predictor variables were correlated with conviction, including the presence of DNA evidence ($r = .41$). Indeed, DNA evidence was the single strongest predictor of jury verdict, even better than a defendant confession ($r = .25$). A multivariate analysis predicting jury verdict using the five best predictors (victim sex, fingerprint evidence, DNA evidence, defendant confession, and defendant denial) revealed a huge effect for DNA evidence, with the odds of conviction estimated to be twenty-three times greater when DNA evidence was presented by the prosecution than when not presented. DNA evidence had a larger effect than a defendant confession or defendant denial (but, oddly enough, not fingerprint evidence). Briody's study therefore provides support for the notion that DNA has a powerful effect on real juries.

Is There a CSI Effect?

The enduring popularity of TV shows centered on the idealized processing of forensic evidence (particularly DNA) in criminal cases (e.g., the original "Crime Scene Investigation" and its many spin-offs) has raised widespread concern among legal professionals that venirepersons who regularly watch such shows will have unrealistically high expectations for the evidence they encounter at trial. There has been a great deal of hype associated with the so-called *CSI effect* but rather little good data. Mancini (2011) reviewed the six published studies relevant to the CSI effect and noted that only one yielded a significant association between forensic-science TV viewing and juror verdicts, although there was some indication that viewership was related to greater expectations regarding the prosecution's evidence. Unfortunately, all these studies suffer from some notable limitations, including cursory reference to scientific evidence in brief written trial materials. Mancini added a seventh study to this literature in which 217 students watched footage from a real murder trial and responded to a variety of measures. He found that heavy forensic-science TV viewers reported higher subjective certainty requirements and greater dissatisfaction with the prosecution's evidence than did light viewers, but again there was no detectable relationship between forensic-science TV viewing and juror verdict preferences.

Thus, the existing research—such as it is—does not support the existence of a CSI effect or the associated fear that heavy forensic-science TV viewing will corrupt jurors to the extent that they are unwilling to convict without pristine scientific evidence. Extensive exposure to unrealistic TV programs involving forensic evidence may raise evidentiary expectations somewhat, but this does not appear to translate directly into pro-acquittal verdicts. More than anything, future research on the impact of forensic-science TV programming needs to utilize more realistic trial materials and case types other than homicide, better distinguish forensic TV *viewing* and forensic science *knowledge*, and involve deliberating groups.

Summary

Drawing these threads together, the research on scientific evidence yields several conclusions. First, evidence of an incriminating match against the defendant—particularly when it involves DNA evidence—is very powerful. Interestingly though, exonerating DNA test results are not necessarily interpreted as strong evidence of innocence. Second, jurors do not appear to be very sensitive to variations in the reported incidence rates of characteristics used to match the defendant to a crime. Third, most jurors do not use statistical information in an optimal fashion, tending to underweight it relative to the impact it should have according to the Bayesian model, and fail to combine probabilities in an ideal manner. Unfortunately, instructions and visual aids aimed at improving comprehension of Bayes's theorem do not seem to help very much, but they may in some circumstances. Fourth, decision makers are sensitive to the manner in which RMP information is conveyed, particularly the ease with which it brings to mind the possibility of coincidental matches. Specifically, fewer convictions result when reference is made to the possibility of multiple matching individuals and the relevant population is large. Fifth, jurors are likely to vary in their untutored beliefs about the likelihood of RMP and LE as a function of their life experiences. Sixth, LE information appears to have less impact on jurors than RMP despite the former being much more likely. Overall, the research on scientific evidence suggests that scientific test results are powerful (particularly with regard to DNA), but perhaps not as much as they should be, and regardless they are not processed by jurors in an optimal fashion.

Confession Evidence

Researchers can probably be forgiven for directing relatively little attention to the impact of confession evidence on jurors. After all, why study something that seems obvious? Some jurors might even wonder why a trial is necessary in the wake of a confession by the defendant. The presumptive finality of confession evidence may be largely responsible for the lack of empirical attention it has received from researchers. Only a few studies have examined juror verdicts in the context of a mock trial featuring some form of confession evidence, but they all point to the conclusion that confession evidence is very powerful and difficult for jurors to set aside even if it was obtained under questionable circumstances.

In the first such study, Kassin and Neumann (1997) examined the relative impact of various forms of evidence, including confession. In their initial experiment, mock jurors read four case summaries involving different types of charges (murder, rape, assault, and automobile theft). Each summary contained circumstantial evidence along with one of the following: a confession, an eyewitness identification, negative character testimony, or nothing else. In all but the theft case, confession evidence produced conviction rates 16–40 percent higher than the next-best form of evidence. Their second experiment used only the assault scenario but included multiple forms of evidence, and participants were given handheld electronic devices to record their perceptions of evidence strength at regular intervals as they read through the case summary. The confession evidence was viewed as more incriminating than any of the other types of evidence and was the most-often cited type of decisive evidence by those who convicted (in contrast to the eyewitness testimony, which was reported to be the decisive factor most often by those who acquitted). The findings of this second experiment were then replicated in a third using a different type of case (i.e., rape).

Kassin and Sukel (1997) further demonstrated the power of confession evidence—even when the statement is coerced. Mock jurors were presented with an extensive written transcript that included (for most) a confession by the defendant. In the experimental conditions, the confession was elicited via either a high-pressure or low-pressure interrogation, and ruled as either admissible or inadmissible by the judge. Mock jurors in the control condition did not read anything about a confession. The interrogation pressure manipulation involved the defendant either confessing immediately at the start of questioning (low pressure) or after being subjected to physical discomfort, yelling, and the menacing display of a firearm (high pressure). Those exposed to a confession tended to convict more often, although the difference between conviction rates for the four experimental conditions and the control condition became significant only when verdicts were weighted by verdict confidence in order to create a more sensitive continuous variable. The prosecution's evidence was strengthened in a second experiment and the initial findings replicated. Participants who learned of a confession— regardless of whether it was ruled admissible or not—convicted 25–44 percent more often than those who did not hear of a confession. Mock jurors generally reported that they discounted the confession evidence when it was elicited under high pressure—as they should have—but the lack of effect for the pressure manipulation on verdicts suggests otherwise. In essence, these studies show that confession evidence is powerful and has influence even when the jurors are aware that it should not.

A third study on confession evidence by Neuschatz, Lawson, Swanner, Meissner, and Neuschatz (2008) showed that confession evidence is powerful even when it does not come directly from the defendant. In this study, a key component of the prosecution's murder case was a secondhand confession provided by a "cooperating" witness. This individual was described as either a criminal accomplice present at the crime, a convicted criminal who heard the defendant confess in a correctional facility, or a school classmate of the defendant who heard the defendant confess in a card game. In addition to varying the cooperating witness's identity, half of the participants were told the witness had an incentive to testify in the form of either a reduced sentence or a monetary reward, whereas the other half were told the witness was testifying out of civic duty. Similar to Kassin and Sukel (1997), mock jurors exposed to a confession in *any* form convicted more often than those who did not, and more convictions resulted when the confession was introduced at trial by a cooperating witness who supposedly testified out of civic duty as opposed to when this person was portrayed as an accomplice or a jailhouse snitch. A second study with an additional incentive condition replicated the higher conviction rate (29–39%) for all experimental conditions relative to the control group that heard no confession evidence, and again failed to produce an effect for witness incentive—suggesting jurors are insensitive to the motive underlying secondary confessions.

Thus, confession evidence appears to be very powerful regardless of how jurors come to know of it. This conclusion is consistent with research on fundamental attribution error in which observers favor dispositional attributions for behavior and tend to discount the situational context. It is also consistent with the Story model in that learning the defendant personally admitted to the alleged behavior makes for a story that is short, sweet, and ultimately difficult to dismiss. Future research on confession evidence that varies the substantive content of the confession (e.g., the degree of admission) and/or its consistency with the rest of the evidence would be useful.

Demonstrative Visual Evidence
Gruesome Images

Exposure to photos or scenes of graphic violence is unsettling to many people. In the context of a trial, the relevant question is: Does exposure to gruesome visual stimuli cause jurors to be harsher on defendants? There is certainly reason to believe that this might occur. Evidence that produces an agitated, upset juror could result in more verdicts against the defendant for several reasons (Bright & Goodman-Delahunty, 2006). These include jurors confusing their emotional reactions with factual information, adopting a heuristic processing style, discounting exculpatory evidence, or desiring to blame someone for their negative feelings. For their part, the data tend to corroborate the notion that gruesome images work against the defendant.

Two studies have examined the display of gruesome physical evidence in simulated civil trials involving serious injury. One study manipulated the presence of four color slides showing victim injuries resulting from a farming accident (Oliver & Griffitt, 1976), whereas another varied the presence and nature of a single photo (i.e., black/white v. color v. no photo) of a child victim's body at the scene of an accident (Whalen & Blanchard, 1982). Both of these studies suggest that graphic visual evidence may increase the size of damage awards, at least under some conditions. Larger damage awards tended to be made by those who saw the slides (Oliver & Griffitt, 1976) and those who saw a color photo (as opposed to no photo or a black-and-white shot), but only when there was strong evidence of culpability and severe victim injury (Whalen & Blanchard, 1982).

Five studies have examined gruesome visual evidence in criminal trials, and they collectively indicate prejudicial effects despite some inconsistency in their results. With regard to verdicts, two of these studies yielded a substantially higher conviction rate for gruesome visual evidence (Bright & Goodman-Delahunty, 2006; Douglas, Lyon, & Ogloff, 1997), whereas two others produced no impact (Kassin & Garfield, 1991; Nemeth, 2002). In one of the studies that produced an effect, participants who saw three graphic autopsy photos convicted roughly twice as often as those who saw no photographs, regardless of whether the photos were in color or black/white (Douglas et al., 1997). In the other study, by Bright and Goodman-Delahunty (2006), verbal evidence (gruesome v. not gruesome) was manipulated separately from visual evidence (none, neutral photos, gruesome photos). Participants saw either five carefully selected gruesome photos from a real murder trial, five neutral photos, or no photographs at all. The conviction rate for those who saw the gruesome photos was over four times higher than those who saw no photographs (41% v. 9%), but it was also elevated for those who saw the neutral photos (38%). Follow-up analyses suggested the effect of the gruesome photos on verdicts may have been due to the higher levels of anger elicited by the photos. On the other hand, although verdicts did not differ, participants who saw the relevant crime-scene videotape used in the Kassin and Garfield (1991) study did report lower confidence thresholds required to convict, and the Nemeth (2002) study involved a weak manipulation of gruesomeness. Most recently, participants who saw one color photo of a murder victim tended to assign greater punishments than those who saw no photo in a study conducted in France (Finkelstein & Bastounis, 2010). On balance, exposure to gruesome visual evidence seems to increase the likelihood of conviction in criminal trials as a result of the negative emotion it elicits (specifically, anger toward the defendant).

Computer Simulation

Although the use of computer animation in court is becoming increasingly common, there is very little research to date on its impact (Nemeth, 2011). Consistent with clichés about one picture being worth a thousand words, we might expect computer-generated depictions to produce a decided advantage for the side that presents them. The three studies that have examined the effect of computer simulation evidence on juror verdicts, however, do not present a clear pattern of findings. In the first study on the topic, Kassin and Dunn (1997) observed that different computerized simulations of a falling body had considerable effect on mock juror verdicts and more impact than oral testimony, but it also showed that a computer simulation could bias verdicts when partisan versions were introduced by either side that were inconsistent with the undisputed physical evidence. In contrast, two other studies hint that the effect of computer simulations may depend on jurors' familiarity with the simulated event. A study by Dunn, Salovey, and Feigenson (2006) found an effect for computer simulation in one trial involving a plane crash, but no effect in a second trial in which a car accident was depicted. Similarly, in a highly realistic study on the topic, Bennett and his colleagues observed no greater impact of a computer simulation compared with traditional oral testimony plus graphics on judgments of responsibility or the damage awards of six-person juries deciding another automobile accident case (Bennett, Leibman, & Fetter, 1999). Presumably, jurors are more familiar with car accidents than plane crashes, ameliorating the informational value of a simulated depiction of the auto accident. Thus, initial work implies that computer simulations *may* have greater influence than traditional demonstrative exhibits, but any superiority could be limited to situations where jurors are unfamiliar with the simulated event(s).

Neuroimaging Tests

A variety of technologies exist that produce computer-generated images relevant to assessing the status and functioning of the human brain. At present, these technologies include CAT, PET, MRI, and fMRI—and there may be more on the way. It is increasingly common for the results of neuroimaging tests to be presented in court, and concerns have been raised that test-result images will be inordinately powerful because they allow attorneys to point to a picture and say to jurors, "See, *this* is the reason for the defendant's behavior" (Dumit, 1999; Kulynych, 1997). Research on the impact of neuroimaging evidence is just beginning, but the mixed results at present provide little basis for the fears expressed. On one hand, an initial study by Gurley and Marcus (2008) *did* find that defendants in an insanity case were more likely to be found NGRI if the defense presented MRI results showing a brain lesion. On the other hand, a recent major study revealed no impact of fMRI neuroimages on verdicts or sentences across four tightly controlled experiments that employed a large, representative sample of jury-eligible members of the community (Schweitzer et al., 2011). These experiments are notable for including several different control conditions in order to distinguish any effect of the neuroscience images from effects associated with the expert (i.e., mode of examination, testimony, and conclusion), as well as the presentation of visual evidence per se. No experiment produced the expected results, and even a mini-meta-analysis conducted on the accumulated results of the four studies revealed no effect—a result that clearly surprised and puzzled the authors. Thus, it is too early to say whether neuroscience images have a reliable impact on jurors, or whether any influence depends on other factors, but at this point the data are not consistent with the existence of a strong general effect.

Closing: When Is Evidence "Strong?"

The amassed research on various aspects of the evidence leads to one fairly straightforward conclusion: Strong evidence is that which makes for a good story. Confessions are very powerful because they offer a ready-made story with little need for any other information. Similarly, eyewitness testimony is also very powerful because it typically comes in the form of a firsthand narrative and supplies critical story-related information about the perpetrator's identity and/or actions. The impact of expert testimony will vary, but experts appear to have more influence when they apply their knowledge to the specific facts of the case at hand and provide information that jurors do not already possess—in other words, when they can help jurors' to flesh out a story for the present trial. Scientific evidence is at times part of an expert witness's testimony, and is most powerful when it definitively addresses a fundamental issue in jurors' stories—the identity of the main actor. Jurors clearly do not reason according to Bayes's model, but this should come as no surprise given that the model is very much at odds with the notion of sifting through the evidence to create a narrative explanation for trial-related events. When jurors have a difficult time comprehending an expert's message, they may use heuristic cues such as the expert's gender, credentials, or financial incentives for testifying in order to decide whether the expert's sub-story is plausible. Finally, demonstrative visual evidence likely influences jurors by literally making it easier for them to envision certain stories.

Heading into deliberation, jurors may have formed the evidence into a satisfactory story of the trial, or they may still be struggling with it. It remains to be seen what the other jurors are thinking.

7

Deliberation

Most jury trials are not so lopsided that views of the "correct" verdict are shared by all jurors at trial's end. Consensus must typically be forged through the deliberation process, which, reduced to its essence, involves one or more jurors changing their mind. This chapter reviews what has been learned about social influence in the context of deliberation.

Theories of Social Influence

Social influence can be viewed as a change in attitude, belief, or behavior triggered by the words, actions, or even mere presence of another individual. Change in underlying attitudes or beliefs has been called acceptance, persuasion, or internalization; behavioral change without accompanying attitudinal or belief change has been referred to as conformity or compliance. Deutsch and Gerard (1955) further distinguish between two types of social influence, informational and normative. *Informational influence* arises from the communication of ideas, facts, impressions, data, and so on; it represents change attributable to the content of a message and a desire to be correct in one's beliefs. *Normative influence* stems from a desire to feel included by others and avoid standing apart from the rest of the group. In essence, normative influence arises from a desire for people to be in agreement or harmony with others and a corresponding recognition of the social costs associated with overt disagreement. Given that these costs are incurred due to their "public" nature, normative influence may result in behavioral change (i.e., compliance) without necessarily producing an underlying change in attitude or belief. In other words, jurors may change their preferred verdict to be in overt accord with other jurors without necessarily believing their new position is the correct one. In contrast, informational influence tends to result in real cognitive change.

Another important distinction in the literature on social influence is between majority and minority factions. Moscovici (1980; 1985) argued that majority and minority factions within groups have differential access to these two types of influence. *Majority factions* contain more individuals than minority factions and thus can exert relatively large amounts of both normative influence and informational influence. Lacking numbers, *minority factions* can exert relatively little normative influence and are relegated primarily to informational influence. In other words, the largest faction within a jury can cause members of the smaller faction to change via the number and quality of the arguments they put forth, as well as the subtle (or sometimes not-so-subtle) pressure they can apply for the smaller faction to "fall in line." Conversely, smaller factions must rely primarily on the force of their arguments to convert the larger faction. Since 1980, several theoretical models have been offered to explain the operation of majority and minority influence during group decision making (Tindale, Davis, Vollrath, Nagao, & Hinsz, 1990). These models differ in their fine details, but all converge on the notion that the influence exerted by any faction is a positive but decelerating function of its size, with each additional member increasing faction influence by a smaller and smaller amount (Latane & Wolf, 1981; Mullen, 1983; Tanford & Penrod, 1984).

What Is Deliberation Like?

Only a small portion of the empirical literature on jury decision making has involved the intensive study of the deliberation process (Devine et al., 2001), perhaps 5–10 percent, but these studies provide a general portrait of deliberation in which data from real juries cohere fairly well with data from mock juries. Juries generally receive little in the way of instruction from the judge regarding how they are to arrive at their decisions, so jury deliberations are characterized by a fair amount of procedural diversity.

One thing most if not all juries are specifically told to do is select a foreperson, which is often their first formal task. After this, there is no general sequence that all juries follow. Jurors *do* spend a good portion of their time sitting around a table listening to a single speaker, although parallel conversations sometimes take place as people turn to those nearby and engage in sidebar interactions. Jurors get up and move around from time to time, and the conversation doesn't necessarily stop while some members are gone. Group discussion is often characterized by a certain amount of nonlinearity, with some jumping around and cycling back when it comes to the topic. Of course, there are often moments of disagreement and occasionally outright conflict. In the only large-scale study to involve the videotaping of real deliberations, Diamond and her colleagues (2003) noted numerous similarities between jury deliberations and committee meetings in non-legal settings.

Polls

Most deliberations include one or more nonbinding straw polls (or informal votes) at some point, particularly when jurors sense they are getting close to consensus. These polls are often taken in the open with a show of hands, but sometimes anonymously using slips of paper. Real juries generally report taking their first vote somewhere between twenty minutes and forty-five minutes of entering the deliberation room (Sandys & Dillehay, 1995; Hans et al., 2003). One study by Diamond et al. (2003) had the unique ability to assess first-vote timing in forty Arizona civil juries by actually "going to the tape." On average, these juries took their first vote twenty-one minutes into deliberation, although first-vote timing may have been affected somewhat by whether jurors were allowed to talk about the case before the end of the trial, with juries allowed to discuss the evidence prior to deliberation more likely to take their vote within the first ten minutes of deliberation than those not permitted (39% v. 17%).

Foreperson Selection and Characteristics

One might expect juries to carefully choose their formal leader, but the limited research available suggests they generally do not. Instead, the foreperson selection process appears often to be brief and even perfunctory, seemingly driven more by a desire to pick someone and get on with things rather than identify the best person for the role. Much of the time, the foreperson is determined quickly and harmoniously by someone volunteering or accepting the nomination of another juror (Bridgeman & Marlowe, 1979; Devine et al., 2004; Ellsworth, 1989; Hawkins, 1962). In one realistic simulation study where mock deliberations were recorded, 90 percent of forepersons were chosen within twenty statements of the start of deliberation (Diamond & Casper, 1992). Accordingly, forepersons tend to share some rather mundane characteristics. They are often the first to speak (Sannito & Arnolds, 1982) or the first to mention the need to choose a foreperson (Boster, Hunter, & Hale, 1991; Ellsworth, 1989). Forepersons also tend to sit in more visible places such as at the ends of rectangular tables (Diamond & Casper, 1992; Dillehay & Nietzel, 1985; Ellsworth, 1989; Strodtbeck & Lipinski, 1985; Velasco, 1995). Occasionally, two or more jurors express a desire for the job, and this may be when one task-relevant characteristic of forepersons—previous experience as a juror—plays a role as tiebreaker (Ellsworth, 1989; Kerr et al., 1982; Strodtbeck & Lipinski, 1985). Forepersons also have a particular demographic profile. In the United States, they tend to be better educated (Foley & Pigott, 1997b; Hastie et al., 1983; 1998; Strodtbeck & Lipinski, 1985), White (Boster et al., 1991; Devine et al., 2009; Lynch & Haney, 2011), and—most especially—male (Beckham & Aronson, 1978; Boster et al., 1991; Devine et al., 2009; Dillehay & Nietzel, 1985; Ellsworth, 1989; Hastie et al., 1998; Kerr et al., 1982; Lynch & Haney, 2011; Sannito & Arnolds, 1982). In terms of personality, forepersons also tend to be more extraverted than the typical juror (Clark, Boccaccini, Caillouet, & Chaplin, 2007; Rotenberg, Hewlett, & Siegwart, 1998).

Juror Participation

Turning to the spoken contributions of members, two early mock jury experiments associated with the Chicago Jury Project produced several findings leading to the overall conclusion that juror speaking during deliberation is neither a systematic or egalitarian process (Hawkins, 1962; James, 1959; Simon, 1967; Strodtbeck et al., 1957; Strodtbeck & Mann, 1956). First and most clearly, men generally spoke more often than women. Second, using a fairly crude measure of occupational status, individuals working in more prestigious occupations tended to speak more often than jurors in less prestigious occupations. Third, participation was not equal across jurors—a few members tended to do the lion's share of the talking while other members said little or nothing throughout deliberation. Indeed, in one study, the top three participants accounted for roughly half of the speaking entries in most juries. Fourth, forepersons took more than their share of speaking turns during deliberation, accounting for 25–30 percent of the speaking acts in a twelve-person jury. Fifth, the probability of a mock juror speaking was found to be inversely related to the size of the faction they were part of, with individuals in small factions—and a few representatives of large factions—doing most of the talking.

Subsequent research has shown these findings to be robust. One early study of deliberation involving twenty-eight mixed-gender mock juries found men to initiate more speaking acts (particularly with regard to giving suggestions, opinions, and information), and also to be the target of more speaking actions by other jurors (Nemeth, Endicott, & Wachtler, 1976). Based on their very thorough analysis of the deliberations of sixty-nine mock juries, Hastie et al. (1983) observed that males generated 40 percent more speaking acts than women, high-SES jurors spoke more often than low-SES jurors, members of factions tended to speak less in proportion to their faction's size, and forepersons generated 25 percent of the speaking acts during deliberation—three times as many as the average juror. Similarly, forepersons said more than twice as much as the average juror in a study of the deliberations of sixty mock juries determining damage awards in a price-fixing civil case (Diamond & Casper, 1992). In one study conducted in Spain, forepersons spoke the most often in 56 percent of mock juries composed of Spanish students (Velasco, 1995). Finally, in studies of real juries in the United States, forepersons have been reported to be more talkative than other jurors (Bridgeman & Marlowe, 1979; Sannito & Arnolds, 1982), and high-SES jurors have been found to speak more often than other jurors (York & Cornwell, 2006).

Deliberation Style

The vast majority of jury deliberations result in a decision of some sort, but the path taken to get to that point can vary. Hastie et al. (1983) coined the term *deliberation style* to refer to the jury's general approach to their task, and identified two styles in particular: *verdict-driven* juries organize their discussion around choosing a verdict, whereas *evidence-driven* juries focus their efforts on going over the testimony and exhibits to establish the facts of the case as best they can. According to Hastie et al., verdict-driven deliberations are characterized by several markers: an early public vote on the appropriate verdict, jurors acting as advocates for particular verdicts and citing evidence to support it, common mention of preferred verdicts by members, and frequent polling of the jury. In contrast, evidence-driven juries tend to defer their first vote until fairly late in the proceedings, sometimes the very end of deliberation. Individual jurors do not publicly commit to preferred

verdicts and the jury's explicit focus is on reviewing the evidence and establishing the facts of the case without discussing their verdict implications. In
essence, evidence-driven juries focus on constructing a narrative regarding
the events leading up to trial and only after the facts of the case have been
established and assembled into a coherent framework is an effort made to
link the "story" to a verdict.

Although deliberation style represents a fairly broad construct, in practice, inferences about a jury's deliberation style have been based primarily
on jurors' reports of the timing of their first vote. Based on this criterion,
Hastie et al. (1983) classified 28 percent of their jury deliberations as verdict-
driven, 35 percent as evidence-driven, and 38 percent as a mix of the two. A
subsequent study with a small number of mock juries suggested that up to 50
percent of juries may take a preliminary poll before discussing the evidence
(Ellsworth, 1989), but several field studies point toward a lower incidence
rate for the verdict-driven approach in real juries, with estimates between 6
percent and 31 percent (Devine et al., 2004; 2007; Sandys & Dillehay, 1995).
These same studies suggest that the evidence-driven approach is adopted in
31–40 percent of deliberations (Devine et al., 2007; Sandys & Dillehay, 1995),
with the remaining proportion engaging in some mix of the two. Thus, both
deliberation styles seem fairly common but, due to the reliance on first-
vote timing as a proxy measure, it is difficult to say which one is used more
frequently.

Duration

The amount of time a jury spends in the deliberation room is easy enough to
measure but difficult to interpret. It presumably reflects the amount of effort
and energy expended by jurors in reviewing the case evidence, but this proposition has been very difficult to test due to the long-standing prohibition
against direct observation of deliberation. As a result, deliberation length has
probably been of more interest to practitioners and court-watchers than jury
scholars.

Over the years, numerous field studies have reported the mean amount
of time taken by actual juries to deliberate, and they collectively imply that
most deliberations last from two to four hours, with the majority falling
between two-and-a-half and three-and-a-half hours (Clark et al., 2007;
Devine et al., 2004; Diamond et al., 2003; Heuer & Penrod, 1989; 1994b;
Moran & Comfort, 1986; Kalven & Zeisel, 1966; Werner et al., 1985; Zeisel
& Diamond, 1978). The last word on how long the typical jury deliber-
ates, however, should go to Gregory Mize and his colleagues (2007), who

surveyed judges and attorneys about their most recent jury trial and obtained reports of deliberation duration for a whopping 11,752 jury trials. They calculated a mean time of 2.77 hours for a "referent" deliberation associated with a civil trial heard in state court where the relevant evidence and law were rated as "not complex," and twelve jurors were required to reach a unanimous decision. However, deliberation duration was strongly associated with several case characteristics, including *type of case* (criminal v. civil), *court system* (state v. federal), and *trial complexity* (evidentiary as well as legal), but only slightly related to various courtroom procedures and practices. Most striking was the additional time taken by juries to deliberate in the federal court system for criminal trials—a discrepancy that increased with the seriousness of the case (i.e., on average, adding one-half hour for misdemeanor cases, one hour for felonies and civil trials, and four hours for death-penalty cases). In addition, the impact of trial complexity was quite large for both *evidentiary complexity* (on average, adding 112 minutes for moderately complex evidence and 223 minutes for extremely complex evidence) and *legal complexity* (+55 minutes for moderate complexity and +109 minutes for extreme complexity). In contrast, several courtroom practices had little impact on deliberation length, including using juries of different sizes, requiring unanimity, allowing jurors to take notes, providing juries with written instructions, and allowing juries to discuss the evidence prior to deliberation. These relatively small differentials suggest that courtroom efficiency is not strongly affected by many potential reforms and should not be a primary consideration regarding their adoption.

Initial Verdict Preference Distributions and Jury Verdicts
Faction Size Effect

Regardless of the specific relationship or proposed mechanism, theories of social influence converge on the notion that there is strength in numbers. During deliberations, larger factions should exert more influence than smaller factions, whether that influence is normative, informational, or some combination. The theories further agree that factions exert influence in proportion to their relative size, with each additional member increasing its "pull." Ultimately, larger factions should be more effective at converting members from other factions, leading the verdicts favored by larger factions to be more likely chosen as the jury's final verdict.

Theory and data definitely agree on this point. Research has consistently shown a strong and robust relationship between the verdict preferred by the majority of jurors at the start of deliberation and the jury's ultimate verdict. This has been observed in numerous experimental studies where mock jurors were asked to indicate their preferred personal verdict prior to deliberation, and then jury verdicts were recorded after deliberation. In an early meta-analysis, MacCoun and Kerr (1988) examined the relationship between the distribution of predeliberation verdict preferences and jury verdicts in twelve such studies with mock juries, and found the size of the majority faction to be very predictive of the jury's ultimate verdict. In particular, their analysis suggested a critical "success" threshold for factions once they consisted of twice as many members as the competing faction, which is to say that the probability of a faction "winning" deliberation increases with each additional member and becomes very high once a two-thirds majority exists.

The strong relationship between the distribution of individual juror preferences and jury verdicts has also been noted in several field studies with real juries wherein the distribution of votes on the first poll was used to approximate the initial verdict preference distribution (Devine et al., 2004; 2007; Hannaford-Agor, Hans, Mott, & Munsterman, 2002; Kalven & Zeisel, 1966; Sandys & Dillehay, 1995). In the watershed study on this topic, Kalven and Zeisel (1966) reconstructed the first vote taken during deliberation in 225 criminal jury trials based on post-trial interviews with the jurors. In the 156 deliberations with a non-unanimous majority on the first vote, the jury's final verdict corresponded to the majority's preference in 91 percent of the forty-one cases where the first vote favored acquittal and in 86 percent of the 105 cases where the first vote favored conviction. When there was an even split, juries convicted half of the time and acquitted the other half. Thus, in 91 percent of the 215 trials in which the first vote was not evenly divided, the jury ended up choosing the verdict favored by the majority on the first vote. These data led Kalven and Zeisel to a conclusion that has shaped research on deliberation ever since:

> However, in the instances where there is an initial majority either for conviction or acquittal, the jury in roughly nine out of ten cases decides in the direction of the initial majority. Only with extreme infrequency does the minority succeed in persuading the majority to change its mind during the deliberation. But this is only to say that with very few exceptions the first ballot decides the outcome of the verdict. And if this is true, then the real decision is often made before the deliberation begins. The upshot is a radical hunch about the function of the deliberation process. Perhaps it does not so much decide the case as bring about the consensus, the outcome of which has been made highly likely by the distribution of first ballot votes.

The deliberation process might well be likened to what the developer does for an exposed film: it brings out the picture, but the outcome is pre-determined. (pp. 488–489)

Several subsequent field studies have produced remarkably similar estimates of the "win rate" for initial majorities. In a study based on interviews with sixty-five jurors from ten criminal jury trials in California, Bridgeman and Marlowe (1979) concluded that in no instance did the final trial outcome differ from the majority preference on the first vote, although it is not clear if any of these juries were evenly split at first. Sandys and Dillehay (1995) interviewed three or more jurors from forty-three criminal juries in Kentucky and determined that 90 percent of the jury verdicts were consistent with the majority's preference on the first vote. In an excellent field study of jury decision making involving criminal trials held in Washington, DC, Maricopa County, Phoenix, the Bronx, and Los Angeles, final verdicts coincided with the majority preference on the first vote in 80 percent of the 256 juries that were not evenly split (Hannaford-Agor et al., 2002; Hans et al., 2003). Finally, two of my own studies produced similar results with Indiana criminal juries. In the first, sixty-two of seventy juries (89%) reached a verdict consistent with the first-vote majority (Devine et al., 2004); in the second study, eighty-one of ninety-six juries (84%) eventually chose the verdict preferred by the majority on the first vote (Devine et al., 2007). Thus, a "majority wins" decision scheme characterizes the workings of actual juries as well as mock juries.

In 2001, my students and I conducted a second meta-analysis of the relationship between the initial verdict preference distribution within juries and their verdicts (Devine et al., 2001). We sought to update and extend the earlier work of MacCoun and Kerr (1988) and were able to gather a database of twenty-five studies that included two studies of actual juries where the split on the jury's first vote was used to estimate the initial verdict preference distribution. As expected, this larger meta-analysis revealed a very strong positive association between the faction size and the probability of a faction's preferred verdict being the jury's ultimate verdict. In other words, the chance of a faction "winning" (i.e., having its preferred verdict chosen as the jury's ultimate verdict) is greater for each additional juror in the faction at the start of deliberation.

There is even indication of a faction size effect for the weightiest jury decision of all—whether to take a life. Analyzing data from fifty-three South Carolina juries deciding on a sentence of life in prison versus death in the penalty phase of a capital trial, Theodore Eisenberg, Stephen Garvey, and Martin

Wells (2001) observed results strikingly similar to those seen with verdicts related to guilt. In the twenty-one cases where *66 percent or less* of the jury supported death on the first vote, the jury always opted for life in prison. Conversely, in the twenty-one cases where *76 percent or more* of the jury favored the death penalty on the first vote, the ultimate sentence was always for death. Only in the narrow range where two-thirds to three-fourths of the jury favored death on the first vote (eleven cases) was there any (retrospective) uncertainty about the jury's ultimate decision, with these juries opting for a death sentence 63 percent of the time. Across all cases, 79 percent of the jury sentencing decisions were consistent with the first-vote majority.

Overall, the many experimental laboratory studies along with the corroborating data from real juries demonstrate convincingly that the number of jurors who favor a particular verdict early in deliberation is a very good predictor of the final verdict. Put simply, initial majority factions usually "win" deliberation. This well-established finding does, however, come with some fine print—very little attention has been devoted to factions in civil juries, trials involving multiple charges against the same defendant, or trials involving verdict options other than the traditional G/NG dichotomy (e.g., lesser charges, NGRI, GBMI). When there are multiple charges against the defendant and/or more than two verdict options available (e.g., conviction on a lesser charge), the number of relevant preference distributions goes up exponentially. In such situations, there will undoubtedly be times when no majority exists within the jury. What happens when the largest faction is only a plurality and there are verdict options available other than guilty or not guilty? At this point, we have little idea.

Defendant Leniency Effect

A fundamental principle of the American criminal justice system is that a defendant's guilt must be proven beyond a reasonable doubt before a jury convicts. In essence, the bar—the standard of proof—is set intentionally high so that the evidence must be overwhelming before the state is allowed to deprive individuals of their liberty or their life. The behavioral implication of this principle is straightforward—jurors should vote to acquit unless they are very confident of the defendant's guilt. Combining this principle with the faction-size effect, we might expect juries to opt for the verdict preferred by the majority of their members and, if there is no clear majority, give the benefit of the doubt to the defendant. In other words, juries should decide in favor of the defendant in cases where the evidence does not clearly meet the standard of proof.

After the initial wave of research on social decision schemes subsided, MacCoun and Kerr (1988) examined this issue using meta-analytic techniques and data from twelve studies employing primarily six-person mock juries. Across all twelve studies, juries that were evenly split at the start of deliberation were four times more likely to acquit than convict. Focusing on just those juries with an exact two-thirds majority (e.g., 4–2 or 2–4) that did not hang, MacCoun and Kerr found that initial pro-conviction majorities succeeded 67 percent of the time whereas initial pro-acquittal majorities succeeded at a whopping 94 percent rate. Thus, consistent with a "defendant protection" norm, juries without a strong majority at the start of deliberation were much more likely to acquit than convict. MacCoun and Kerr then replicated this finding in two studies of their own where mock juries were composed with an even split, although the leniency effect was not as pronounced for members of the community as for students, and all but disappeared when a "preponderance of the evidence" standard was used as opposed to "beyond reasonable doubt." We obtained similar results in our later meta-analysis using data from over twice as many studies (Devine et al., 2001). For six-person juries that ultimately reached a verdict, we calculated success rates of 70 percent for two-thirds majorities favoring conviction and 96 percent for two-thirds majorities favoring acquittal, whereas evenly split juries convicted only 22 percent of the time. Fewer studies used twelve-person juries, and the available data were more spread out across verdict preference distributions, but the overall pattern was very similar. Thus, despite the diversity of studies involved, our analyses also support a leniency effect in criminal juries.

It is interesting to note, however, that the evidence for a leniency effect in actual juries is much weaker than in mock juries. Considering data from five field studies that reconstructed the first-vote preference distribution in real juries deciding non-capital cases (Devine et al., 2004; 2007; Hannaford-Agor et al., 2002; Kalven & Zeisel, 1966; Sandys & Dillehay, 1995), there was a 51 percent conviction rate across eighty-two evenly divided juries—a value that seems inconsistent with giving the defendant the benefit of the doubt. It is possible that these real-world data reflect some measurement "noise" (i.e., pre-vote change, conviction on lesser charges), but it appears the leniency effect is weaker or less reliable in actual juries than studies using mock juries would suggest.

Combining a strong faction-size effect with a defendant-leniency effect, the research on verdict preference distributions in criminal juries suggests the relationship between the size of the pro-conviction faction and the probability of the jury convicting is nonlinear. Specifically, its shape resembles a stretched-out "S." The probability of conviction begins at essentially zero when no jurors initially favor guilt, and it remains very low as the percentage of jurors favoring conviction increases from 0 to 33 percent (i.e., one-third of the jury), rising just a little bit along the way. Around the 33 percent mark, the probability of conviction begins to go up in a more-or-less linear fashion until the 75 percent mark (i.e., three-fourths of the jury), reaching the 50 percent probability threshold somewhere between an evenly divided jury and one in which two-thirds of the members initially favor guilt. Once 75 percent or more of the jury favors conviction, the probability of a guilty verdict becomes very high and remains high as the faction size moves toward 100 percent. Of course, other variables may have some impact on the overall shape of the curve or shift it somewhat to the left or right, including the wording of the instructions given by the judge and perhaps the nature of the crime. The graph for pro-acquittal faction size would look about the same as mentioned but, given the defendant leniency effect, would be shifted to the left (i.e., a greater chance of a pro-acquittal faction "winning" at every size relative to a pro-conviction faction). Although very little research has been conducted on social decision schemes in civil juries, the general shape of the function relating initial faction size and jury verdict might be expected to be similar for civil juries but without the shift for defendant leniency.

Informational Influence

Ideally, what jurors say during deliberation *should* be largely responsible for any opinion change that takes place. However, relatively few studies have focused on informational influence associated with the content of deliberation because of the formidable practical hurdles involved. Coding audiotapes or videotapes of deliberation is a time-consuming, labor-intensive activity that first requires figuring out what will be coded as well as what will count as an instance of each code. Transcripts can run to hundreds of pages in length, and all of those statements must be classified. Even when good coding schemes are paired with rigorous observer training, the level of interrater agreement can be discouragingly low. The difficulties associated with coding deliberation go a long way toward explaining why these studies are fairly rare.

Despite these obstacles, good studies have been done, and they show that deliberation content can and does influence jury decisions. For instance, using a clever design that disentangled normative and informational influence, Stasser, Stella, Hanna, and Colella (1984) manipulated the number of supporters for a particular verdict independent of the number of persons advocating for that verdict. They accomplished this by composing six-person mock juries so that each would have a two-thirds majority favoring conviction or acquittal, and then *assigning* four persons to argue for one verdict and two for the other. In two of the four study conditions, mock jurors were told to advocate for their own preferred verdict, but in the other two conditions a majority of persons (i.e., four people) were told to argue for the verdict favored by the minority (i.e., two people). In other words, some conditions contained devil's advocates assigned to argue for a verdict they did not personally favor. Consistent with the legal ideal, individual preference change after fifteen minutes of deliberation was found to be a function of the number of persons arguing for a particular verdict (i.e., informational influence) as opposed to the number of persons who actually favored it (i.e., normative influence).

Another study supporting the impact of juror discussion featured one hundred mock juries composed primarily of persons recruited from jury pool rosters who heard a case involving three charges: assault, burglary, and armed robbery (Tanford & Penrod, 1986). Deliberations were videotaped and coded using thirty-four categories that captured both the topic and evaluative nature (i.e., positive, neutral, or negative) of each statement. Analyses were focused on predicting jurors' postdeliberation verdicts based on the number of comments made during deliberation from each category. In general, the deliberation content codes were able to account for 26–50 percent of the variance in jurors' postdeliberation votes. Various content categories correlated significantly with final juror verdict preferences as expected, with the strongest relationships observed for case facts and verdict statements. Although it was unclear how much variance was uniquely attributable to the various deliberation content variables, the general picture that emerges suggests that what is said during deliberation is the mechanism through which the initial preference distribution influences the jury's final decision.

Hastie, Schkade, and Payne (1998) conducted a similar experiment with jury-eligible residents of Colorado using four civil-case scenarios in which the jury was charged with determining the appropriateness and amount of punitive damages. Jury deliberations were videotaped and transcribed, with each statement subsequently coded into one of sixty-three categories. Multi-step regression analyses were conducted to predict whether the jury would find the defendant liable for punitive damages. In the first step, control variables reflecting the case (i.e., variations in the strength of evidence) and the predeliberation preference distribution within the jury accounted for 42 percent of the variance in final jury-level judgments. In addition, fifteen deliberation content variables selected by the computer were able to increase the percentage of variance explained to 76 percent (68% using only the best eight). The thoroughness of jury deliberation was also coded using an index that counted whether the jury (1) discussed and (2) reached a formal decision on each of the five legal criteria relevant to punitive damages. In the real-life version of each case, punitive damages had been ruled inappropriate by an appeals court; in the study, mock juries that awarded punitive damages were significantly less thorough in addressing the relevant legal criteria. Thus, in this study, deliberation content variables helped account for jury decisions over and above the characteristics of the case and the jury's predeliberation vote distribution, with juries that were more thorough in discussing relevant criteria more likely to arrive at the legally appropriate decision.

Finally, another intriguing study directly highlights the important role of narrative stories in deliberation (Holstein, 1985). Forty-eight mock juries composed of Michigan ex-jurors were shown a simulated trial involving the alleged theft of bricks from a construction site. Deliberations were audiotaped, transcribed, and coded for the number of schematic interpretations of the evidence articulated during group discussion. A "schematic interpretation" was defined as "any juror's attempt to specify what he or she thought was happening in the situation in question" (p.88). In other words, a schematic interpretation was basically a story. Several interesting findings emerged from this study. Every deliberation produced from one to five schematic interpretations (2.3 on average); new interpretations tended to occur earlier in deliberation rather than later; and the more interpretations articulated, the longer deliberation lasted. Most interesting was the relationship between the number of articulated schematic interpretations and final jury-level outcomes. Every deliberation involving only one proposed "story" (i.e., interpretation) ended in a verdict, whereas 28 percent of those involving two stories yielded a hung jury, and 72 percent of those featuring three or more stories ended with the jury unable to reach a decision. Further, the existence of multiple stories supporting a particular verdict was associated with a *lower* likelihood of that verdict being chosen by the jury. In the fifteen deliberations where three or more interpretations were articulated and one of the verdicts was supported by a majority of the stories, only one deliberation produced a unanimous verdict consistent with the multiple stories. In contrast, three of these deliberations yielded a verdict consistent with the "singleton" story. In essence, the existence of multiple stories supporting a particular verdict may have created doubt about the correctness of *any* of them. The more stories offered, the more difficult it was for juries to reach a verdict—even when multiple stories supported the same verdict.

Interpersonal Influence: Roles and Individual Differences

Social influence in groups can stem from individual difference variables as well as situational characteristics associated with the role that an individual takes or is forced to adopt. Researchers have focused on the foreperson role whereas other potentially influential roles such as faction leader have garnered much less interest. Although a number of studies have measured juror participation, only a few attempted to measure influence per se. Those that have done so used several strategies for identifying influential individuals, including self reports, peer nominations or ratings, and correlations between individual juror's preferred verdicts or damage awards and final jury verdicts or awards.

These studies show that jurors who are reported to have the most influence during deliberation tend to be male and have high SES. In one of the best early studies of influence, Hastie et al. (1983) reported a number of demographic characteristics to be positively associated with ratings of persuasiveness, including education level, occupational status, income, and gender (i.e., being male). These results are consistent with several field studies involving actual juries. In a survey of ex-jurors by Mills and Bohannon (1980), only 26 percent of responding female jurors felt they were responsible for changing other jurors' decisions in contrast to 43 percent of male jurors (although this result held only for White jurors). Similarly, participants in Marcus, Lyons, and Guyton's (2000) study reported that male jurors were more likely than female jurors to have influenced them personally (and also said the same thing about jurors who were tall). However, York and Cornwell (2006) observed only a slight tendency for men to be identified as influential more often than women during deliberation but did find support for the importance of SES. Roughly 39 percent of the upper-class jurors in their study were nominated as influential, compared with 38 percent of upper-middle-class jurors, 13 percent of middle-class jurors, and only 8 percent of lower-class jurors. Further, jurors in the two highest categories (upper-class and upper-middle-class) were about 3.5 times more likely to be viewed as influential compared with lower-class jurors.

Not surprisingly, jurors who are identified as more persuasive or influential also tend to participate more than others (Diamond & Casper, 1992; Hastie et al., 1983; York & Cornwell, 2006). In their comprehensive analysis of the deliberations of sixty-nine mock juries, Hastie et al. (1983) found the amount of speaking by each of their 828 mock jurors was strongly related to their rated persuasiveness, with those in the upper quartile of persuasiveness credited on average with over 3.5 times as many statements as those in the lowest quartile. In York and Cornwell's (2006) study, about 40 percent of jurors who participated "much more" than others were nominated as influential compared with only 14 percent of those who spoke "much less" than others. However, in an excellent study of sixty mock jury deliberations, Diamond and Casper (1992) obtained peer ratings of influence along with objective measures of participation (i.e., number of words spoken) and found that the amount of speaking by a juror explained *some* of the variance in their rated influence, but only a modest amount (14%). So it appears there is more to influence than simply how much a juror talks.

Several other studies indicate that juror personality characteristics play a role as well. Most notably, jurors perceived as highly influential tend to be extraverted (Clark et al., 2007; Marcus et al., 2000; Rotenberg et al., 1998). In their study of dyadic influence among eighty-six jurors who took part in eight twelve-person jury trials (seven of which were criminal), Marcus and his colleagues (2000) asked respondents to rate their own influence on other members and indicate who they felt had influenced them personally. Extraverted jurors tended to be viewed by their peers as having more influence during deliberation, whereas jurors who scored relatively high on conscientiousness tended to report being the most influenced by others. Surprisingly, individuals who scored highly on openness to experience reported being the least influenced by other jurors. In a similar study, Clark et al. (2007) had 764 venirepersons complete a personality inventory before undergoing voir dire and tracked those individuals who later deliberated in one of seventeen different jury trials (eleven civil, six criminal). In the criminal trial deliberations, jurors who reported higher levels of influence on others tended to score higher on extraversion and openness as well as lower on neuroticism. In the civil trial deliberations, jurors with greater self-reported levels of influence tended to be higher on extraversion and conscientiousness.

Finally, need for cognition (NC) may be yet another important personality characteristic. In a study by Shestowsky and Horowitz (2004) involving four-person mock juries, individuals who were classified as high-NC spoke more often and were rated as more assertive, talkative, and persuasive than low-NC individuals by themselves, peers, independent coders, and interacting confederates. At the same time, the arguments they produced across two studies were not judged to be more valid or stronger than low-NC individuals. In a complementary fashion, low-NC jurors were more receptive to influence, more likely to change their position, and, perhaps most importantly, better at discriminating strong and weak arguments regarding the evidence. Thus, extraversion, conscientiousness, and need for cognition may be important for understanding who influences who in jury deliberations.

Foreperson

As the only formal role within the jury, there has been a fair amount of interest in the degree of influence associated with being a foreperson. Most but not all studies of deliberation influence that kept track of foreperson status have concluded that forepersons are more influential than the typical juror (Bridgeman & Marlowe, 1979; Foley & Pigott, 1997b; York & Cornwell, 2006). One of the best studies was conducted by Diamond and Casper (1992) who used several converging methods to measure influence. In general, forepersons were rated as more influential than other jurors and foreperson status explained variation in influence ratings above and beyond mere participation. There was also indirect support for the influence of the foreperson in that the foreperson's predeliberation award preference was strongly correlated with the jury's ultimate damage award, and this correlation was notably larger than the corresponding correlation between the predeliberation preferred awards of other jurors and the jury's ultimate award. Finally, the foreperson's preferred damage award prior to deliberation explained additional variation in jury damage awards beyond the single-best predictor of the jury's award—the median of the individual members' predeliberation awards.

Data from actual juries also underscores the suspected influence of the foreperson. In an analysis of data on 605 dyads from fourteen real juries that controlled for a variety of demographic characteristics and participation, forepersons were more than twice as likely as non-forepersons to be judged as the most influential juror (York & Cornwell, 2006). In addition, in one of my studies, we found that the foreperson's initial verdict stance (guilty, uncertain, not guilty) was a very strong predictor of jury verdicts in a post-trial survey of 179 criminal juries *even* when the strength of evidence was statistically controlled—implying foreperson influence was important and not simply an artifact of representing the stronger side (Devine et al., 2007). Consistent with this, in another field study, forepersons were rated as especially influential in two criminal cases that yielded acquittals compared with four trials that produced convictions (Clark et al., 2007). Not all of the data agree on this issue, though, with two mock-jury studies conducted by Reid Hastie and his colleagues producing no indication that forepersons were more influential than other jurors (Hastie et al., 1983; 1998). These latter results may be anomalous or may signal that the amount of influence exerted by the foreperson depends on other variables such as the deliberation style used by the jury or the size of the foreperson's faction.

Faction Leaders

Although foreperson is the only formal role in most juries, informal roles may develop over the course of deliberation that have consequences for speaking turns, prestige, and ultimately who is influential. In our study of 179 Indiana criminal juries, we asked jurors to indicate whether any individual emerged during deliberation as a clear leader of either the pro-conviction or pro-acquittal factions (Devine et al., 2007). Surprisingly, the presence of an identifiable pro-conviction faction leader was not correlated with jury verdicts, but the presence of a pro-acquittal faction leader was. In essence, NG verdicts were much more likely when responding jurors reported that there was a clear leader of those favoring acquittal. These data suggest that a key event in deliberations which eventually produce acquittals is the emergence of a faction leader who can actively argue their side's viewpoint and rally others to the cause.

Summary

Tying together the threads from the preceding discussion, the most influential jurors tend to be talkative, male, high SES, extraverted, and occupy the foreperson role. Those jurors who are most influenced by others appear to be higher on conscientiousness and lower in terms of need for cognition. Considerable attention has been devoted to forepersons, but more attention should be devoted to informal roles that emerge during deliberation (e.g., faction leaders).

Procedural Mechanisms
Polling

The power of the initial majority is considerable, but what happens when the majority viewpoint is not obvious to the jurors? In such instances, normative influence might be exerted by a minority faction that (at least temporarily) *appears* to represent the majority within the jury. This intriguing notion was examined in several studies by James Davis and his colleagues via the mechanism of straw polling (i.e., voting).

In their first study, Davis, Stasson, Ono, and Zimmerman (1988) had mock jurors watch a videotaped trial simulation involving assault, and then formed them into 105 six-person juries that were evenly divided in terms of their initial distribution of verdict preferences (i.e., 3G–3NG). Jurors were seated such that all three members of a particular verdict faction were adjacent to each other and voted in succession. Some juries took public votes with the acquittal faction going first, others took public votes with the conviction faction going first, and still others voted privately (and simultaneously) in order to serve as a baseline condition. In addition, half of the juries were instructed to take a first vote immediately at the start of deliberation whereas the other half were told to take their first vote after five minutes of discussion. In the simultaneous-voting (baseline) juries, mock jurors were much more likely to switch their preferred verdict from G to NG, especially when the first vote occurred after five minutes of discussion. In the sequential-voting juries, there was clear indication of normative influence associated with public polling—but only when the first vote was taken early. When the straw poll was taken before discussion and the three members of the pro-conviction faction voted first, critical fourth jurors from the opposing (pro-acquittal) faction were over six times more likely to switch their verdict preference to conviction compared with the corresponding rate of spontaneous preference change in the private, simultaneous juries (i.e., 32% v. 5%). When the straw poll was taken before discussion and the first three votes were for NG, critical fourth jurors who initially favored conviction switched their votes to NG somewhat more often than the corresponding change rate in the simultaneous juries (27% v. 15%). In contrast, there was no effect of the initial voting sequence on critical fourth voters after five minutes of discussion regardless of which side voted first, presumably because the lack of consensus within the jury had become apparent by then. In terms of impact on the final verdict, juries in which the first three jurors voted NG ended up acquitting the defendant 75 percent of the time in comparison to a 61 percent acquittal rate for juries in which the first three votes were cast for conviction (and a 69% acquittal rate for privately voting juries). Thus, a 14 percent difference in NG verdicts arose from a seemingly trivial source—the first three votes in the first deliberation poll.

This intriguing finding was replicated and extended in a follow-up study by Davis, Kameda, Parks, Stasson, and Zimmerman (1989) using the same trial materials and 130 six-person juries composed of jurors with known verdict preferences. This time, however, juries with a two-thirds majority favoring conviction (i.e., 4–2) were examined in addition to evenly split (3–3) juries, and all juries were instructed to take their first poll before any discussion. Relative to the low rates of spontaneous change in juries that voted simultaneously (i.e., 0–4%), critical jurors (i.e., the first juror to vote in the second faction) in both the 4–2 and 3–3 sequentially voting juries changed their votes much more often than would be expected by chance (i.e., 19–29%). Normative influence was even apparent in the 4–2 juries when the two individuals favoring acquittal voted first, causing 23 percent of the first voters in the pro-conviction faction to switch to NG. This latter finding is especially intriguing in that it stemmed from the vote of only two members who were in fact a minority within the jury.

The effects of polling may depend on other factors, however. In particular, Davis et al. (1993) were unable to replicate the effects of poll timing and voting sequence in a civil trial where mock jurors made judgments about damage awards. Voting sequence was manipulated by arranging six-person juries so that preferred amounts were expressed in an *ascending* order (each successive vote was for a larger amount than the last) or *descending* order (each successive vote was for a smaller amount). Unlike the earlier studies, the voting sequence did not effect the dichotomous decisions of juries to award damages or the mean amount awarded by those juries that found the defendant liable, but juries polled after five minutes of deliberation on average awarded 33 percent more than juries who took their first poll before any discussion. Nevertheless, these studies by Davis and his colleagues highlight another procedural mechanism that can influence jury decisions—straw polling.

Deliberation Style

Hastie and his colleagues first identified deliberation style as a potentially important variable in their classic 1983 study, but Kameda (1991) remains one of the few who actually manipulated it. This was done in the context of two civil cases, one that required *either* of two factual criteria to exist in order to award damages to the plaintiff (the disjunctive case), and the other that required *both* criteria to be met before a damage award was appropriate (the conjunctive case). Deliberation style was manipulated by instructing half of the juries to reach an individual decision on each criterion and then aggregate these opinions to reach a personal verdict for the case before any discussion (compound style), whereas the other half of the juries were told to withhold making any personal decisions, discuss the case, make a consensus judgment about each relevant criterion as a group, and then reach a final collective decision (elemental style). Juries using the compound style took a public vote before any discussion; elemental-style juries did not. These two deliberation styles are essentially analogous to the verdict-driven (compound) and evidence-driven (elemental) styles identified by Hastie et al. (1983) and mentioned earlier.

Based on a formal mathematical model, Kameda (1991) predicted juries using the compound (i.e., verdict-driven) style would be more likely to find the defendant liable than juries using the elemental (evidence-driven) style in the disjunctive case, but just the opposite for the conjunctive case. This is indeed what transpired. Compound-style juries found the defendant liable 25 percent more often than elemental-style juries in the disjunctive case, but 25 percent less often in the conjunctive case. A follow-up experiment replicated this interaction almost exactly using four-person mock juries composed of Japanese participants and two versions of a single criminal case involving fraud. In fact, the results were almost identical to the first study, with the compound style producing 21 percent more convictions with the conjunctive version of the case but 24 percent fewer convictions with the disjunctive version. This intriguing interaction—predicted and found in both studies—strongly suggests the general approach used by the juries to reach a collective decision can affect final verdicts.

There is also reason to believe that deliberation style may be associated with deliberation quality. In particular, two studies suggest that a verdict-driven style tends to result in a less thorough examination of the evidence, more normative pressure and conflict, more hung juries, and lower juror satisfaction (Devine et al., 2007; Hastie et al., 1983). In a third study, juries that eventually hung took their first votes earlier than juries that reached a verdict (Hannaford-Agor et al., 2002). Thus, an evidence-driven style appears to be more in keeping with the legal ideal associated with deliberation and would seem to be the preferred style for juries to employ.

Jury Discussion Structure

Yet another demonstration of the power of sequencing was made by Kameda and Sugimori (1995). Six-person mock juries were composed such that they consisted of four members who supported the death penalty in an infanticide case and two members who opposed it. Half of the juries operated in the traditional manner the other half used a two-stage procedure where they were first divided into two three-person subgroups, one of which contained the two members who opposed the death penalty (thus constituting a *local majority* in that subgroup). The verdicts of the traditional single-stage juries reflected the well-established power of the majority—64 percent decided the death penalty was appropriate, 18 percent decided the death penalty was not appropriate, and 18 percent hung. The two-stage juries showed a different pattern, one highlighting the potential influence of local majorities. No two-stage jury decided the death penalty was appropriate whereas 21 percent decided against it and a whopping 79 percent hung. At the individual level, opinion change over the course of deliberation was much higher among the local minority jurors who favored the death penalty than it was for pro-death jurors in the single-stage juries. A follow-up study was undertaken to replicate these findings using six-person juries that were not composed in any particular fashion but presumably featured pro-death majorities given prevailing attitudes. The results of this second study were very consistent with the first: 63 percent of single-stage juries opted for the death penalty, 21 percent decided against it, and 17 percent hung, compared with corresponding rates of 35 percent, 22 percent, and 43 percent (respectively) for the two-stage juries. Thus, both studies suggest local majorities can substantially disrupt traditional majority influence processes.

Charge Consideration Order

In addition to polling, deliberation style, and subgrouping, it is also possible for juries to be influenced simply by the order in which they consider charges in those trials where the defendant is faced with multiple charges or claims. Specifically, in deciding the first charge, jurors might basically determine the "story" they believe is most plausible for the case as a whole—a story that will then be applied to the evaluation of other charges or claims. What is most intriguing is that the story constructed by jurors might depend in part on which charge or claim is evaluated first, as focusing on some aspects of a case may lend itself to the creation of a story that would not have been generated if other aspects of the case had been more salient. In effect, this reasoning suggests that *charge sequence* is important, and two experimental studies investigated its effects in deliberating groups.

In the first of these, Nagao and Davis (1980) had six-person mock juries consider two independent cases in the same session: rape and vandalism. Participants read a trial summary for one of the cases, deliberated to a verdict, then repeated the process for the second case. Half of the juries received the rape case first and then the vandalism case; the other half received the cases in the opposite order. Focusing on the predeliberation conviction rates for the two cases, the results were consistent with a contrast effect. In essence, the preference for conviction on the more serious case (rape) was 11 percent greater when that case was decided first, whereas preference for conviction on the less serious case (vandalism) was 12 percent lower when that case was decided first. The authors explained the observed order effect by speculating that the consequences of conviction for the defendant seemed inordinately heavy to jurors when a rape charge was considered after vandalism, but inordinately light when vandalism was considered after rape.

Davis, Tindale, Nagao, Hinsz, and Robertson (1984) followed up this study with another involving more mock juries and a single case featuring three independent charges against the same defendant. The three charges differed in seriousness, ranging from reckless homicide (most serious) to aggravated battery to criminal property damage (least serious). Participants watched a videotaped trial simulation that presented all the evidence at once and then deliberated in six-person juries. The order in which the charges were to be decided was the only experimental manipulation. One-third of the juries were told to decide the charges in *descending* order of seriousness (i.e., reckless homicide first, then aggravated battery, and then criminal property damage), one-third were told to tackle them in *ascending* order, and the last third were not given a specified order of consideration. The focal outcome was the difference in conviction rates for ascending-order and descending-order juries on the aggravated battery charge, which was resolved second in both of the specified orders. Again, the data lined up squarely behind a contrast effect for both individual jurors and juries as a whole, with 22 percent of the descending-order juries convicting on aggravated battery compared with only 4 percent of the ascending-order juries. In other words, the conviction rate on the focal (middle) charge was more than *five times higher* when resolved after the more serious charge compared with the less serious charge.

Another apparent sequence effect is a tendency for juries to spend less time talking about later charges compared with the initial charge. In their 1986 study, Tanford and Penrod noted stronger relationships between the initial jury-level vote and jurors' final verdict preferences for the second and third charges as opposed to the first. In a corresponding fashion, they also observed weaker relationships between the deliberation content variables and jurors' final verdict preferences for the later charges. These findings are consistent with the notion that jurors—as individuals or collectively—will decide on a single story that has fairly obvious implications for verdicts associated with all the charges. Once jurors have arrived at a story in the process of deciding the first charge or claim, there is simply much less to talk about. Alternatively, jurors may become fatigued over the course of deliberation and simply be less willing to engage in critical analysis and/or confrontation, relying more and more on the precedent established by their earlier verdicts. Both mechanisms (i.e., creating stories and fatigue) would suggest that jury verdicts on multiple charges will be strongly correlated with one another, and field studies that have recorded verdicts for multiple charges have found this to be true (e.g., Devine et al., 2009).

Overall, studies of procedural influence are consistent with the Story model and indicate that the timing and sequence of events during deliberation (such as the order of charge consideration) may have an impact on jury verdicts aside from the more well-established faction size and defendant leniency effects.

Damage Awards Decisions

When a jury finds a defendant liable for damages in a civil trial, it typically must then decide how much money to award the plaintiff. Civil juries have been studied less than criminal juries in general, and damage awards in turn have been studied less than judgments of liability. One reason for this is simple math: only a small percentage of civil cases—less than 5 percent in most jurisdictions—actually make it to a jury and then only about half of those result in a damage award. So for every one hundred civil cases initiated, there are about two or three jury damage awards. Damage awards that do occur are also not distributed in an optimal (bell-shaped) fashion but instead tend to be heavily skewed, making it harder to find significant associations with other variables. Further, of the research that has addressed civil jury decisions, only a small fraction has involved deliberating groups and focused on the dynamics of damage-award decisions. Many existing studies of civil juries are archival in nature and involve only basic information about the case, litigants, and outcomes of civil jury trials (e.g., Daniels & Martin, 1990; Eisenberg, Goerdt, Ostrom, & Rottman, 1996; Ostrom, Rottman, & Goerdt, 1996; Peterson, 1987). These studies provide a descriptive portrait regarding how often damages are awarded and the typical amount of the award, but shed little light on how juries reached their decisions.

Nonetheless, it is apparent that a number of variables influence the frequency and magnitude of damage awards (Devine et al., 2001; Levett et al., 2005; see Greene & Bornstein, 2003, for an excellent review). First, more than any other variable, the severity of injury to the plaintiff(s) drives jury damage awards. Across both well-controlled lab experiments and archival studies with actual juries, plaintiffs who are more severely injured tend to be compensated more than those who are less seriously injured. Second, damage awards definitely vary by the type of case as well, although for the most part this is probably a reflection of reliable differences in the nature and extent of injuries suffered in different types of cases. Third, and very logically, jury damage awards are influenced by the dollar amounts that the plaintiff requests—so-called *ad damnum* amounts—as well as the amount countered by the defense if applicable. Fourth, damage awards are sometimes influenced by the conduct of the parties, especially the defendant. Relevant to the issue of liability, reprehensible conduct by one party or the other should not affect the size of awards but sometimes it does. Finally, the act of deliberating tends to increase jury awards in relation to the mean of jurors' predeliberation amount preferences.

But *how* do juries arrive at dollar amounts? A handful of excellent studies of damage awards have involved either the observation of mock jury deliberations (e.g., Diamond & Casper, 1992; Greene, Hayman, & Motyl, 2008; Hastie et al., 1998) or interviews with actual civil jurors in the wake of real cases that produced a damage award (e.g., Hans & Lofquist, 1992; Mott, Hans, & Simpson, 2000). Perhaps the best single study of civil juries, however, was a field experiment conducted in Arizona to evaluate a reform initiative allowing juries to discuss the evidence presented in a case prior to deliberation (Diamond et al., 2003). In this instance, trials were randomly assigned to experimental conditions (early discussion allowed or no early discussion), and just as importantly, the researchers were allowed to videotape the juries as they deliberated. Taken together, these relatively few intensive studies of civil jury deliberation give a preliminary sense of how juries go about determining damage awards.

One clear finding from this work is that all juries do not follow the same path in reaching their judgments. Most jurors do not go into deliberation with a particular dollar figure in mind (Mott et al., 2000). Although there is considerable support for the effect of specific requests by the plaintiff (sometimes countered by a specific amount offered by the defense) on the jury's final award (Greene & Bornstein, 2003), juries do not seem to simply accept those numbers at face value and ratify them with little or no discussion (Greene, Downey, & Goodman-Delahunty, 1999). Rather, there are two general approaches that juries use to arrive at damage award figures (Greene, 1989; Mott et al., 2000). The *component sums* approach is reductionist in nature and involves determining an appropriate amount for each component of a claim via collective discussion, with the final award calculated by summing the component values. The *gestalt* approach entails a back-and-forth discussion of total award amount values in an effort to settle on one value that seems appropriate. Here the focus is on identifying an appropriate overall amount that "feels right." Consistent with this holistic strategy, aggregated measures of the total award preferred by individual jurors prior to deliberation are good predictors of the final award made by the jury (Boster et al., 1991; Davis, Au, Hulbert, Chen, & Zarnoth, 1997; Diamond & Casper, 1992; Hulbert, Parks, Chen, Nam, & Davis, 1999). In particular, the *mean* of individual award preferences correlates fairly well with final jury awards (Diamond & Casper, 1992), the *median* of the individual award preferences correlates as well as the mean if not better, and a *"trimmed" median* calculated after discarding the single-most outlying value in the jury may be even better (Davis et al., 1997; Hulbert et al., 1999). Despite the predictive ability of these aggregate measures of central tendency, juries do not appear to actually calculate them very often (Mott et al., 2000), suggesting the combination of member preferences occurs implicitly when using this approach.

It is also apparent that juries often discuss topics that they are not supposed to consider. Jurors are usually not informed about such things as attorney fees, defendant insurance, taxes, and other post-trial adjustments to the awards because they are deemed to be irrelevant to the determination of damage awards. Although the law is "silent" on these issues, they come up in many deliberations (Diamond & Casper, 1992; Diamond & Vidmar, 2001; Greene et al., 2008; Mott, et al., 2000). For example, studies of the deliberations of actual civil juries indicate that attorney fees are discussed by 80–85 percent of juries whereas the question of insurance by either or both parties comes up less often but still frequently (Diamond & Vidmar, 2001; Mott et al., 2000). Similarly, in their content analysis of the deliberations of fifty-six mock juries, Greene et al. (2008) found that 84 percent of their juries discussed the plaintiff's insurance, 75 percent discussed the defendant's insurance, 48 percent talked about attorney fees, and 23 percent spoke of pretrial settlements. Indeed, only two of fifty-six juries refrained from talking about any of the forbidden topics. All this talk about forbidden subjects does not necessarily translate into a strong effect on the final award, though. After controlling for several important variables (i.e., the severity of the plaintiff's injury, the reprehensibility of the defendant's conduct, and overall deliberation time), Greene et al. (2008) determined that the mean number of times these "silent" topics were mentioned explained only a small amount of additional variation in damage awards. The frequency with which "silent" topics come up seems to suggest that jurors want to know the impact of their award and how it will be received—in other words, they want to know the whole *story*.

Does Deliberation Reduce—or Inflate—Individual Bias?

There is a long history of scholarly interest in the effects of deliberation. Perhaps the most important question that has been examined is whether group discussion ameliorates or exacerbates the biases that individual jurors bring to deliberation. There are two perspectives on this. On one hand, deliberation could cause jurors to examine the evidence more actively and critically, increasing the chance that juries arrive at the "correct" decision in relation to their constituent members. According to this view, the biases and prejudices of individual members will tend to cancel out during deliberation. On the other hand, deliberation could potentially make matters worse, amplifying and propagating the biases of their members. To determine which of these possibilities is a better description of reality, jury researchers have employed two methodological approaches. Some studies have compared deliberating and non-deliberating jurors, whereas others have compared the decisions of a single group of mock jurors before and after deliberation. A wide variety of outcomes have been examined, including juror attitudes, instructional comprehension, evidence recall, critical thinking, verdicts, and damage awards.

In terms of its effect on individual jurors, the findings point toward a moderate beneficial effect of deliberation for some outcomes. Jurors generally appreciate the opportunity to deliberate and come away more satisfied, more confident in their verdicts, and more positive about the legal system (Gastil, Burkhalter, & Black, 2007). Deliberating jurors tend to recall more of the evidence presented at trial than non-deliberating jurors and be fairly good at catching and correcting errant statements by their members about the evidence (Ellsworth, 1989; Hastie et al., 1983). There is also some indication that deliberation causes jurors to think more critically about the evidence than those who do not deliberate (McCoy, Nunez, & Dammeyer, 1999). Conversely, deliberation appears to have only a minor positive impact on jurors' comprehension of their instructions (Ellsworth, 1989; Elwork, Alfini, & Sales, 1982; Severance, Greene, & Loftus, 1984), and even less effect when it comes to improving comprehension in the sentencing phase of capital trials (Diamond & Levi, 1996; Lynch & Haney, 2009; Wiener et al., 2004).

All of this is perhaps subordinate to the fundamental question of whether deliberation yields better jury decisions. In other words, does deliberation serve to negate or exaggerate bias associated with such things as demographic prejudice, exposure to pretrial publicity, and inadmissible evidence? Here it appears the effect of deliberation is not reliable, instead depending on other factors such as the strength of the evidence and maybe even the distribution of bias within the jury (e.g., the extent of racial bias or exposure to pretrial publicity). Overall, more studies than not have shown that deliberating juries (or postdeliberation jurors) do better than non-deliberating (or predeliberation) jurors. Perhaps the most notable investigation underscoring the fears of jury critics was conducted by Kramer, Kerr, and Carroll (1990). In a large, well-designed, and realistic study with six-person mock juries, they manipulated exposure to two different types of pretrial publicity (factual v. emotionally arousing) and the use of three common legal remedies (judicial instructions, continuance of the trial, and the opportunity to deliberate). Although there was negligible difference in predeliberation verdict preferences, juries exposed to emotional publicity convicted 20 percent more often than juries that did not encounter it. An analysis of deliberation content further revealed the jury-level effect of PTP on verdicts was not mediated by group discussion of it either.

In contrast, deliberation had the desired dampening effect in several studies examining exposure to extraneous or otherwise inadmissible factors (Kaplan & Miller, 1978; Kerwin & Shaffer, 1994; London & Nunez, 2000), and four other studies revealed some qualified improvement with regard to lessened bias in juror verdicts following group deliberation (Carretta & Moreland, 1983; Ruva et al., 2007; Shaw & Skolnick, 2004; Thompson, Fong, & Rosenhan, 1981). One of the most well-known studies supporting the positive effect of deliberation on juror-level bias was conducted by Martin Kaplan and Lynn Miller (1978). In one of their experiments, they manipulated obnoxious behavior by one or the other of the attorneys, or the judge, using two versions of a criminal trial, one which involved stronger evidence and one weaker evidence. Predeliberation differences on guilt ratings due to the obnoxious (but legally irrelevant) behavior were evident at both levels of case strength but disappeared after deliberation, with mean postdeliberation guilt ratings increasing in all of the stronger-evidence conditions and decreasing in all of the weaker-evidence conditions. In other words, the polarization of postdeliberation ratings in the direction of the evidence strength suggests deliberation had a focusing effect that helped juries disregard the noise associated with the irritating (yet irrelevant) behavior of the legal professionals.

Despite the predominance of findings suggesting that deliberation tends to tamp down the effects of individual bias, Kerr, Niedermeier, and Kaplan (1999) made a compelling case for the existence of an interaction between bias, deliberation, and the strength of evidence. They argued that whether deliberation produces attenuation or amplification of individual-level bias depends on the strength of the evidence. Their hypothesis was that deliberation would *decrease* bias existing in predeliberation preferences when evidence strength was extreme in either direction (i.e., very weak or very strong), but *exacerbate* individual bias when the evidence was ambiguous (i.e., moderate). Data were collected from eighty four-person mock juries to examine this possibility, and the authors did indeed find support for their hypothesis at both the juror and jury levels of analysis. This finding helps to explain some of the inconsistencies regarding the effects of deliberation observed in the literature—deliberation may ameliorate individual bias when the evidence strongly favors one side, but amplify it when the evidence is only moderately strong.

Deliberation Matters

Decades ago, Kalven and Zeisel (1966) noted that about 90 percent of jury verdicts are consistent with the verdict preferred by the majority faction on the first vote during deliberation, and they likened the deliberation process to that of darkroom photo development—the image (i.e., decision) is essentially set when the picture is taken (i.e., the trial ends) but must be developed behind closed doors (deliberation). The vivid imagery used to convey this finding—along with the prohibition against directly observing the deliberation of real juries—probably suppressed interest in the study of deliberation for decades.

This is unfortunate. We now know that there is much more to deliberation than simply waiting for the initial majority to manifest itself. An evidence-driven style, a local majority that emerges during speaking or polling, the articulation of alternative "stories" supported by the evidence, discussion of "forbidden" topics, the presence of faction leaders (particularly for the defense), the appearance of local majorities that obscure the size of majority factions—one or more of these phenomena may play a key role in many trials. Further, the well-established prediction rule associated with early majorities may not even apply in the many trials that involve something other than one defendant facing one charge with only the two traditional verdict options available to the jury. In contrast to almost every study examining the predictive ability of faction size, many real-world trials feature multiple charges or civil claims, lesser included charges, nontraditional verdict options, or special verdict forms. What do juries do in situations where there is no initial majority? In addition, many civil juries must make quantitative decisions about dollar amounts, and some criminal juries make life-or-death decisions about punishment. Little is known about the operative social decision schemes in these lesser-studied circumstances. Moving forward, it will be important for researchers to continue to examine how juries go about reaching their decisions via deliberation.

8

An Integrative Multi-Level Theory
of Jury Decision Making

The focus of the previous chapters was on identifying what we know about jury decision making. This chapter builds on those research findings in order to present an integrative Multi-Level theory that weaves together the threads from the empirical literature. As in any area of science, a good integrative theory of jury decision making should meet several criteria. First, it should incorporate the major empirical findings on jurors and juries. Second, it should be consistent with established conceptual models and theoretical frameworks, and not involve assumptions contrary to these perspectives without justifiable reason. Third, it should address decisions made by jurors as well as juries. Fourth, it should extend the current literature by contributing something new in the way of scientific understanding or practical application. Specifically, it should yield interesting propositions that can be tested and have practical implications for improving jury performance. This chapter presents a theory developed with these criteria in mind. I begin by highlighting several themes that emerge from the empirical research, then provide a brief overview of the entire theory, and conclude with a detailed discussion of the theory's major components.

Building Blocks: Empirical Themes

The study of jury decision making has produced many findings, but several general themes emerge from the previous literature review. Table 8.1 summarizes these findings and indicates the strength of each effect along with the level of support for it present in the literature. The latter is a function of the number of studies that found the effect as well as the number that did not find an effect. From these findings, it is possible to extract several substantive themes that in turn will be incorporated into the integrative theory.

Individual Differences Matter

It is abundantly clear that jurors are not tabula rasa, carte blanche, or any other exotic-sounding phrase implying emptiness waiting to be filled up by the evidence at trial. Individual differences are perhaps most apparent at the beginning of deliberation in the many trials that fail to produce a unanimous view of the appropriate verdict. Jurors hear and see the same evidence but often come to different conclusions about the appropriate decision, in which case it *must* be something about the individual jurors that is responsible. The persons serving on a jury will differ in terms of their genetic makeup and come from different social backgrounds that produce varied life experiences. These biological and social factors form the basis for enduring dispositional tendencies to perceive and react to situations in particular ways via the development of various cognitive structures, including *person-related categories* (e.g., stereotypes) and *event-related categories* (e.g., scripts). Once activated in the context of a trial, these structures influence what jurors attend to, how they interpret testimony and exhibits, who they find credible, what they recall later on, and what stories they form to explain the evidence. Differences will also emerge during deliberation in terms of what jurors say and do.

There is nothing radical about the claim that individual differences are important to understanding juries, but singling out a small number that are most critical is another matter. Most theories of juror or jury decision making have treated jurors as essentially interchangeable. Generality may have been necessary thirty years ago due to the limits of the literature, but no longer. Hundreds of studies on the characteristics of trial participants allow for at least the preliminary identification of a set relevant to jury decision making. Given limited resources associated with the study of juries, narrowing our focus to a smaller set of focal individual

Table 8.1: Summary of Major Findings in the Empirical Literature on Juries.

Finding	Effect Size	Literature Support
Jurors more likely to favor guilt or liability when:		
Death qualified (Ch. 3)	Small	Considerable
Exposed to negative PTP (Ch. 4)	Small-medium	Overwhelming
Trial is "joined" in some fashion (Ch. 4)	Small-medium	Considerable
Trial is unitary (i.e., not bifurcated) (Ch. 4)	Small	Decent
Standard of proof is defined leniently (Ch. 4)	Medium	Decent
Exposed to anti-defendant information challenged and/or ruled inadmissible during trial (Ch. 4)	Small-medium	Overwhelming
Defendant is low socioeconomic status (Ch. 5)	Small	Decent
Defendant is known to have a prior conviction for similar offense (Ch.5)	Medium	Considerable
Defendant is physically unattractive (Ch. 5)	Small	Considerable
Defendant is of a different race than the juror (Ch. 5)	Depends	Considerable
Female, and the case involves sexual assault or child victims (Ch. 5)	Small-medium	Overwhelming
High socioeconomic status (Ch. 5)	Small	Decent
High on legal authoritarianism (Ch. 5)	Small-medium	Considerable
The defendant is identified by a very confident eyewitness (Ch. 6)	Medium-Large	Considerable
Prosecution/plaintiff presents a confession by the defendant (Ch. 6)	Large	Considerable
Prosecution/plaintiff presents DNA evidence implicating defendant (Ch. 6)	Large	Considerable
Expert witness presents case-specific testimony for the prosecution/plaintiff (Ch. 6)	Small	Considerable
Prosecution/plaintiff presents graphic visual evidence of injury (Ch. 6)	Medium	Some
Jurors understand their instructions better when:		
Simplified instructions are used instead of standard (pattern) instructions (Ch. 3)	Small-Medium	Overwhelming
Allowed to take notes in complex trials (Ch. 3)	Small-Medium	Some
Case does not involve the death penalty (Ch. 3)	Medium	Considerable
Jurors deliberate better when:		
Jury size is larger (Ch. 3)	Small	Decent
Required to reach unanimity (Ch. 3)	Small-medium	Decent
Demographically diverse (Ch. 5)	Small-medium	Some
Evidence-driven deliberation style adopted (Ch. 7)	Medium	Some

differences could pay dividends in future research and ultimately practical application.

Jurors Use Relevant Information Regardless of Its Source

Stories require information, and the largely subconscious, automatic, associative nature of human cognition is not conducive to placing limits on what can and cannot be used. When jurors are exposed to pretrial publicity or inadmissible evidence at trial, they are typically instructed by judges to set it aside, give it no weight, and treat it as if it did not exist. Underlying this legal practice is a rosy view of human cognition, one that assumes jurors can isolate and remove the effects of selected bits of information the way a surgeon can find and remove a tumor. Unfortunately, jurors simply cannot do this very well if at all. Study after study on the effect of exposure to pretrial publicity (PTP) or in-court inadmissible evidence (ICIE) shows that these forms of legally inappropriate information have a reliable influence on jurors. The heart of the problem seems to be that jurors exposed to extralegal information may simply lose track of where it came from and incorporate it into their emerging narrative along with the admissible evidence. Although the influence of extralegal information may be lessened under some conditions, it appears difficult to stamp out entirely. If jurors are exposed to information that helps them form a coherent story, there is every reason to believe they will use it—regardless of its source or what they are told they can or cannot do with it.

Jurors Do Not Keep Things Separate

Another mistaken assumption of the legal system is that jurors can compartmentalize their thought processes. This is most apparent in the instructions that juries receive, which presume that jurors can parse the evidence as it comes in and use some for this purpose and some for that. In contrast, decades of research in cognitive psychology have shown that human cognition is dynamic, fluid, and adaptive. Knowledge is organized in associative networks, with information acquired through the senses in turn activating portions of that stored knowledge in a rapid, effortless, automatic fashion almost entirely beyond conscious control. Information that achieves a certain level of activation may then influence whatever cognitive task is underway regardless of its logical (or legal) relevance. Research on the effects of trial-related practices such as joinder and bifurcation shows consistent spill-over effects that are not rectified by limiting instructions. Spill-over contamination is especially likely in complex trials that involve multiple charges, defendants, or plaintiffs. In short, there is little reason to expect that jurors divvy up the evidence and use it to construct multiple independent stories for each charge and each defendant—and telling jurors to use information for restricted purposes does not fix the problem.

Jurors Create Stories

The previous themes converge on this larger "meta" theme. The notion that jurors sift through the evidence in order to fashion a narrative out of it may have seemed a tad whimsical when introduced in the late 1970s, but the Story model has emerged as the juror-level model of choice in part because it is so psychologically plausible. Stories play an important role in helping people make sense of daily life, and there is every reason to believe jurors use these same cognitive tools when it comes to comprehending what they encounter in a trial context. Listen to a former juror discussing his or her case and you will probably be able to glean the makings of a story. The role of stories has also been demonstrated in a number of empirical studies, whereas alternative mathematical theories that proffer "mental meters" and "weighing" the evidence have little basis in cognitive science. Although jurors may occasionally attempt to assign numerical weights to different aspects of the evidence or otherwise tote it up in some "spreadsheet" format, this probably occurs when efforts to create a compelling story have failed. The default decision-making device at trial appears to be a narrative organization of causally linked events—a story.

Deliberation Is Not a Democracy

Many words could be used to characterize the deliberation process, but "equal" and "egalitarian" are probably not good choices. Juries begin their work essentially unstructured but, as in most groups, social structure emerges quickly to impose some degree of order and predictability on discussion. Participation is not equal across jurors either. A few speak a great deal, most speak a moderate amount, and several often say little or nothing. Who speaks during deliberation is far from random, being largely determined by roles within the group and individual differences. Forepersons, men, those who are more extraverted, and those with higher social status tend to speak more often in deliberation. Influence within the jury ultimately depends on the characteristics of those who speak and the merits of what they say, as well as the attributes of those who are listening and their arrangement into subgroups.

Majority Factions Are Usually Successful

The data on jury decision making are adamant about one thing: Deliberation is no free-for-all where any verdict is as likely as another. Rather, the
jury's final decision is consistent with the early majority faction's preference
in about 90 percent of trials—a result observed in many studies with mock
juries as well as actual juries. To reach consensus during deliberation, usually
some jurors must change their minds. Sometimes jurors change their minds
because of what they hear (informational influence), but sometimes they do
so simply to avoid standing apart from the others in their jury (normative
influence). Larger factions usually succeed because they have more proponents and can marshal more arguments along with more pressure to conform. Those occasions when the majority's preference is not the jury's ultimate verdict (i.e., a "reversal") presumably come about when the minority is
able to fully mobilize its informational resources while the majority is unable
for some reason to exert maximal informational or normative influence.

Local Majorities Can Be Important

Local majorities occur when a minority faction (or, more specifically, its viewpoint) *appears* to represent a majority—at least temporarily. A number of studies demonstrate the impact local majorities can have during deliberation. Sometimes local majorities emerge as the result of polling. Two aspects of polling
that are most relevant to the formation of local majorities are the timing of the
first poll and whether individual opinions are provided privately (i.e., anonymously). Studies show that public polling can be a source of normative influence when a minority view is overrepresented in the early part of the sequence.
This is especially true when the poll is taken relatively early in the process.
Other research shows that local majorities can arise through non-representative
discussion (i.e., the formation of subgroups). Local majorities may be one of the
mechanisms that explain those instances when initial majorities do not prevail.

Overview: A Multi-Level Theory of Jury Decision Making

The Multi-Level theory integrates decision making on two levels—the individual juror and the jury as a whole. Each level corresponds to a distinct
model of decision making within the larger theory, with the final product of
the juror-level model serving as the starting point for the jury-level model.

The Director's Cut model is concerned with the decisions of individual
jurors prior to deliberation (see Fig. 8.1). The primary metaphor underlying

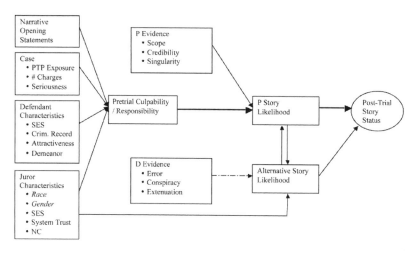

Figure 8.1: "Director's Cut" Model of Juror Decision Making

the model is that of a film director. Much as a director assembles the footage from many scenes into a cohesive narrative, jurors work with the evidence presented at trial in an effort to formulate a satisfying narrative account of the events preceding it. Prior to the trial, jurors will have a "shooting script" to guide them in the form of any existing knowledge of the case, their own beliefs and assumptions activated at trial, and the opening statements. As the trial proceeds, jurors will form mental pictures of the events leading up to the trial, ultimately crafting a "final cut" representing their personal view of what happened. In the end, some of the footage (evidence) may not fit into the final cut and thus end up on the cutting-room floor. Ambivalence regarding how everything fits together may trigger the consideration of alternate endings (alternative stories).

The cognitive foundation for juror stories is a mental representation of the trial and its precipitating events. Construction of this representation involves a fundamental interaction between what is seen and heard in the courtroom and what jurors already "know." Much of the information in a juror's representation will come from the trial proceedings, but some will be retrieved from memory via the activation of cognitive scripts and stereotypes. This reciprocal process underscores the importance of individual differences among jurors. Jurors will vary in terms of the scripts and stereotypes they possess due to their diverse life experiences. Learning the type of case to be tried and seeing the parties involved (e.g., the defendant's appearance) may activate schema-based beliefs and assumptions that are used to flesh out the motives, actions, and behavioral consequences associated with the parties involved. Opening statements are important in that they offer a relatively unfettered opportunity for each side to present its version of events in a cohesive narrative fashion. Along with script- and stereotype-activated information, they provide the substance for the initial representation in many trials. What is perceived or learned during the trial itself is added to the initial representation, which is adjusted as needed to accommodate the incoming information. In the end, the updated representation is translated into a mental model (often visual in nature) to evaluate the plausibility of potential story explanations. Jurors can then be viewed as being in one of four cognitive states when the trial concludes: (1) favoring the prosecution/plaintiff's story (a *believer*), (2) favoring an alternative story offered or implied by the defense (a *doubter*), (3) trying to choose between two or more stories deemed to be equally plausible (a *muller*), or (4) unable to formulate any story that provides a satisfactory account of the evidence (a *puzzler*).

When deliberation begins, the focus shifts to the jury as a whole and the Story Sampling model (see Fig. 8.2). Each juror enters deliberation with a stored constellation of case-related impressions, facts, inferences, and stories. During deliberation, jurors "sample" from the contents of their memory and share items with the other jurors. Depending on their personal characteristics, cognitive state, and role within the group, jurors will vary greatly in terms of how much they participate in the discussion. Participation comes

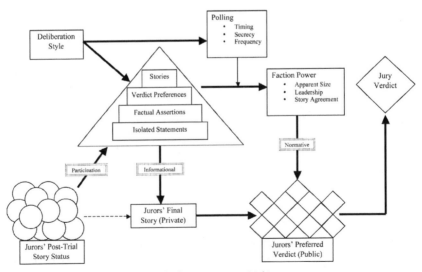

Figure 8.2: "Story Sampling" Model of Jury Decision Making

in the form of spoken contributions that fall in a hierarchy ranging from iso-lated statements to full-fledged stories. The frequency of different types of contributions is expected to be inversely related to their informational influ-ence. In other words, the more frequent types of spoken contributions (i.e., isolated statements) will have little or no effect on other jurors, whereas the rarest contributions (i.e., complete stories) have the potential for consider-able impact. The most critical aspect of deliberation is thus the number and quality of stories offered by jurors to explain the evidence.

Deliberation provides an opportunity for both normative and infor-mational influence, with jury decisions generally viewed as a function of both. Informational influence results from the content of discussion, spe-cifically factual assertions and articulated stories (in whole and in part). Normative influence arises from the perception of factions within the jury. A faction will exert more normative influence to the extent that it is per-ceived to be relatively large, effectively led by one or more individuals, and united in terms of belief in an underlying story. Through a combination of normative and informational influence, large majority factions will usu-ally succeed—when they exist, that is—unless some relatively rare critical event occurs. Critical events include disproportionate speaking by mem-bers of the minority faction, persuasive articulation of alternative stories, emergence of a strong minority faction leader to galvanize resistance, or the manifestation of dissension within the majority faction. Procedural mechanisms (e.g., polling) may also intentionally or inadvertently affect the manifestation of normative influence via the revelation of local majori-ties. In essence, majority factions will occasionally fail because of strong informational influence from the minority or a failure to exert maximal normative influence.

The Multi-Level theory thus consists of two separate but linked mod-els—the Director's Cut model dealing with the formation and evaluation of stories by individual jurors, and the Story Sampling model addressing deci-sions made by the jury as a whole. The remainder of this chapter reviews the components of each model in more detail, beginning with the processes that underlie juror decisions.

Director's Cut Model of Juror Decision Making
Story Beginnings: Initial Mental Representations

Extensive research in social cognition shows that humans comprehend their surroundings by using various cognitive structures that represent catego-ries of people, objects, and events—*schemas*. The most compelling evidence for the existence and influence of these schemas comes in the form of recall errors: people often "remember" schema-consistent information that was never presented to them and fail to recall schema-inconsistent information that was. In trial contexts, jurors acquire information relevant to their decisions from a variety of sources—both internal and external—and use this information to form a mental representation of the events that precipitated the trial.

Two types of cognitive structures that play a fundamental role in constructing trial representations are scripts and stereotypes. These schemas serve to organize incoming information, activate stored knowledge and beliefs, help us comprehend our present situation, and generate expectations about what will happen in the future. *Scripts* are event-centered cognitive structures that involve a series of actions occurring in a causal sequence. *Stereotypes* are person-centered cognitive structures consisting of a category label and a set of associated characteristics. Although unsavory, there is no doubt that we all possess stereotypes associated with different types of persons or that, in many ways, these categories allow for efficient cognitive processing. At trial, jurors' scripts and stereotypes may be activated by learning the nature of the case and seeing the parties involved (e.g., defendants, victims, and plaintiffs). The features associated with cognitive categories that become activated in court may then be used to flesh out the emerging mental representation of the trial (e.g., "resident," "ER," and "surgery" in a malpractice lawsuit).

According to the Director's Cut model, jurors may begin forming their initial representation of a trial—the shooting script—even before the trial begins. Most of the time, venirepersons arrive for jury duty without advance knowledge of their case but on occasion (such as a high-profile trial), a fair number of venirepersons will have been exposed to detailed reports about the case through the media. PTP almost always casts defendants in a negative light, and its consistent prejudicial effects are likely due to the activation of scripts and stereotypes. PTP effects are difficult to stamp out because information gained through the media is very likely to form the basis of the initial mental representation of the trial.

Simply learning the nature (or type) of case to be decided will also provide information. In the world of movies there are a number of common film types, or genres. Movie genres have fairly standard plotlines, character types, and event sequences. They focus attention on key actions, generate plot expectations, and supply missing information about character motives and off-screen behavior. For jurors, case types may function like movie genres. Jurors will be familiar with various types of legal cases via their life experiences, and learning the type of case they will hear may activate an associated script that brings to mind assumptions, beliefs, images, and expectations about what the evidence will show. Critically, core features of the case-type script may be integrated into the mental representation unless contradicted directly by the evidence, whereas evidence that is inconsistent with the script might be more likely to be discarded when the final narrative is formed.

Knowledge of the case type to be tried may also influence the content of initial representations by serving to trigger strong negative emotions that affect the activation of other cognitive structures or provide a mindset for subsequent interpretation of the evidence. For example, some types of cases may produce strong feelings of anger or revulsion (e.g., child molestation, gruesome homicide, brutal sexual assault) that elicit a desire on the part of jurors to blame someone—with the defendant being the obvious first choice.

The features of jurors' scripts and stereotypes will be heavily shaped by their life experiences, which in turn tend to be associated with several individual difference variables. Four characteristics of *jurors* have emerged as particularly important in the literature: (1) race, (2) gender, (3) socioeconomic status, and (4) trust in the legal system. In general, jurors are more likely to see defendants as culpable (i.e., guilty in a criminal context or responsible in a civil) when the juror is of a different race than the defendant, female (for some types of cases), high socioeconomic status, and very trusting of the legal system. All four characteristics are likely associated with differences in the way that jurors perceive and process trial-related information.

Race and *gender* are two of the "usual suspects" when it comes to extra-legal bias, apparently with some reason. The most important thing about a defendant's race is whether it is the same as a juror's: social psychological theory on ingroup/outgroup bias and a growing number of empirical studies suggest a systematic tendency for White and Black jurors to be more lenient toward defendants of their own race. A potential exception to this pattern is when the defendant is clearly culpable and the behavior in question is morally reprehensible—the black sheep effect. Similar to race, the impact of gender depends on something else—the *type* of case. In dozens of studies, women have been more likely to convict when trials involve sexual crimes against women or child victims. This finding may be due to a greater concern that women have for their physical safety in general and being the target of sexual assault in particular, making it easier for female jurors to empathize with the victims of sexual crimes. Women are also more likely than men to be the primary caregiver for a child, and crimes against children may more readily elicit a role-related protective mentality.

Socioeconomic status (SES) has not been studied as often as race or gender—or measured consistently—but there is sufficient convergence in the literature to conclude that jurors who are fairly well-to-do will be somewhat more likely to view criminal defendants as culpable. In essence, the experiences that lead high-SES jurors to be successful in life may prime them to be on the lookout for those who would unfairly take from others and disrupt the social order. This rationale would suggest a stronger effect of jurors' SES in trials involving burglary, theft, robbery, fraud, and societal delinquency. The same logic would also suggest that high-SES jurors may tend to favor the defense in civil trials, but juror SES has not been studied extensively in this context and the existing findings are mixed.

Trust in the legal system refers to the degree to which jurors view the human elements of the legal system as fair and competent. It represents a new construct that captures the essence of several overlapping constructs (i.e., legal authoritarianism, dogmatism, and juror "bias"), all of which seem fundamentally grounded in a juror's faith in the accuracy of legal system operations. As a result of differences in their life experiences, jurors will vary in terms of their beliefs about the competence and integrity of the police, the accuracy and honesty of eyewitnesses, the motives of expert witnesses, the trustworthiness of scientific tests, and so on.

Turning to defendants, the perception by jurors of certain characteristics of the accused may also routinely trigger assumptions and beliefs relevant to culpability. Four defendant characteristics in particular have emerged in the empirical literature and may play an instrumental role in juror's construction of an initial mental representation: (1) SES, (2) prior criminal history, (3) physical attractiveness, and (4) display of emotion. Basically, jurors may associate certain characteristics with legal culpability—being poor, unemployed, homeless, and uneducated (i.e., low SES); having a criminal record (especially for a similar charge); being physically unattractive; and showing little or no sympathy toward victims. These characteristics are likely to be featured in jurors' stereotypes of lawbreakers and their activation at trial may lead jurors to *feel* that the defendant is the kind of person who would commit a crime or be responsible for some injury.

Many jurors probably have stereotypes of criminals that include characteristics associated with being poor (i.e., low SES). These associations are particularly likely to be activated in cases where the defendant is charged with doing something illegal to obtain money or acquire someone else's property.

Of the focal defendant characteristics, knowledge of *prior criminal history* probably has the strongest impact on jurors, particularly when the defendant has one or more previous convictions for a similar offense. Research has consistently shown that conviction rates are higher when jurors learn that the defendant has a criminal record, and the logic is fairly straightforward: If he did it before, why wouldn't he do it again? The perception of behavioral continuity on the part of the defendant lends itself readily to the creation of a story centered on a criminal disposition.

Assessing *physical attractiveness* appears to be fundamental to human nature, occurring rapidly and automatically. Accordingly, perceptions of attractiveness have been associated with favorable outcomes across many studies, including more lenient decisions by jurors when attractive defendants are being tried. It does appear that we tend to assume, at least to some extent, that what is beautiful is also good. At the same time, the effects of defendant physical attractiveness may vary somewhat within juries given that the perception of physical attractiveness is somewhat subjective.

As noted previously, defendant race is most important in terms of whether it matches the race of jurors, but research also suggests that race may be a feature in jurors' scripts for various crimes. Put bluntly, when jurors think of certain types of illegal behaviors (e.g., drug-dealing), they may envision a person of a particular race. At a subconscious level, jurors may tend to assume that certain crimes are more likely to be committed by people of a certain race and draw inferences about likely culpability based on the degree of match.

These characteristics of the defendant almost certainly play a role by influencing what is recalled by jurors from memory and used to construct a mental representation of trial events. However, it is important to recognize that juror schemas are not the source of all or even most of the information that jurors will have at their disposal—we have not yet even considered what information jurors encounter through the proceedings of the trial itself.

Opening Statements

Preliminary remarks are offered by the attorneys in almost every jury trial and yet they have received little attention from researchers. This is unfortunate in that, in most trials, opening statements probably have a considerable impact on jurors' initial mental representations. There is also an interesting asymmetry with regard to opening statements. The side with something to prove (i.e., the government in a criminal trial or the plaintiff in a civil trial) will often try to outline a specific story in their opening statement, but the defense has more flexibility. It can offer an alternative version of the events leading up to the trial (i.e., a counterstory), argue that the real story is unknown and could be one of several, or simply argue that the other side's story is incorrect without offering an alternative. Given jurors' predilection for narrative explanation, it seems likely that good opening statements will mimic good stories. One particular characteristic of opening statements that should have a positive impact on jurors is a chronological structure, as opposed to some other organizational scheme.

In addition to providing a broad outline of one side's version of the events leading up to trial, opening statements may provide specific details that essentially represent factual assertions. Jurors are instructed not to treat opening statements as evidence, but they may not be able to reliably "tag" factual assertions in the opening statements and set them aside later on if they are not substantiated during the trial. Indeed, some of the factual assertions embedded in opening statements may never be supported by a shred of evidence, but it is unclear if and when jurors notice such occurrences or how they respond. Modest discrepancies may be overlooked by jurors, whereas major deviations may provoke conscious awareness and a negative reaction.

Thus, using information available from various sources, jurors will have an initial mental representation of the case as the trial begins. This mental representation is a nexus of information obtained from pretrial publicity, the preliminary legal proceedings, perceptions of the defendant and the nature of the case, along with stored information that enters working memory through "backdoor" cognitive channels (i.e., case-related scripts and person-related stereotypes). The initial representation is usually not equivalent to a fleshed-out story, though, because it is missing something important—the evidence.

"P" Story Construction: Prosecution/Plaintiff

Although there are some notable differences between the prosecution in a criminal trial and the plaintiff in a civil trial, they both share the burden of persuasion. The side that wants something (i.e., a conviction or damage award) must convince jurors of a particular version of events and hope they draw the appropriate inference when it comes to their legal decision. As such, the "instigating" side (or the "P" side—for prosecution or plaintiff) will almost certainly try to fashion the evidence it presents into a single compelling narrative. Given the nature of stories, "strong" evidence by the instigating side should be a function of three things: (1) scope, in terms of providing the basis for a precise, detailed narrative account, (2) credibility, in terms of the believability of the various story elements, and (3) singularity, in terms of converging on one—and only one—story.

Scope basically concerns the richness of the evidence and the degree of detail in the main story. It pertains to the level of precision associated with the actions of the presumed perpetrator (i.e., the defendant), and the extent to which the motive or mindsets of the actors are understood—even in situations when not legally required. This represents an important divergence between human nature and the law. For example, it may be legally sufficient in a theft trial to show that the defendant physically stole $10 from someone else's wallet and knew what he was doing, but due to an inherent desire to make sense of the world, jurors may want to know why someone who makes $500,000 a year would do such a thing. If the prosecution offers no rationale for the defendant's behavior, jurors may be unable to formulate a convincing story and thus be reluctant to convict even though the legal criteria have been met. Jurors may even generate separate mini-stories (or subplots) for key witnesses to account for their presence in court. A good deal of the information for subplots may come from stereotypes activated by heuristic cues associated with the witnesses. Scope is thus not concerned with the degree to which the evidence satisfies the legal criteria for finding the defendant culpable, but rather the degree to which the emerging story can answer the questions that jurors naturally have about the case. Evidence with good scope should leave jurors with the impression that everything has been laid out in front of them and there is nothing left to ponder.

Credibility has to do with the trustworthiness or believability of the major evidentiary elements in the prosecution/plaintiff's story. A premise of the Director's Cut model is that factual assertions at trial will be accepted as true unless one of the following conditions exists: (1) the assertion comes from a witness who is not seen as credible, (2) the assertion is incompatible with the juror's beliefs about how the world works, or (3) the assertion is disputed at trial by one or more credible sources. In other words, factual assertions will be incorporated into jurors' mental representations unless there is a good reason to do otherwise. Regarding the first condition, extensive research suggests that judgments of witness credibility are driven largely by perceptions of cognitive competence and trustworthiness. Presumably if witnesses are clearly lacking in cognitive capacity *or* attempting to be deceptive, their assertions will be discounted. With regard to perceived trustworthiness, jurors may be particularly sensitive to the reason a witness is testifying and may discount the assertions of witnesses who have an obvious motive to be deceptive (e.g., family loyalty, friendship, financial interests, avoiding public embarrassment, etc.). Regarding the second condition, juror beliefs about the way the world operates should serve as a check on the acceptability of some assertions, with those viewed as outlandish being rejected. Regarding the third condition, when multiple credible sources disagree on a factual assertion, some mechanism must be used to resolve the issue. At least two strategies are possible: The most credible source could be believed, or the number of credible sources behind each assertion could be considered. Thus, one important determinant of credibility is likely the degree to which evidentiary elements are corroborated by multiple trustworthy sources.

Singularity refers to the extent to which the prosecution/plaintiff's evidence converges on *one* story. Singularity is low when many factual assertions do not fit well into the main storyline and are thus suggestive of alternative stories; singularity is high when all the evidence fits together nicely and there are no leftover pieces. Jurors' desire for singularity represents another potential divergence between human nature and the law. For example, if the plaintiff in an auto accident case attempts to show that the defendant was driving aggressively *and* distracted by continually text-messaging during the trip, this might seem to give jurors more than enough reason to find the defendant liable. However, these two potential storylines (i.e., innate aggressiveness and situational distraction) *might* be viewed as somewhat contradictory, leading jurors to conclude that it is unclear what the defendant was really doing before the accident. Low singularity may lead jurors to the same question that arises from assembling something in the real world and finding extra parts at the end—what is wrong here? Thus, more is not necessarily better when it comes to the prosecution/plaintiff's evidence.

Alternative Story Construction: The Defense

As noted earlier, the defense in a jury trial has a choice of story-related strategies: It can present an alternative version of events that counters (i.e., contradicts) the other side's story, suggest the possibility of multiple stories and the impossibility of knowing which is the correct one, or try to show that the story offered by the prosecution/plaintiff is not the right one without identifying any alternative. There are several major categories of alternative stories that can be offered: (1) *wrong defendant,* (2) *wrong actions,* (3) *wrong mindset,* and (4) *wrong consequences.*

The first and most basic type of alternative story maintains that the defendant was not present or involved in the illegal activity (i.e., wrong defendant). Stories of this type basically argue that the defendant was misidentified as the perpetrator due to one or more errors, mistakes, or lies. Most alibi defenses would fall into this category. Alternative stories in the second category acknowledge the defendant's presence and/or involvement but assert that the defendant did not commit the illegal activity (i.e., wrong action). Exemplars include arguing that someone other than the defendant committed the alleged offense (e.g., the defendant's friend) or that what the defendant did was not illegal. Alternative stories from these first two categories are likely to involve the assertion of mistaken eyewitnesses, lying eyewitnesses, inaccurate scientific test results, coincidental physical evidence, or police framing.

If there is no uncertainty regarding the defendant's identity or actions, alternative stories will likely come from the two categories that focus on what the defendant was thinking (i.e., wrong mindset) or what actually resulted (i.e., wrong consequence). Alternative stories of the former type acknowledge the defendant's actions but assert that the defendant intended to do something else (e.g., an accident), thought he/she was doing something else (e.g., a misunderstanding), was unaware of committing the action (e.g., due to distraction, drugs/alcohol, or mental illness), was provoked by someone else (e.g., the victim), or committed the act for a good reason (e.g., self-defense). Essentially, these stories revolve around the idea that there are extenuating circumstances that reduce or eliminate the defendant's culpability. Another type of alternative story relevant when the defendant's actions are not in dispute involves the claim that no harm resulted from those actions (i.e., wrong consequence). This type of story will be relevant most often in civil trials, particularly when the defense suspects malingering on the part of the plaintiff.

A few comments are in order about the alternative story possibilities. First, the nature of the case will constrain the viable alternative stories in a given trial, and the facts of the specific case will make some of these more attractive than others. The defense cannot simply select whatever alternative story seems best without regard for what the evidence will show, but in some cases there may be choices about which type of story to present. Second, jurors may well vary in their receptivity to different types of alternative stories based on their personal characteristics. For example, in the United States, jurors who are non-White or low SES are more likely to have had negative experiences with the legal system (police officers in particular) and probably more willing to believe that the police might tamper with evidence in the interests of securing a conviction. Jurors with very low levels of education might be more likely to discount the results of scientific tests or believe that the expert could make them out to say whatever is desired, whereas highly knowledgeable jurors might be more cognizant of errors that can occur during testing and thus more receptive to alternative stories involving mistaken test results. Third, other things being equal, *all* jurors might be more receptive to some types of alternative stories than others. In particular, jurors may react more positively to alternative stories that contest the defendant's involvement as opposed to stories that acknowledge the defendant's role in the activity. Fear of punishing the wrong person may be a fundamental concern for many jurors, and if the defendant's involvement is clear, jurors do not have to worry about this possibility. Knowing that the right person is on trial and clearly did something wrong may lead jurors to be less concerned with whether the prosecution met its burden on any particular legal charge. Jurors may also be more favorably disposed to alternative stories that involve *one* mistake or lying witness as opposed to *multiple* mistakes or a conspiracy involving several deceptive individuals simply because these stories lack parsimony, which may be used as a heuristic for likelihood.

A major question for the defense in many trials is whether to present an alternative story or simply try to undermine the story offered by the other side. "Poking holes" in the other side's story may be a permissible strategy in the courtroom (and, in some cases, the only one available), but psychologically it leaves much to be desired. The primary problem is that the "poking holes" strategy does not offer an explanation for what actually happened—it just implies that the prosecution/plaintiff's story is not correct (or, even worse, implies it is true but not legally adequate). Jurors will likely adhere to the conventions of everyday dispute resolution and expect each side to present its own version of the events. Outside the courtroom, if only one story is put forward in a dispute, there is nothing to argue about—only in a criminal trial can a person say nothing in his or her own defense and expect to have any chance of winning. In general, then, jurors should be more positively disposed toward *any* plausible alternative story offered by the defense than an effort to undermine the prosecution's evidence. It would seem difficult for jurors to avoid drawing the inference that a counterstory was not offered because the "P" story is basically true. On the other hand, it is unclear how jurors would react to defense efforts to raise the possibility of *multiple* alternative stories as opposed to just one. Unlike the prosecution/plaintiff, the defense does not have to prove a particular version of events. Hinting at or directly offering multiple alternative stories would certainly seem likely to raise reasonable doubt, but it could also agitate jurors and lead them to conclude that the defense is using a "kitchen sink" strategy out of desperation. Thus, for the defense, the strongest evidence would seem to be that which directly points toward a single alternative story.

Independent of what the defense offers in the way of an alternative story, jurors may spontaneously generate and consider alternative stories on their own. Jurors with low levels of trust in the legal system should be especially inclined by nature to consider alternative story possibilities that involve mistakes or conspiracies by eyewitnesses, the police, or testing labs. Spontaneous construction of an alternative story may also be more likely when elements of the case call to mind similar life experiences in which the jurors found themselves (e.g., being distracted while driving). Of note, jurors with high levels of NC should be more likely to consider self-generated alternatives by nature. How much time and energy jurors put into the consideration of alternative stories will likely be a function of the defense's evidence along with various individual differences. Strong evidence of an alternative, high NC, and low trust in the legal system should all factor into the amount of time a juror is willing to spend considering alternative stories.

Story Evaluation: Assessing the Possibilities

How do jurors choose between the primary story offered by the instigating side and an alternative story offered (or implied) by the defense? A fundamental premise of the Director's Cut model is that in most cases jurors will construct mental models to provide an overall test of *story likelihood*. Although not widely known outside of cognitive psychology, mental models have considerable empirical support (Johnson-Laird, 1983; Radvansky, Spieler, & Zacks, 1993; Wyer, 2007) and may serve as the primary cognitive mechanism for evaluating stories. Different mental models can be generated and evaluated based on different sets of factual premises. In the end, the perceived likelihood of a story should correspond to how well its underlying mental model can account for a particular version of events.

Mental models can exist in a text-based *propositional modality* or an image-based *visual modality*, with their form in any given situation depending in large part on the task at hand and the modality of relevant information. Given our general human reliance on the visual sense, most mental models created by jurors are probably based in the visual modality. Visual mental models are essentially imaginary simulations of some event or sequence of events based on beliefs about the way the world operates (e.g., how a car skids through an intersection or a body falls off a building). Jurors may evaluate stories by constructing a mental model based on a set of factual assertions and then "run" it, which is to say imagine the outcome when belief-based rules are applied. For instance, a juror might create a mental model in order to "see" how an assailant hides in an apartment and then springs on a victim, how a driver trying to send a text-message might inadvertently drift into another lane of traffic, or how a perpetrator might gain access to a home by entering through an open window on the second floor. Running a mental model is analogous to assembling and watching the "rough cut" of a film—only a mental model uses images and scenes that are created in the mind based on the evidence. Inability to create a mental model that can satisfactorily capture a story should lead to the story's rejection, whereas a good-fitting mental model might result in the phrase, "Yeah, I can see that."

When it comes to choosing among stories that pass some threshold of likelihood, jurors are presumed to prefer simpler stories and those that involve dispositional attributions about the focal characters (e.g., the defendant). Other things being equal, simpler stories are probably more attractive than complex stories in that they will seem more plausible as a result of having fewer moving parts. For one, simpler stories should be easier to test using mental models. Jurors also likely prefer stories that explain human actions in terms of dispositional tendencies. Considerable research on the fundamental attribution error shows that we tend to attribute the behavior of others to stable, internal motives (although paradoxically we are more likely to acknowledge the effects of situational influences on our own behavior). Particularly when the allegations against the defendant involve violence, a desire to see consistency and purpose in the behavior of others may lead jurors to innately favor stories where the defendant is viewed as a "bad" or "evil" person who is fundamentally different from other people.

Jurors are also probably not willing to conduct intensive comparisons of alternative stories. Research on decision making shows that, in a wide variety of domains, people tend to *satisfice*, or choose the first acceptable option. Multiple social psychological theories converge on the notion that we generally do not evaluate alternatives by conducting systematic, point-to-point comparisons due to the excessive cognitive load it would impose. On top of this, cognitive dissonance theory suggests it is stressful to remain in a state of suspended judgment and that we find states of uncertainty to be aversive. Pulling these threads together, jurors should try to settle on an acceptable story as quickly as possible, avoid systematic comparisons of the alternatives, and stop evaluating alternatives (at least temporarily) when a story with high likelihood is identified.

Predeliberation Cognitive States

At the conclusion of the trial, jurors can be classified into one of four categories based on their favored story status. Some jurors may feel the story offered by the instigating side (the "P" story) has a high likelihood of being true; these are the *believers*. Other jurors may come to the conclusion that the "P" story is implausible and a specific alternative story is more likely; these are the *doubters*. Still other jurors may see multiple stories as viable and be uncertain as to which one is most likely; these jurors can be referred to as *mullers*. Finally, some jurors may be confused and unable to identify any satisfactory story; these jurors can be said to be *puzzlers*. Jurors' need for cognition may be an important determinant of how much effort they are willing to expend formulating and running mental models consistent with alternative stories, and how long they are willing to go before settling on a single story and dismissing the rest from active consideration. Thus, heading into deliberation, some jurors will have a single preferred story in mind, some may be actively pondering the merits of multiple stories (probably two), and some may still be struggling to fit the evidence together into a coherent story. The stage is thus set for jurors to talk it out in deliberation.

The Story Sampling Model of Jury Decision Making
Participation and "Sampling" Juror Contributions

Most existing models of jury decision making focus on the relationship between an initial distribution of verdict preferences and the jury's ultimate verdict but have little to say about the underlying process by which juries arrive at their decisions. In contrast, two models of group decision making developed by Garold Stasser address the process of discussion (Stasser 1988; 1992). As depicted in these models, discussion is a mechanism for "sampling" the inputs of group members from the pool of task-relevant information they possess. Sampling basically refers to sharing (i.e., mentioning aloud) a particular piece of information with other members of the group. Applied to juries, deliberation can be viewed as a process where the spoken contributions of individual jurors are sampled by the jury over a period of time. Spoken contributions can come in a variety of forms, including isolated statements, factual assertions, verdict preferences, and even full-fledged stories that purport to explain the evidence.

Individual differences relevant to deliberation. It is clear from the literature that jurors will not contribute equally to the discussion, and the amount spoken by the individuals within a jury will often vary considerably. Four critical individual difference variables pertinent to deliberation are a juror's: (1) extraversion, (2) gender, (3) socioeconomic status/SES, and (4) need for cognition/NC. Who participates and how much they say will be largely dependent on these variables, along with an individual's role within the jury. Specifically, studies have shown that jurors who exert more influence during deliberation tend to be male and have higher levels of NC, extraversion, and SES. Forepersons tend to be inordinately participative and influential as well. These characteristics will determine how much each juror speaks, how much influence they exert, and how much they are influenced by others.

There is good theoretical and empirical support for the importance of all these characteristics. *Extraversion* is a well-established trait included in nearly every major model of human personality. It has obvious implications for a juror's willingness to speak during deliberation, and several studies of jury decision making have revealed an association between extraversion and influence exerted during deliberation. Research has repeatedly found that *gender* is relevant to deliberation as well. Women tend to speak less often than men during deliberation, and women tend to report being influenced by others more often than men. These tendencies are consistent with stereo-typical gender roles, but those may change over time. SES corresponds to a juror's standing in the social hierarchy outside the jury room. It is reflected in a juror's education level, occupational prestige, personal wealth, and annual income, and imparted to other jurors through speech quality, mannerisms, clothing style, and disclosure of life details. As with extraversion, studies have found that jurors with high levels of SES tend to be more talkative and influential during deliberation. High-SES jurors are likely to have had more experience with leadership roles and may be more comfortable than low-SES jurors when it comes to addressing groups; high-SES jurors may also be per-ceived as more knowledgeable based on their apparent success in life, and therefore invited to speak more often by other jurors. When they do con-tribute, high-SES jurors may be more likely to organize and articulate their thoughts in ways that other jurors can understand, and to assert their views more confidently. Finally, *need for cognition* refers to a juror's willingness to think. Initial investigations of juror NC in the context of deliberation suggest that those with high NC tend to be more influential but also less open to the ideas of others, whereas those low in NC speak less, contemplate more, and are more willing to change their position.

Deliberation content: The pyramid of spoken contributions. Another funda-mental premise of the Story Sampling model is the existence of a hierarchical structure to spoken juror contributions. In a nutshell, the frequency of dif-ferent types of contributions is expected to be inversely proportional to their informational influence on other jurors. At the base of the pyramid—least influential but most common—are *isolated statements*. Spoken contributions in this category include scattered thoughts or observations that jurors might have about different aspects of the trial, as well as a variety of questions. Iso-lated statements may be the product of confusion, distraction, or thinking out loud, but they are distinguished by being disconnected from any narra-tive explanation of the evidence.

Less frequent but potentially more influential are *factual assertions* about what is true in the context of the case. These statements are not necessarily true but are represented as such by the speaker and do have a basis in reality. Some factual assertions are fairly straightforward whereas others will represent inferences based on premises that may or may not be articulated. They may involve repeating something asserted to be true by one or more witnesses, declaring a belief about something that was disputed or ambiguous at trial, or drawing an inference about what must have been true given other "facts." Factual assertions are important in that they represent the building blocks of potential stories.

Yet another type of spoken contribution is the *preferred verdict*. Basically, this category consists of statements that convey the speaker's opinion of the appropriate decision. Sometimes these statements may come on the heels of one or more factual assertions, but other times the speaker's reasoning may be far from obvious or missing entirely. These statements are important in that they indicate where a juror stands in relation to other jurors, but they have little or no informational value because they are not set in a narrative context and do not explain why a juror prefers the verdict.

Finally, the rarest but potentially most influential type of spoken contribution is the *story*. A story represents a juror's attempt to provide a narrative explanation for the events leading up to trial—in other words, bracketing the most critical aspects of the evidence, deciding what is true from a factual standpoint, and assembling those "facts" into a coherent, causal sequence. Stories will vary in terms of their comprehensiveness, with a *complete* story accounting for the defendant's intentions and a sequence of linked actions, in contrast to *partial* stories that will only have some of those elements. Stories probably vary in terms of how consciously aware jurors are of them as well as the extent to which jurors can articulate them. The stories that jurors have in their heads are not necessarily the ones that come out of their mouths. Stories in the mind (or *cognitive* stories) will likely diverge to some extent from *conveyed* stories that a juror actually shares aloud due to "slippage"—something lost in translation—in the form of omissions, confusing syntax, poor word choice, interruption, and the like. Straightforward trials with limited evidence may yield fairly simple stories that are easily conveyed; complex trials featuring many actors and linked actions may foster stories that are relatively difficult to convey. In any case, to the extent that something is lost in the telling, conveyed stories should be less powerful and influential than their underlying cognitive stories.

A conveyed story may or may not represent the story actually favored by a juror at the time it is offered, but most of the time it probably does and, perhaps more importantly, other jurors will probably assume that it does. Jurors may express support for a strong conveyed story when it has the same verdict implications as their favored (but undisclosed) cognitive story simply as a matter of expediency or because they wish to hide the real reason for preferring a story (e.g., racial bias). Putting all the evidentiary pieces together and articulating a compelling story is probably not an easy thing to do in most trials. As a result, conveyed stories are probably fairly rare but also potentially very influential—particularly when expressed well by a high-status juror. Indeed, the persuasive articulation of an alternative story may help to explain those times when the majority's preference is not the jury's ultimate verdict.

Deliberation Style

Deliberation essentially involves the sampling of individual juror contributions. Two major approaches (or styles) have been identified in the literature that juries may take as they go about doing this.

When the jury adopts a *verdict-driven style*, the focus of deliberation is on reaching a consensus about the correct decision. A straw poll is usually taken early in the process, sometimes before any substantive discussion. This is ostensibly a means of gauging the degree of consensus within a jury, but it also exposes the size of different factions within the jury and so facilitates application of normative pressure. The ensuing deliberation then basically amounts to a "battle of the factions," with discussion featuring a disproportionately large number of preferred verdict statements and relatively few factual assertions. Full-fledged stories may not emerge immediately, but they likely have more impact the earlier they are conveyed. The key jurors in verdict-driven deliberations are those who enter deliberation without a preferred story or those who are trying to choose between multiple stories— in other words, those who don't belong to a faction. These undecided individuals may take a back seat during the discussion, listening and hoping to be convinced by something they hear. For them, the first compelling story offered may be decisive. At some point, the jury may collectively review the discussion, including the stories offered. The manner in which this is done may serve to make some stories seem more plausible or accepted within the jury.

In contrast, deliberation should play out quite differently when juries employ an *evidence-driven style*. This approach is characterized by the deferral of a straw poll in favor of a systematic, group-level review of the evidence in order to establish the "facts" of the case and determine what actually happened. Only after this has been done is an effort made to fit the facts to the relevant law and identify an appropriate verdict. Relative to verdict-driven juries, the nature of discussion should differ, with relatively more isolated statements and factual assertions and markedly fewer verdict preference statements. Conveyed stories are probably less frequent, particularly early on, and more likely to be partial when offered.

One phenomenon that may occur in a pure evidence-driven deliberation is the construction of a jury-level story. This process would involve cycles of factual assertions followed by attendant discussion concerning their veracity. "Facts" seem likely to be established in juries the same way they usually are in everyday life—by being asserted and not contested. Social norms dictate that disagreements be noted and resolved when they arise. There is probably a window of opportunity for disputing assertions that, once closed, becomes difficult to reopen. During deliberation, a factual assertion that is not contested may be accepted—implicitly or explicitly—as true by the jury. Each additional reference to the assertion may then further increase jurors' confidence in its truth. This implicit process highlights the importance of wording, as descriptive terms included in the original assertion may be treated as factual as well. For example, if a juror characterizes a victim's death as "vicious and cold-blooded" and no one disputes this characterization, jurors may interpret this as indicating that everyone agrees the killing was indeed vicious and cold-blooded. The terms "vicious and cold-blooded" might then be built into jurors' mental representations of the killing and affect the images used in any visual mental model. As the "facts" are established, they take their place in an emerging narrative framework and serve as premises for later factual assertions. Given the social costs involved, it probably takes an exceptionally self-assured (or agitated) individual to be willing to halt forward progress and dispute a factual assertion after it has been mentioned and implicitly accepted as true by the rest of the jury.

At some point, the fact-determination process will be interrupted or terminated, and one or more jurors will attempt to articulate a story based on the collectively determined facts. This is probably a critical moment in a true evidence-driven deliberation, as subtle nuances in the form of framing and word choice associated with the initial articulation of the "jury's story" may be decisive in cases where the evidence is somewhat ambiguous. Not every juror will necessarily agree with the jury's collective story as articulated, but it is probably more difficult to dissent the longer the collective fact-determination process has continued. Alternative stories based on the same facts may be offered at this time as well. Afterwards, the remaining discussion may take on the characteristics of a verdict-driven deliberation, but in general, the more cooperative and congenial atmosphere of an evidence-driven deliberation should minimize normative influence relative to verdict-driven juries. Indeed, the construction of a jury-level story may coincide with those times when jurors report taking only one unanimous vote at the very end of deliberation, essentially ratifying the straightforward implications of the jury's collective story.

No research exists on how juries determine what deliberation style to use, but verdict-driven deliberation styles may be more likely when the evidence clearly favors one side (i.e., very weak or very strong), or when the trial is relatively straightforward with few facts in dispute. In other words, a verdict-driven approach should be more attractive when most jurors enter deliberation with a high degree of confidence in a particular story. Jurors may expect other jurors to feel the same way and believe that a quick vote will reveal this to be true.

Verdict Determination

As shown in figure 8.2, jurors' final verdicts are expected to be a function of both informational influence and normative influence. Informational influence will arise to some extent from factual assertions but primarily from conveyed stories. It is important to note that informational influence occurs at the dyadic level—between two jurors. In other words, the spoken contributions of jurors will differentially affect other members of the jury. Throughout deliberation, some jurors will participate more than others, and the impact of their contributions will depend on their personal characteristics as well as those listening. In general, the informational influence associated with a particular juror during deliberation is viewed as follows:

Juror Informational Influence = Conveyed Story Quality * Prestige

In other words, a juror's influence on other members of the jury is viewed as a joint function of the quality of any story they articulate along with their standing in the group (i.e., prestige). *Conveyed story quality* is defined as the degree to which a juror contributes to the articulation of a story. This contribution need not occur all at once, nor involve the articulation of a complete story. A low level of conveyed story quality might equate to a juror making a few factual assertions during deliberation that could serve as elements for some story. The highest level of conveyed story quality would exist when a juror eloquently and persuasively offers a complete, well-articulated story. *Prestige* is viewed as a composite construct reflecting how highly a juror is thought of by others in the jury. Perceptions of prestige will be determined by such things as a juror's SES, perceived case-specific expertise (particularly in civil trials), and role within the group (e.g., foreperson). It is expected that the components of prestige will combine in an additive fashion. The proposed multiplicative relationship between the two primary components of informational influence reflects the belief that the impact of a juror's conveyed story quality will depend on the juror's prestige—complete stories conveyed by those with higher standing in the jury should have the most impact on other jurors' thinking and, ultimately, the jury's verdict.

Normative influence during deliberation, on the other hand, is associated with the existence of verdict-favoring factions. In the Story Sampling model, a faction's normative influence is basically seen as a function of its power. A faction's *power* in turn is essentially a synergistic combination of its apparent size, the effectiveness of its leadership, and the degree of story agreement among its members:

Faction Power = Apparent Faction Size * Faction Leadership * Story Agreement

Apparent faction size refers to the perceived number of jurors who support a particular verdict. In many instances, the apparent size of a verdict faction will correspond closely to its actual size—but not always. Apparent and actual faction size should be closest when juries take many polls, particularly in the open, where members can determine not only the size of each faction but which individuals are in each one.

Faction leadership refers to whether a faction includes at least one individual willing and able to speak for its members and advocate effectively for their view. Such individuals are instrumental in articulating key factual assertions, sharing and defending faction-preferred stories, and responding to points made by members of the opposing faction. Faction leadership may range from nonexistent to very strong. The ideal faction leader would be extraverted, high in status, high-NC, and a good speaker. Such a person might also possess some case-relevant knowledge (or be perceived to possess it). Factions can also be led by two or more individuals, but whether this can be done effectively depends on how well the would-be leaders can get along and coordinate their efforts.

Story agreement reflects the extent to which the members of a verdict faction are in accord with respect to their preferred narrative explanation of the evidence. A premise of the Story Sampling model is that the normative power of a faction will be weaker when subgroups exist within it, each adhering to a different version of events even though they favor the same verdict. The extent of disagreement among members can vary of course, but serious divergence among faction members should make it difficult to present a united front that represents the psychological foundation of conformity pressure.

Overall, the relationship among the three components of faction power is presumed to be multiplicative in nature such that if *any* component is low, the faction's normative influence will also be relatively low. Conversely, the model predicts that factions will be most powerful when they are perceived as large, effectively led, and their members agree on a story.

Which type of influence will have more impact in any given jury trial will likely depend on the deliberation style adopted. When an evidence-driven style is adopted, informational influence will be the primary determinant of the jury's final verdict. Normative influence will not be irrelevant and factions will probably still exist, but they should be more difficult to discern given the constraints of the discussion structure and thus operate primarily in the background. In these situations, informational influence exerted by the individual jurors should be more predictive of the ultimate jury verdict. When a verdict-driven style is adopted, jury verdicts will likely be determined by both informational and normative influence. As a result, faction power should be a strong predictor of the jury's final verdict when a verdict-driven style is used but much less so when an evidence-driven style is adopted.

When a majority faction exists within the jury, the default expectation is that its preferred verdict will be the jury's eventual choice. However, several circumstances may increase the likelihood of a minority faction's preference becoming the jury's eventual verdict—a "reversal" of the majority. These circumstances include: (1) the existence of a relatively large minority faction, (2) consensus within the minority faction regarding the underlying story, (3) strong minority faction leadership, (4) disagreement within the majority faction regarding the underlying story, (5) weak or nonexistent majority faction leadership, (6) adoption of an evidence-driven deliberation style or private polling that obscures the contours of the majority faction, and (7) the availability of a compromise verdict option. Each of these circumstances should increase the likelihood of the majority's preferred verdict *not* being the jury's ultimate choice, and there may be interactions among them as well. In fact, reversals of the majority are known to be infrequent and may require a *combination* of circumstances.

Of course, there will also be times when there is no clear majority faction within the jury. This may occur because of an even split over the two traditional verdict options (i.e., guilty v. not guilty; liable v. not liable), or the existence of nontraditional options that represent a *compromise verdict* of some type. Most often these will come in the form of the opportunity for criminal juries to convict on a lesser charge, but other options will some-times be available as well (e.g., NGRI, GBMI, NP). The defining feature of a compromise verdict is its more central position on the continuum of cul-pability—somewhere between the two traditional options. Compromise verdicts are expected to be particularly likely when there is no majority faction within the group (i.e., no faction has more than a plurality), no fac-tion is substantially stronger than any other, and the factions are internally united with regard to agreement on a narrative explanation of the underly-ing events. Of particular note, compromise verdicts may be especially likely when the actions of the defendant are in agreement but there is division with regard to the defendant's mindset or motive.

Defendants are often faced with multiple charges in criminal cases and usually, through joinder, the same jury decides them. Several studies focus-ing on deliberation suggest juries spend the majority of their time discussing the first charge (often the most serious), progressively less time on successive charges, and variables representing the content of deliberation are better pre-dictors of the verdict on the first charge than verdicts on subsequent charges. Verdicts reached by the same jury on multiple charges tend to be similar despite the fact that the charges themselves may be quite unrelated. In other words, if a jury convicts on one charge against a defendant, they are likely to convict on the others. The Story Sampling model provides a straightforward explanation for these findings in asserting that most jury decisions are based on a single story. In deciding their initial verdict, jurors (and possibly the entire jury) will construct a story. This story, along with its associated factual premises, serves as a constraint on subsequent decisions. In some cases, the implications of the story may be so obvious that jurors see little need to dis-cuss the evidence further before deciding the remaining charges. Extensive discussion after the first verdict is probably limited to situations where: (1) the defendant is facing very different charges/claims involving actions that seem largely independent, (2) there are conflicts among the stories that indi-vidual jurors favor, or (3) it is unclear how to apply the law to subsequent charges given what has been established.

Summary

The Multi-Level theory consists of two models operating at different hierar-chical levels and incorporates numerous empirical findings. The Director's Cut model deals with individual jurors and builds on the well-established Story model of juror decision making. Unlike earlier models, jurors are not seen as interchangeable but instead differ in terms of several important characteristics that affect how they process trial-related information, as well as how they formulate and evaluate stories. Jurors will construct an initial mental representation of a trial based on what they see and hear in court as well as information drawn from memory via activated scripts and stereotypes. When the trial begins, the instigating side (i.e., the prosecution or plaintiff) will attempt to offer one story, with the strength of its evidence being a function of the degree to which it leads jurors to form one (and *only* one) thorough, detailed, and plausible version of events. The defense has the option to present an alternative story, suggest that multiple stories are possible, or poke holes in the other side's story. Jurors will update their mental representations as the evidence comes in, ultimately constructing and running mental models to assess the likelihood of different possible stories that could account for the evidence. Heading into deliberation, jurors are presumed to be in one of four cognitive states with regard to their preferred story (i.e., believer, doubter, muller, or puzzler).

According to the Story Sampling model, deliberation represents an information-sampling process that involves both informational influence and normative influence. Jurors will vary in terms of how much they speak and what kinds of things they say, with contributions ranging in form from isolated statements to complete narrative explanations of what happened—stories. Informational influence will come primarily in the form of conveyed stories shared with other jurors. Normative influence will result from the perception of verdict factions within the jury, with factions having greater normative power to the extent that they are perceived as large, well-led, and united on a story. Juries may adopt an evidence-driven style or a verdict-driven style, with corresponding implications for the importance of these two types of influence. Informational influence should be the primary determinant of jury verdicts when an evidence-driven style is used; both informational and normative influence should be critical when a verdict-driven style is adopted. Majority factions will usually succeed when they exist, but minority factions may prevail under some circumstances—when they are (relatively) large, effectively led, and internally unified; and when the majority faction is not. Thus, the Multi-Level theory helps explain when we will see the real-life version of Henry Fonda's performance in *Twelve Angry Men*.

9

So What? Implications and Future Directions

It has been said that there is nothing so practical as a good theory. Among other things, theory can do two things that empirical findings cannot— explain *why* something happens and predict when it will happen in the future. Over the last half-century, jury researchers have generated thousands of empirical studies, but much of the research has been driven by relatively narrow questions concerning whether some trial-related practice influences jury verdicts or not. We now have answers to many of those questions, but they are only pieces of a larger puzzle. After more than fifty years of research, it is time to consolidate what we have learned about jury decision making and place that knowledge in a broader theoretical framework. The Multi-Level theory attempts to do this, and this chapter offers a reflection on how well it succeeds.

Contributions of the Multi-Level Theory
Broad Applicability

The Multi-Level theory is intended to apply to all juries—not just those deciding a particular kind of case, located in the United States, or dealing with a criminal (as opposed to civil) matter of law. This is not to deny important differences across jurisdictions and nations that may affect jury decisions in some way (e.g., the standard of proof, the nature of the parties involved, or the sanctions against defendants), but there is nothing in the research to suggest that the fundamental role of the *story* is altered by these variables. Story making appears to be a basic cognitive process used in a wide variety of everyday circumstances, and relatively minor differences in the trial context should not change that. Jurors in both civil and criminal trials have essentially the same underlying task—to make sense of the evidence. It would certainly be possible to construct a theory of jury decision making specifically targeted at criminal or civil juries, but it is unclear how much would be gained in terms of explanatory power in return for the loss of parsimony.

That said, civil juries do have one important function not shared with criminal juries—determining monetary damage awards. Although stories seem well-suited to helping jurors decide on *verdicts* in civil trials, they do not seem as useful for generating precise numerical figures. A few studies have examined how civil juries arrive at monetary amounts, but much remains to be learned. As more research becomes available, it may be possible to develop a more detailed theoretical account of how juries decide how much to award in damages as a complement to theories such as the Multi-Level theory that focus primarily on categorical decisions.

Specification of Underlying Cognitive Structures

The Multi-Level theory builds on research findings from cognitive psychology in order to specify with more precision how juror and jury decisions are linked to underlying cognitive structures. In particular, the Director's Cut model highlights the importance of scripts associated with case type, stereotypes associated with person categories, and mental models. When the Story model was first developed in the late 1970s and 1980s, the study of these cognitive structures was still in its infancy, and the model does not go into detail with regard to cognitive structures. Ultimately, improved understanding of the nature and relationships among these mediating cognitive variables should benefit the scientific study of juror and jury decision processes, and may be helpful for determining how extralegal bias can be reduced through changes in courtroom practices or jury instructions.

Mental models play an especially important role in the Director's Cut model in that they serve as the primary cognitive mechanism for evaluating alternative stories. They have been used to explain and predict performance on a variety of mental tasks, and there is plenty of empirical support for their existence. They are employed in the model because they seem especially well-suited to decision making in court—specifically, they represent dynamic structures created in real time and capable of being used to evaluate different cognitive scenarios (i.e., stories). A particular point of emphasis is the *visual* nature of many mental models used at trial. Jurors clearly have the capability to form visual representations and simulate their operation in order to project likely outcomes. Much remains to be learned about the nature of mental models, but many are probably based on stored representations of visual stimuli encountered in real life. Jurors may be especially likely to use visual images observed frequently in their daily lives, or seen in movies or on TV.

Identifying Focal Individual Differences

The literature on jury decision making features many psychological variables. However, some of these variables overlap with each other, some are of questionable importance, and some probably play a role only in very specific trial circumstances. One function of theory is to call attention to selected variables and, in doing so, divert attention from others. The Multi-Level theory highlights a relatively small number of characteristics associated with jurors and defendants that should play a role in *most* trials. By omission, it also suggests that other individual difference variables are of lesser or only occasional importance. Table 9.1 lists these focal individual-difference variables and indicates the time period when each characteristic is most relevant.

At the juror level, the Director's Cut model underscores the importance of several juror demographic characteristics (i.e., race, gender, and SES) and two personality traits (extraversion and need for cognition). Relevant defendant characteristics include physical attractiveness, criminal history, and SES. The characteristics of other trial participants—attorneys and judges especially—may be important, but there is very little research on these participant types at present. The location of these juror and defendant characteristics in the Director's Cut model helps to explain why strong relationships with verdict preferences have generally not been observed in the literature—their effects occur relatively early in a complex decision process. They influence the retrieval of stored information from memory and how the evidence is interpreted, but numerous other variables play an important role as well. In addition to these well-established demographic characteristics, two lesser-known participant characteristics are featured in the Multi-Level theory. *Legal system trust* is a multidimensional construct capturing a juror's fundamental beliefs about the motives and competence of the people involved in the legal system. It shares some similarity with two classic constructs—legal

Table 9.1: Key Individual Differences in the Multi-Level Theory

	Relevant to:	
Individual Difference Variable	**Story Generation & Preferred Verdict**	**Deliberation**
Defendant Characteristics:		
Physical Attractiveness	x	
SES	x	
Race	x	
Prior Criminal Record	x	
Demeanor	x	
Juror Characteristics:		
Race	x	
SES	x	x
Gender	x	x
Legal System Trust	x	
Extraversion		x
Need for Cognition	x	x

authoritarianism and juror "bias"—but is broader than both of these and more concerned with perceived competence. Several recent measures (i.e., the Pretrial Juror Attitude Questionnaire and the Attitudes Toward the Criminal Legal System) appear to correspond fairly closely to the definition of legal system trust and may provide good operational measures of this construct. *Defendant demeanor* refers to the display of emotion (e.g., sadness, sorrow, or remorse) in front of the jury. Existing studies on the expression of emotion by defendants have focused primarily on sentencing decisions in capital trials, but a consistent finding is that jurors in a variety of case types are affected by signs that the defendant "has a heart"—specifically, when sympathetic emotion is shown for victims. In short, stony detachment or arrogant haughtiness may activate stereotypes of hardened criminals, increasing the likelihood of a guilty (or liable) verdict.

At the jury level, the Story Sampling model also calls attention to several personal characteristics relevant to interpersonal influence during deliberation. There has not been nearly as much interest in how individual differences affect the deliberation process as opposed to their relationship with predeliberation verdict preferences, but there is enough. Two of the focal characteristics identified here as important to deliberation were discovered by the Chicago Jury Project more than fifty years ago—gender and SES. More recently, extraversion emerged with the development of the Big Five framework of personality, and need for cognition (NC) has received a good deal of attention from scholars in the wake of dual-processing theories of persuasive communication. Both extraversion and NC account for the willingness of some jurors to think and speak more than others, something with obvious implications for influence during deliberation. Two additional variables may be relevant to a juror's informational influence but have thus far received little or no research attention—speaking ability and charisma. *Oral communication ability* would seem to be an obvious mediator of influence during deliberation—perhaps too obvious—but there is no easy way to measure it, which may explain the dearth of studies on it. Similarly, no research has examined the *charisma* of jurors, but the extensive literature on transformational leadership in workgroups underscores the potential value of including measures of this characteristic in future study.

Several considerations should be noted about the individual difference characteristics identified in the Multi-Level theory. First, there are relatively few of them on purpose. Parsimony is a value in all areas of science and was viewed as important in the derivation of any integrative theory. Additional characteristics can certainly be added in the future if subsequent empirical research suggests there is value in doing so. Second, identifying a focal set of individual difference variables is not meant to imply that no other individual difference characteristic is ever relevant to jury decision making. In particular, case-specific attitudes may be good predictors of pretrial culpability and preferred stories in cases involving controversial legal concepts (e.g., insanity) or practices (e.g., capital punishment). Case-specific attitudes are not featured in the Director's Cut model simply because they are not germane in most trials, even though they will be highly relevant in some. Third, although not depicted as such in figures 8.1 and 8.2, the impact of some focal individual differences will likely depend somewhat on other variables such as the type of case, the strength of the evidence, or other individual difference variables. These interactions are not depicted for the sake of simplicity, but have been discussed. In general, though, the participant characteristics specified in the Multi-Level theory are expected to play a role in most trial contexts.

Case Type

Charges and claims will differ in terms of their legal requirements regarding what the evidence must show in order for the jury to find a defendant culpable, but the importance of case type goes beyond this. Case type probably makes a substantial contribution to the initial mental representation that jurors form, activating stored information from memory in the form of assumed event sequences, perpetrator motives, victim reactions, images, and so forth. The impact of case type is most clearly evident in the scattered experimental studies that attempted to hold the evidence constant while varying the nature of the charge against a criminal defendant. Conviction rates *should* be very similar across conditions, but sometimes they are not. The most likely explanation for this is the existence of scripts associated with different types of cases and the incorporation of script-related features into the juror's mental representation.

With regard to the inclusion of charge seriousness in the Director's Cut model, it is fair to say that the existing literature provides only lukewarm support. Basically, charge seriousness is included in the model because several field studies show an increased likelihood of culpability (guilt or liability) for more serious cases, and there is a good rationale for its effect—our robust human tendency to point fingers when something bad happens. The worse that "something" is, the more we want to pin responsibility for it on someone. In addition, actual criminal jurors need be concerned about a frightening proposition—sending violent perpetrators back into the community with an errant acquittal. Jurors deciding a case where the defendant is charged with possession of marijuana probably experience much less pressure to keep that individual out of society than jurors involved in a capital trial where the defendant is charged with several brutal murders. Put bluntly, jurors seem likely to err on the side of public safety in cases involving serious wrongdoing, particularly when the defendant is known to have committed the behavior or at least been involved in some fashion.

"Strong" Evidence

In trying to decide how to handle a case, many a trial attorney has probably wondered how jurors evaluate the evidence, and no doubt many rubrics and personal formulae exist for determining when evidence is "strong." Three factors are identified in the Director's Cut model as primarily responsible for determining how positively the evidence for the instigating side (i.e., the prosecution or plaintiff) will be received by jurors—scope, credibility, and singularity. In essence, "strong" evidence is that which can be easily fashioned into one detailed and plausible story that explains the actions and motives of the various players.

Scope refers to the comprehensiveness of the evidence in terms of detail and explanatory power. A key element of scope is the ability to explain why the players in the story acted as they did (or are doing). Even though jurors in some cases will need to make decisions based only on a narrow set of facts, they will usually desire to understand the perpetrator's history and motives and will always prefer a rich, detailed story that includes the motives of the individuals involved.

Credibility is a term familiar to legal professionals and jury researchers but used here a little differently than usual. In the Multi-Level model, credibility is attached to the distinct elements of the main story rather than an individual witness. In general, undisputed factual assertions are assumed to be true unless they are seen as coming from a noncredible source or completely outlandish. When a factual assertion is disputed by two or more sources, jurors may assume that the correct interpretation is the one asserted by the most credible source or the one with the greatest number of corroborating sources. Corroboration is likely to be important because jurors undoubtedly know from life experiences that people make mistakes and sometimes lie, so the number of witnesses attesting to something can serve as a potential indicator of an assertion's veracity. Of course, it is possible for multiple individuals to be mistaken about the same thing and for multiple people to conspire to lie about something, but these interpretations are probably not very attractive to most jurors because they imply intricate and convoluted stories. Put differently, jurors prefer explanations that are short and sweet.

Finally, *singularity* pertains to how well the evidence converges on a single story. Here the predictions of the story-based models diverge from other conceptualizations of evidence in that "more" is not always "better" when it comes to the amount of evidence presented. Jurors will try to fashion one compelling story from the evidence, and evidentiary elements that cannot be incorporated neatly should be discounted (at best) or possibly serve to trigger consideration of alternative stories (at worst).

On the other side of the courtroom, strong evidence for the defense is presumed to be that which facilitates the formation of alternative stories. A premise of the Director's Cut model is that, although there are many types of charges and claims that can be leveled against defendants, there are only a limited number of basic explanations that can be offered in defense. The model specifically proposes four major types (see chap. 8) of alternative stories: (1) *wrong defendant* (the defendant was not present/involved), (2) *wrong actions* (the defendant did something culpable, but not what was alleged), (3) *wrong mindset* (the defendant acted as charged but extenuating

Table 9.2: Research Hypotheses Associated with the Director's Cut Model

Hypothesis & Prediction

1   Narrative organization of opening statements will be correlated with pretrial perceptions of culpability/responsibility:

    • Prosecution/plaintiff (+)

    • Defense (-)

2   Exposure to anti-defendant PTP will be positively correlated with perceptions of pretrial culpability/responsibility

3   The following case characteristics will be positively correlated with pretrial perceptions of culpability/responsibility:

    • The seriousness of the primary charge/claim against the defendant

    • The number of charges/claims against the defendant

4   Defendants will be viewed as more culpable/responsible prior to trial when perceived to have:

    • Low socioeconomic status

    • Prior conviction(s) for similar offense

    • Low physical attractiveness

    • Stony or haughty demeanor

5   Jurors will perceive defendants as more culpable/responsible prior to trial when the juror is:

    • A different race than the defendant

    • Female (in cases involving sexual assault or a child victim)

    • High socioeconomic status

    • Highly trusting of the legal system

6   (a) Characteristics of the opening statements, (b) the case, and (c) the trial participants will each explain unique variance in pretrial ratings of culpability/responsibility

7   Pretrial ratings of culpability/responsibility will be positively correlated with the perceived likelihood of the prosecution/plaintiff's story

8   The following characteristics of the prosecution/plaintiff's evidence will be positively correlated with the perceived likelihood of the prosecution/plaintiff's story:

    • Scope

    • Credibility

    • Singularity

Hypothesis & Prediction

9   Construction of a plausible visual-based mental model will be positively associated with perceived likelihood of the prosecution/plaintiff's story

10   (a) Characteristics of the prosecution/plaintiff's evidence, (b) pretrial ratings of culpability/responsibility, and (c) the perceived likelihood of an alternative story will each explain unique variance in the perceived likelihood of the prosecution / plaintiff's story

11   The following will be correlated with the perceived likelihood of an alternative story:

• Perceived likelihood of the prosecution/plaintiff's story (-)

• Defense evidence of error, conspiracy, or extenuation (+)

• Juror need for cognition (+)

• Juror trust in the legal system (-)

12   (a) Defense evidence suggesting error, conspiracy, or extenuation, (b) perceived likelihood of the prosecution/plaintiff's story, (c) juror need for cognition, and (d) juror trust in the legal system will each explain unique variance in the perceived likelihood of an alternative story

13   The perceived likelihood of the prosecution/plaintiff's story and the perceived likelihood of an alternative story will interact to predict juror post-trial story status

circumstances exist), and (4) *wrong consequences* (the defendant's actions did not produce the alleged harm).

The strongest type of alternative story is probably the *wrong defendant*, because if successful it does not leave the defendant associated with illegal behavior. However, alternative stories of this type fundamentally posit the existence of errors and/or lies, and jurors will differ in their willingness to believe that these may occur. Trust in the legal system probably plays an important role in how plausible jurors will view these sorts of alternative stories. Jurors who are low on legal system trust may readily accept the notion that the police would tamper with the evidence or that scientific tests can be wrong—but jurors who are more trusting of the system might have considerable difficulty "buying" stories that involve these events. In contrast, alternative stories from the *wrong action* or the *wrong mindset* categories are probably easier to argue in most cases but carry the disadvantage of implicating the defendant in questionable behavior. Having no doubt about who committed the illegal act may be the most critical aspect of a juror's willingness to decide against the defendant. Of course, the defense need not offer any story and, at least in criminal trials, present any evidence. However, given jurors' natural desire for a story that explains the evidence in a compelling fashion, this seems like a strategy to be avoided if at all possible. In addition, the defense strategy of "poking holes" in the prosecution/plaintiff's story does not seem ideal in that it may be interpreted as a tacit admission that the prosecution/plaintiff's story is correct, just lacking in some legal (and perhaps discountable) aspect. In the end, jurors may stick with the only story on the table.

Role of Stories in Deliberation

The Story Sampling model is based on two premises: (1) stories are the most important elements of discussion during deliberation, and (2) stories are rarely articulated in one holistic, comprehensive statement. Instead, stories probably emerge in a fragmented and piecemeal fashion, and eloquent, persuasive speeches that lay out an entire story are likely the exception to the rule. Although infrequent, the articulation of a complete story should have considerable impact when it does occur. As such, when the contents of deliberation are coded in research studies, an implication of the Story Sampling model is that the coding scheme should capture the degree to which statements express a story. The challenge for researchers will be to develop schemes that can capture not only when individual jurors share stories but when a story is created through the spoken contributions of multiple jurors. Once story articulation is measured, a second challenge will be determining which jurors adhere to which stories. Experimental studies with mock jurors may usefully employ both close-ended (e.g., agreement with various story-consistent premises and conclusions) and open-ended (e.g., short narrative essay) techniques to measure story preference prior to deliberation, but studies conducted with actual jurors will almost certainly have to rely on retrospective reports that may be influenced by knowledge of how things subsequently turned out. Just because stories are difficult to measure, though, does not mean that they are unimportant or unworthy of study—scholars simply need to think through the potential stories in advance and use multiple strategies that allow them to triangulate on story articulation and adherence.

Dynamics of the Interpersonal Influence

Another noteworthy contribution of the Story Sampling model is its identification of variables underlying the two types of influence that occur during deliberation. Previous models of jury decision making had little to say about the basis for informational influence and treated normative influence simply as a function of faction size. In the Story Sampling model, stories are viewed as the primary conduit of informational influence, and the model can account for differences in participation and influence across jurors. A new construct, faction power, is proposed as the primary source of a faction's normative influence. Faction power in turn is viewed as a function of three components that are synergistically related to each other: apparent faction size, faction leadership, and within-faction story agreement. Operational formulas were offered to quantify informational and normative influence as well. Finally, the Story Sampling model specifies conditions when majority factions will be less likely to succeed in attaining their preferred verdicts, which moves beyond existing models that have little or nothing to say about the likelihood of minority faction success.

Implications for Theory and Research
Testable Predictions

Implicit in the preceding discussion are a number of testable research propositions that could be made explicit. Table 9.2 lists hypotheses that follow from the Director's Cut model; Table 9.3 displays hypotheses associated with the Story Sampling model. Overall, there are two types of predictions inherent in the Multi-Level theory: what causes what, and what does not cause what (see Figs. 8.1 and 8.2). One type of prediction corresponds to causal influence and is depicted by arrows. Arrows in the models essentially represent an expectation that measures of antecedent variables will be directly and meaningfully (i.e., significantly) related to their respective outcome variables. Further, where a *set* of antecedents is specified, each one should have a meaningful relationship with the outcome when the other antecedents have been taken into account (i.e., included in the model and thus statistically controlled). These predictions can be tested through the use of multi-step analytical procedures where the change in the fit of the model is assessed as antecedent variables are entered sequentially. Variables entered at later steps should add incremental validity to the explanation of the outcome over and above already-entered antecedents. A second kind of prediction is implied wherever two variables are *not* connected by an arrow. Basically, "missing" arrows represent a prediction that two variables do *not* have a direct causal relationship. Two variables that are not causally linked could still be correlated with one another via spurious associations, but we would generally not expect to see substantial (or significant) relationships between them.

Table 9.3: Research Hypotheses Associated with the Story Sampling Model

Hypothesis & Prediction

Juror Behavior

1   A juror's participation during deliberation will be positively associated with their:

- Post-trial story status as a believer or doubter

- Being male

- Extraversion

- Socioeconomic status

- Need for cognition

- Being foreperson

2   During deliberation, jurors will express isolated statements most frequently, followed by (in descending order): factual assertions, verdict preferences, partial stories, and then complete stories

3   The degree of informational influence exerted by jurors during deliberation will be positively associated with their:

- Conveyed story quality

- Perceived prestige

4   The degree to which a juror is influenced by the spoken contributions of other jurors will be associated with the focal juror's:

- Post-trial story status as muller or puzzler (+)

- Conscientiousness (+)

- Need for cognition (-)

- Being female (+)

Jury-Level Phenomena

5   Deliberation style will influence the collective frequency of different kinds of spoken contributions during group discussion. Relative to a verdict-driven style, an evidence-driven style will tend to result in:

- More factual assertions

- Fewer verdict preference statements

- Fewer complete stories

6   Faction power will be positively associated with "winning" deliberation (i.e., having the faction's preferred verdict selected as the jury's verdict)

Hypothesis & Prediction

Juror-Level Phenomena

7   Normative influence during deliberation will be negatively associated with:

  • An evidence-driven style

  • Elapsed time before the jury's first poll

  • Private (anonymous) polling

  • The number of polls taken during deliberation

8   Reversal verdicts (i.e, a final verdict other than what was preferred by initial majority faction) will be positively associated with:

  • Collective (summated) informational influence of the minority faction jurors

  • Minority faction power

9   Compromise verdicts will be more likely when:

  • No majority faction exists

  • No faction is substantially more powerful than any other

  • All factions agree internally on the underlying story

  • There is disagreement within the jury as a whole regarding the defendant's mindset

10 The demographic diversity of the jury will be positively correlated with the number of stories articulated during deliberation

11 The number of articulated stories during deliberation will be positively related to the thoroughness of evidence review

Future Research Directions

In addition to testing the specific propositions noted in Tables 9.2 and 9.3, there are several general directions for future research that could be profitable.

First, it would be useful to learn more about common characteristics of jurors' case-related scripts and participant-related stereotypes. Some initial work has been conducted already with regard to assessing prototypes (i.e., stereotypes) of people who are insane and the features of different types of crimes, but we have only scratched the surface in this area. Most notably, little is known about how jurors use mental models to test potential stories.

Qualitative studies featuring in-depth interviews with real jurors (or at least representative samples of jury-eligible adults) could be conducted to identify the common "default" characteristics of different types of crimes, as well as different types of people who commit them (e.g., "drug addict," "child molester," "abusive husband"). Another strategy would be to use "think-aloud" verbal protocols in order to gain a better sense of how jurors construct mental representations in real time.

Second, researchers should examine the distinguishability of individual difference constructs in the domain of legal attitudes. It would be especially valuable to conduct large-sample studies with real jurors that include the various measures of legal attitudes along with measures of constructs that might be determinants of those attitudes (i.e., belief in a just world, locus of control, and authoritarianism). Confirmatory factor analyses could then be used to determine if the constructs are empirically separable and, if so, measured well by existing instruments. Hierarchical regression analyses could also be used to see which measures added incremental validity to the prediction of decisions in various types of cases.

Third, more attention should be given to studying various aspects of the defendant's courtroom demeanor. Existing research has focused on displays of remorse and empathy for the victim, but other aspects of defendant behavior could be examined as well. A useful study would involve manipulating different courtroom behaviors along with different expressed emotions (including positive ones). It will be important to use realistic stimulus materials (e.g., samples of defendant behavior from actual legal proceedings) in any experimental studies. As a complement to better-controlled laboratory research, field studies could also be conducted involving trained courtroom observers who code selected aspects of defendant behavior (and perhaps juror reactions as well), along with recording verdict outcomes.

Fourth, more effort should be devoted to examining the characteristics of opening statements. At this point, little is known about what makes them effective. Given their relative brevity and isolation, it should be fairly easy to manipulate selected aspects of opening statements using realistic trial materials. In addition to assessing effects on jurors' ultimate verdict preferences, researchers could determine if the characteristics of opening statements influence more proximal variables such as pretrial ratings of culpability and preferred stories prior to deliberation. In order to develop a better sense of what aspects of opening statements are most important, qualitative studies could be done with jurors (or mock jurors) asked to "think aloud" as they read through or (even better) watch videotaped opening statements from actual trials.

Fifth, research should examine the role of jury composition with regard to preferred stories. This could be examined in conjunction with such things as the relative size of verdict factions and the availability of nontraditional verdict options. For instance, mock jurors could view a stimulus trial involving a homicide and provide a narrative summary of what they feel happened (i.e., their "story"). Juries could then be composed with known distributions of preferred verdicts and stories. Story heterogeneity within factions could be manipulated by assigning mock jurors to juries based not only on their preferred verdict but also on the story they formulated to explain the evidence. The availability of compromise verdict options could be manipulated by restricting the verdict options to the two traditional choices (i.e., guilty of murder v. not guilty) or allowing additional ones (e.g., the lesser included charge of manslaughter). Participants could be assigned to juries so that factions varied systematically in size, allowing for a better understanding of what happens when there is no majority (i.e., a plurality). Videotaping deliberations would then allow for the coding of potentially critical events (e.g., emergence of strong faction leaders, story articulation, signs of within-faction dissension or teamwork, etc.). To complement this lab-based approach, structured interviews could be done with ex-jurors in the wake of real trials.

Finally, more intensive study is needed to understand the conditions when juries will best *perform* their focal task—thoroughly reviewing the evidence and making reasoned decisions with an appropriate understanding of their instructions. Almost all of the existing research on jurors and juries has been concerned with what decision is reached—guilty v. not guilty, liable v. not liable, life in prison or the death penalty, the amount of damages awarded, and the like. While some of these studies allow us to make inferences about how well juries deliberate, a common problem is that we cannot say what the *correct* decision is. If it is safe to assume that juries that deliberate well are more likely to come to the correct decision, there is clear need for studies that directly examine deliberation quality and its antecedents in cases where the correct verdict is known or can be legally determined. Such data will ultimately be useful in helping to identify and test interventions designed to *improve* jury decision making.

Practical Implications
Juror Selection/Voir Dire

Juror selection in general, and voir dire in particular, is conducted to weed out those individuals who would be unduly partial to one side or the other. It is therefore important for judges and attorneys to recognize that some juror characteristics *do* display a modest association with jurors' beliefs about the appropriate verdict, at least prior to deliberation. First, females are more likely to favor conviction in cases involving sexual assault, child abuse, or a battered woman. Second, males tend to be more willing to give the death penalty in capital cases. Third, people tend to act more favorably toward defendants of their own race. Of particular note, in cases where the victim is White and the defendant is African American, capital juries are *more* likely to mete out the death penalty when they include a critical mass of White male jurors, and they are *less* likely to do so when they include even one African American male. Fourth, jurors who score high on authoritarianism and/ or those who profess attitudes that reflect a high level of trust in the legal system tend to be more likely to prefer conviction. Although not easy to assess quickly, it may be possible for attorneys to gauge these characteristics via a few items on a juror questionnaire or a few choice questions during voir dire.

In addition to these tendencies regarding juror demographic characteristics, attorneys and judges need to be aware of the insidious effects of pretrial publicity (PTP) and the failure of limiting instructions to prevent them. Jurors exposed to case-related PTP tend to view defendants more negatively and are more likely to prefer conviction, and these effects do not necessarily dissipate over time. Under some circumstances, prejudice may even grow stronger. Most legal "remedies" have not been found to work well, but two strategies have shown some promise and should be considered for high-profile cases that receive considerable media attention: individual voir dire and change of venue. Venirepersons are more likely to give honest answers to potentially embarrassing or revealing questions in the judge's chambers than in front of their peers, and studies have shown that media coverage of trials drops off quickly outside the jurisdiction of origin.

Courtroom Practices and Procedures

The Multi-Level theory and underlying research lend themselves to several prescriptions regarding what should be allowed in the courtroom. To begin with, more extensive measures should be allowed during voir dire for cases featuring considerable PTP, including individual questioning. If a large proportion of the venire indicates moderate or high familiarity with a case, motion for change of venue should be allowed. Research and theory converge on the notion that jurors do not keep things separate (in the interests of formulating a comprehensive story) and tend to draw dispositional inferences about defendants. Therefore, motions for severance should be seriously considered, particularly when multiple defendants are involved. The findings to date also suggest no reason to prevent jurors from taking notes or asking questions through the attorneys. Allowing jurors to do these things helps keep them engaged and may improve their comprehension of the evidence, especially in complex cases. Pre-instructing jurors is another practice that has had some beneficial effect, and there again seems to be little reason not to do this. Jurors can be warned that the pre-instructions may not be the final and official word, and they seem to do fine with this knowledge.

Allowing jurors to discuss the evidence as a group prior to the end of the trial is a newer innovation that has been tried in jurisdictions such as Arizona. Some good data have been generated thus far, but the number of studies is small and so it is difficult to say conclusively whether this is a beneficial practice. It may help to improve juror comprehension of the evidence, but juries allowed to discuss the case will apparently do so at times without all their members present. One question that the initial research did not conclusively answer is whether predeliberation discussions promote the early formation of a verdict preference.

Some of the clearest implications for courtroom practice concern the effects of exposure to inadmissible evidence (IE). The long-standing legal remedy for inadvertent exposure has been an instruction from the judge to ignore the inadmissible information, put it aside, and give it no weight. Jurors simply cannot do this well, especially if the IE helps to explain what happened. Judges and attorneys need to recognize this psychological reality, and judges in particular should be willing to declare a mistrial or directed verdict in particularly egregious situations. Obviously, such extreme measures are not feasible for most instances of IE, so the onus falls on preventing juror exposure to it rather than rehabilitating jurors via post hoc instruction. Attorneys should be warned prior to trial that solicitations of inadmissible testimony will not be treated lightly, and questionable material should be vetted in a pretrial hearing or sidebar conference. Given the uncertainties associated with witness testimony, this will not prevent all instances of juror exposure to IE, but pretrial warnings should help. The criterion that should be used to gauge the severity of "contamination" due to exposure to inadmissible information is the degree to which it fits readily into a narrative framework. Judges should be particularly careful with IE forms that have repeatedly been shown to be powerful, including pretrial publicity and confession-related information. Given the difficulty of remediating the effects of exposure to information deemed to be prejudicial, the focus needs to be on preventing it in the first place.

Defendant/Plaintiff Courtroom Appearance and Behavior

The bottom line with regard to defendant appearance and behavior is very consistent with what most attorneys have been doing intuitively all along—make the defendant as physically attractive as possible via clothing, hygiene, and hairstyle. It would also be in defendants' best interests to show respect and humility for the legal process. If the defendant's culpability or liability has already been established or is strongly indicated, displays of real remorse may help jurors to empathize with defendants, but remorse perceived to be insincere could cause a backlash or, manifested prematurely, be viewed as a signal that the defendant is admitting responsibility.

Opening/Story Statements

The Director's Cut theory underscores the importance of establishing a story—the sooner the better—and opening remarks represent the first and best opportunity to do so in most trials. It is difficult to think of a trial where it would not be advantageous to provide an overview of one's case before the jurors start hearing the evidence. Providing a general overview is probably more important than fleshing out specifics, which runs the risk of bogging down and losing jurors to distraction. In general, anything that makes it easier for jurors to compose a narrative framework should be done. Under most circumstances, this would include summarizing points in chronological fashion and identifying the motives of the major characters in the story. In turn, closing statements should include a recap of the story.

Evidence Presentation

For attorneys, perhaps the single most important implication of the Multi-Level theory is the need to structure one's case in a way that fosters a cohesive narrative explanation of what happened. In addition to the obvious importance of the opening statements in this regard, attorneys should consider ways in which their evidence can be presented visually to facilitate the construction and use of mental models. Mental models are particularly important to jurors for assessing events that can be seen in the mind's eye. They can be used to forecast likely outcomes or assess the relative plausibility of different outcomes by providing a context for sequences of behaviors (or events) that play out in space and time. In short, in many trials, it will be difficult for jurors to believe a story that they cannot picture in their minds. Computer-based reconstructions or simulations may be particularly powerful forms of evidence that facilitate the construction of mental models, even substituting for them in some instances. Static representations (such as pictures, flow charts, diagrams, etc.) that are particularly memorable may also facilitate the construction of mental models. These "low-tech" visual aids may be especially important for helping jurors understand and use complex scientific evidence in that they may help jurors to "see" something associated with a process that is inherently hard to visualize (i.e., testing DNA).

Judicial Instructions

Wherever possible, judges should provide instructions to jurors prior to hearing the evidence. Consistent with the principles of human learning, pre-instruction creates a cognitive framework that helps jurors to prioritize and process the evidence during the trial. Although there are relatively few studies on the effects of pre-instruction, the benefits associated with providing learning goals in classroom settings and organizational training situations are well-established and should transfer to the courtroom. In addition, judges should consider including cautionary instructions for some types of evidence. Given widespread appreciation of the problems with eyewitness testimony and the financial burden associated with bringing in expert witnesses to testify to these issues, a judicial instruction that summarizes research findings on eyewitness reliability (e.g., the Telfaire instruction) would be warranted in cases that will hinge on eyewitness testimony. As bodies of knowledge develop in other domains where experts testify, similar instructions could be developed and vetted by the attorneys or appellate courts. Specific instruction regarding the use of complex scientific evidence (perhaps in conjunction with special verdict forms) might be especially helpful given the difficulties that jurors have repeatedly shown.

Finally, and perhaps most critically, pattern instructions should be reviewed for comprehensibility and revised accordingly. It is abundantly clear that many jurors struggle with understanding their instructions, despite what they tell outsiders or even themselves. Lawmakers in some jurisdictions are beginning to act on this reality and rewrite pattern instructions to eliminate the worse aspects of "legalese," but this is not a widespread occurrence as yet. Wherever possible, instructions should be simplified—not dumbed down but revised to be more comprehensible. The key mechanism for bringing this about is using words and sentence structures that make sense to jurors as opposed to attorneys. In jurisdictions where the legislature has not acted proactively to address problems with existing pattern instructions, judges should be willing to do so themselves.

The need for revision is especially apparent in capital cases. The findings from research on the relationship between instruction comprehension and sentencing in capital juries are chilling. Mistaken understanding of the sentencing instructions has been shown to be associated with a belief that the defendant deserves the death penalty. These mistakes include believing that a sentence of "life without parole" will still allow the defendant to be released and that the presence of aggravating factors *requires* the death penalty, as well as failing to consider (or discounting) mitigating factors. Put simply, jurors in death penalty cases need to understand what they are doing, and many apparently do not. Judges should consider addressing these common misperceptions head-on with supplemental instructions in death penalty cases. More radically, judges might also consider calling jurors' attention to lingering inequalities with regard to who gets the death penalty as a function of defendant and victim race. Research suggests that making racial differences more salient may be one strategy for reducing racial discrimination.

A Look Ahead: The Future of Jury Trials and Jury Research

Juries have long played a critical role in the legal system of free societies, and this is very likely to continue into the foreseeable future. At least 150,000 jury trials occur in the United States each year and probably at least several thousand more in the rest of the world. The trend has been for greater use of juries in other countries as well, so we are most definitely not talking about an endangered species when we speak of juries. Indeed, the species has changed remarkably little over the last five hundred or so years. Jury trials are still primarily face-to-face, adversarial events "run" by legal professionals for the benefit of naïve decision makers. It's true, though; there has been some evolution. More kinds of evidence and a wider variety of demonstrative exhibits are now allowed. Persons without direct knowledge of the case appear more frequently nowadays (i.e., expert witnesses). Juries have also gradually (and grudgingly) been allowed to become more active and involved in the trial. Probably the biggest difference is that juries are no longer explicitly charged with determining the relevant law, although they still retain the implicit power to do so. Nonetheless, much has stayed the same. A colonial-era jury from the 1600s transported through time to the viewing area of a modern-day courtroom would still understand what they were watching.

Peering into the crystal ball, we can speculate how jury trials will likely change in the future. First, it would not be surprising to see high-level action taken to limit the use of peremptory challenges during juror selection. There is growing evidence of their misuse and no compelling indication of their value. Second, there will almost certainly be more use of technology in the courtroom to allow for sophisticated displays of visual evidence. Advances in virtual reality may someday revolutionize the presentation of evidence, with three-dimensional projections of key objects, virtual tours of important case-relevant locations, and computer-aided simulations of many events. Third, and relatedly, jurors will likely be given their own workstations in the jury box (i.e., monitor and input devices), and the ability to communicate electronically with the judge and/or attorneys. This would allow jurors to submit questions, take notes, and even signal confusion; it could also provide a means of magnifying, rotating, or reviewing the evidence. Individual workstations could also be used to present instructions and test juror comprehension before proceeding to deliberation.

Going forward, there is reason for optimism among those interested in improving the jury system. Most importantly, we can expect to see more application of what we have learned in the courtroom. We will certainly continue to see more high-quality research on juries. The pace of change continues to accelerate, and technological advances are making it increasingly possible for researchers to conduct tightly controlled experimental studies using authentic trial materials in a realistic context. In addition, we can expect to see more field research with actual juries as well. The last two decades have witnessed a number of collaborative studies involving jury researchers and legal professionals. As the community of jury researchers becomes larger and better connected, it should allow for more high-benefit studies that involve consortiums of researchers pooling their efforts to examine major questions using real juries (e.g., the Capital Jury Project). Even the long-standing taboo against peering in on deliberating juries may be falling by the wayside. In the late 1990s, Arizona became the first major jurisdiction in the United States to allow social scientists to directly observe and record jury deliberation, even if only on a one-time basis. Since researchers poked their noses into the deliberation room, the sun has continued to rise each day and now a precedent has been established; hopefully scientists will be invited back again regularly in the future. Much has been learned about jury decision making in the half-century or so since the groundbreaking work of the Chicago Jury Project in the 1950s. Much more will be learned in the next fifty years about a unique societal institution that may yet represent the best way to make important legal decisions in a world without certainty.

BIBLIOGRAPHY

Abel, M., & Watters, H. (2005). Attributions of guilt and punishment as functions of physical attractiveness and smiling. *Journal of Social Psychology, 145,* 687–702.

Abramson, J. (1994). *We, the jury: The jury system and the ideal of democracy.* New York: Basic Books.

Adams, C., & Bourgeois, M. (2006). Separating compensatory and punitive damage award decisions by trial bifurcation. *Law and Human Behavior, 30,* 11–30.

Adler, F. (1973). Socioeconomic factors influencing jury verdicts. *New York University Review of Law and Social Change, 3,* 1–10.

Adler, S.J. (1994). *The jury: Trial and error in the American courtroom.* New York: Times Books.

Adorno, T., Frenkel-Brunswik, E., Levinson, D., & Sanford, N. (1950). *The authoritarian personality.* New York: Harper.

Allison, M., & Brimacombe, C.A.E. (2010). Alibi believability: The effect of prior convictions and judicial instructions. *Journal of Applied Social Psychology, 40,* 1054–1084.

Allen, M., Mabry, E., & McKelton, D. (1998). Impact of juror attitudes about the death penalty on juror evaluations of guilt and punishment: A meta-analysis. *Law and Human Behavior, 22,* 715–731.

Anderson, N.H. (1981). *Foundations of information integration theory.* New York: Academic Press.

Antonio, M.E. (2006). Arbitrariness and the death penalty: How the defendant's appearance during trial influences capital jurors' punishment decision. *Behavioral Sciences and the Law, 24,* 215–234.

Apodaca, Cooper, & Madden v. Oregon, 406 U.S. 404 (1972).

Arbuthnot, J., Myers, B., & Leach, J. (2002). Linking pretrial knowledge and juror prejudgment: Some methodological considerations. *American Journal of Forensic Psychology, 20,* 53–71.

Bailis, D.S., Darley, J.M., Waxman, T.L., & Robinson, P.H. (1995). Community standards of criminal liability and the insanity defense. *Law and Human Behavior, 19,* 425–446.

Baldus, D.C., Pulaski, C., & Woodworth, G. (1983). Comparative review of death sentences: An empirical study of the Georgia experience. *Journal of Criminal Law and Criminology, 74,* 661–753.

Baldus, D.C., Woodworth, G., Zuckerman, D., Weiner, N.A., & Broffit, B. (1998). Racial discrimination and the death penalty in the post-Furman era: An empirical and legal overview with recent findings from Philadelphia. *Cornell Law Review, 83,* 1630–1770.

Baldwin, J., & McConville, M. (1979). Trial by jury: Some empirical evidence on contested criminal cases in England. *Law and Society Review, 13,* 861–890.

———. (1980). Does the composition of an English jury affect its verdict? *Judicature, 64,* 133–139.

Ballew v. Georgia, 435 U.S. 223 (1978).

Bar-Hillel, M. (1980). The base-rate fallacy in probability judgments. *Acta Psychologica, 44,* 211–233.

Barnett, M.E., Brodsky, S.L., & Davis, C.M. (2004). When mitigation evidence makes a difference: Effects of psychological mitigating evidence on sentencing decisions in capital trials. *Behavioral Sciences and the Law, 22,* 751–770.

Beckham, B., & Aronson, H. (1978). Selection of jury foremen as a measure of the social status of women. *Psychological Reports, 43,* 475–478.

Beckham, C.M., Spray, B.J., & Pietz, C.A. (2007). Jurors' locus of control and defendants' attractiveness in death penalty sentencing. *Journal of Social Psychology, 147,* 285–298.

Bennett, W.L. (1978). Storytelling in criminal trials: A model of social judgment. *Quarterly Journal of Speech, 64,* 1–22.

———. (1979). Rhetorical transformation of evidence in criminal trials: Creating grounds for legal judgment. *Quarterly Journal of Speech, 65,* 311–323.

Bennett, W.S., & Feldman, M.S. (1981). *Reconstructing reality in the courtroom.* New Brunswick, NJ: Rutgers University Press.

Bennett, Jr., R.B., Leibman, J.H., & Fetter, R.E. (1999). Seeing is believing; or is it: An empirical study of computer simulations as evidence. *Wake Forest Law Review, 34,* 257–294.

Bentele, U., & Bowers, W. (2001). How jurors decide on death: Guilt is overwhelming; aggravation requires death; and mitigation is no excuse. *Brooklyn Law Review, 66,* 1011–1079.

Berman, G.L., & Cutler, B.L. (1996). Effects of inconsistencies in eyewitness testimony on mock-juror decision making. *Journal of Applied Psychology, 81,* 170–177.

Berman, G.L., Narby, D.J., & Cutler, B.L. (1995). Effects of inconsistent statements on mock jurors' evaluations of the eyewitness, perceptions of defendant culpability and verdicts. *Law and Human Behavior, 19,* 79–88.

Blankenship, M., Luginbuhl, J., Cullen, F., & Redick, W. (1997). Jurors' comprehension of sentencing instructions: A test of the death penalty process in Tennessee. *Justice Quarterly, 14,* 325–351.

Boehm, V. (1968). Mr. Prejudice, Miss Sympathy and the authoritarian personality: An application of psychological measuring to the problem of jury bias. *Wisconsin Law Review, 1968, 3,* 734–750.

Bordens, K.S., & Horowitz, I.A. (1983). Information processing in joined and severed trials. *Journal of Applied Social Psychology, 13,* 351–370.

———. (1985). Joinder of criminal offenses: A review of the legal and psychological literature. *Law and Human Behavior, 9,* 329–353.

———. (1986). Prejudicial joinder of multiple offenses: Relative effects of cognitive processing and criminal schema. *Basic and Applied Social Psychology, 7,* 243–258.

Bornstein, B.H. (1994). David, Goliath, and Reverend Bayes: Prior beliefs about defendants' status in personal injury cases. *Applied Cognitive Psychology, 8,* 233–258.

———. (1998). From compassion to compensation: The effect of injury severity on mock jurors' liability judgments. *Journal of Applied Social Psychology, 28,* 1477–1502.

———. (2004). The impact of different types of expert scientific testimony on mock jurors' liability verdicts. *Psychology, Crime and Law, 10,* 429–446.

Bornstein, B.H., Rung, L.M., & Miller, M.K. (2002). The effects of defendant remorse on mock juror decisions in a malpractice case. *Behavioral Science and the Law, 20,* 393–409.

Bornstein, B.H., Whisenhunt, B.L., Nemeth, R.J., & Dunaway, D.L. (2002). Pre-trial publicity and civil cases: A two-way street? *Law and Human Behavior, 26,* 3–17.

Boster, F.J., Hunter, J.E., & Hale, J.L. (1991). An information-processing model of jury decision making. *Small Group Research, 18,* 524–547.

Bottoms, B.L., Golding, J.M., Stevenson, M.C., Wiley, T.R., & Yozwiak, J.A. (2007). A review of factors affecting jurors' decisions in child sexual abuse cases. In M. Toglia et al. (Eds.), *The handbook of eyewitness psychology: Volume 1: Memory for events* (pp.509–543). Mawah, NJ: Erlbaum.

Bottoms, B.L., & Goodman, G.S. (1994). Perceptions of children's credibility in sexual assault cases. *Journal of Applied Social Psychology, 24,* 702–732.

Bowers, W. (1995). The Capital Jury Project: Rationale, design, and preview of early findings. *Indiana Law Journal, 70,* 1043–1102.

Bowers, W.J., Steiner, B.D., & Sandys, M.R. (2001). Death sentencing in Black and White: An empirical analysis of the role of jurors' race and jury racial composition. *University of Pennsylvania Journal of Constitutional Law, 3,* 171–275.

Bradfield, A.L., & Wells, G.L. (2000). The perceived validity of eyewitness identification testimony: A test of the five *Biggers* criteria. *Law and Human Behavior, 24,* 581–594.

Bray, R.M., & Noble, A.M. (1978). Authoritarianism and decisions of mock juries: Evidence of jury bias and group polarization. *Journal of Personality and Social Psychology, 36,* 1424–1430.

Bray, R.M., & Kerr, N.L. (1979). Use of the simulation method in the study of jury behavior: Some methodological considerations. *Law and Human Behavior, 3,* 107–119.

Brehm, S.S., & Brehm, J.W. (1981). *Psychological reactance: A theory of freedom and control.* New York: Academic Press.

Brewer, T. (2004). Race and jurors' receptivity to mitigation in capital cases: The effect of jurors', defendants', and victims' race in combination. *Law and Human Behavior, 28,* 529–545.

Brewer, N. (2006). Uses and abuses of eyewitness identification confidence. *Legal and Criminological Psychology, 11,* 3–23.

Brewer, N., & Burke, A. (2002). Effects of testimonial inconsistencies and eyewitness confidence on mock-juror judgments. *Law and Human Behavior, 26,* 353–364.

Brewer, N., & Hupfeld, R.M. (2004). Effects of testimonial inconsistencies and witness group identity on mock-juror judgments. *Journal of Applied Social Psychology, 34,* 493–513.

Brewer, N., & Palmer, M.A. (2010). Eyewitness identification tests. *Legal and Criminological Psychology, 15,* 77–96.

Brewer, N., Weber, N., & Semmler, C. (2005). Eyewitness identification. In N. Brewer & K.D. Williams (Eds.), *Psychology and law: An empirical perspective* (pp. 177–221). New York: Guilford Press.

Bridgeman, D.L., & Marlowe, D. (1979). Jury decision making: An empirical study based on actual felony trials. *Journal of Applied Psychology, 64,* 91–98.

Bright, D.A., & Goodman-Delahunty, J. (2006). Gruesome evidence and emotion: Anger, blame, and jury decision making. *Law and Human Behavior, 30,* 183–202.

Briody, M. (2004). The effects of DNA evidence on homicide cases in court. *Australian and New Zealand Journal of Criminology, 37,* 231–252.

Broeder, D.W. (1958). The University of Chicago jury project. *Nebraska Law Review, 38,* 744–761.

Brunswick, E. (1947). *Systematic and representative design of psychological experiments, with results in physical and social perception.* Berkeley: University of California Press.

Bruschke, J., & Loges, W.E. (1999). Relationship between pretrial publicity and trial outcomes. *Journal of Communication, 49,* 104–120.

Buchanan, R.W., Pryor, B., Taylor, K.P., & Strawn, D.V. (1978). Legal communication: An investigation of juror comprehension of pattern jury instructions. *Communication Quarterly, 26,* 31–35.

Buckhout, R., Weg, S., Reilly, V., & Frohboese, R. (1977). Jury verdicts: Comparison of 6- vs. 12-person juries and unanimous vs. majority decision rule in a murder trial. *Bulletin of the Psychonomic Society, 10,* 175–178.

Bullock, H.A. (1961). Significance of the racial factor in the length of prison sentences. *Journal of Criminal Law, Criminology and Police Science, 52,* 411–417.

Burch v. Louisiana, 441 U.S. 130 (1979).

Butler, B. (2007). The role of death qualification in jurors' susceptibility to pretrial publicity. *Journal of Applied Social Psychology, 37(1),* 115–123.

———. (2008). Racial bias and the death penalty. In B. Cutler (Ed.), *Encyclopedia of psychology and law: Volume 1* (pp. 670–671). Thousand Oaks, CA: Sage.

———. (2010). My client is guilty of 'this,' but not guilty of 'that:' The impact of defense-attorney concession on juror decisions. *American Journal of Forensic Psychology, 28,* 5–19.

Butler, B., & Moran, G. (2007). The impact of death qualification, belief in a just world, legal authoritarianism, and locus of control on venirepersons' evaluations of aggravating and mitigating circumstances in capital trials. *Behavioral Sciences and the Law, 25,* 57–68.

Cacioppo, J.T., & Petty, R.E. (1982). The need for cognition. *Journal of Personality and Social Psychology, 42,* 116–131.

Cacioppo, J.T., Petty, R.E., Feinstein, J.A., & Jarvis, W.B.G. (1996). Dispositional differences in cognitive motivation: The life and times of individuals varying in need for cognition. *Psychological Bulletin, 119,* 197–253.

Cacioppo, J.T., Petty, R.E., & Kao, C.F. (1984). The efficient assessment of need for cognition. *Journal of Personality Assessment, 48,* 306–307.

Cage v. Louisiana, 498 U.S. 39 (1990).

Carlson, S.C., Pasano, M.S., & Jannuzzo, J.A. (1977). The effect of lie detector evidence on jury deliberations: An empirical study. *Journal of Police Sciences and Administration, 5,* 148–154.

Carretta, T.R., & Moreland, R.L. (1983). The direct and indirect effects of inadmissible evidence. *Journal of Applied Social Psychology, 13,* 291–309.

Castelli, P., Goodman, G.S., & Ghetti, S. (2005). Effects of interview style and witness age on jurors' perceptions of children's credibility in sexual abuse cases. *Journal of Applied Social Psychology, 35,* 297–319.

Cavoukian, A., & Heselgrave, R.J. (1980). The admissibility of polygraph evidence in court: Some empirical findings. *Law and Human Behavior, 4,* 117–131.

Chadee, D. (1996). Race, trial evidence and jury decision making. *Caribbean Journal of Criminology and Social Psychology, 1,* 59–86.

Chapdelaine, A., & Griffin, S.F. (1997). Beliefs of guilt and recommended sentence as a function of juror bias in the O.J. Simpson trial. *Journal of Social Issues, 53,* 479–487.

Charrow, R.P., & Charrow, V.R. (1979). Making legal language understandable: A psycholinguistic study of jury instructions. *Columbia Law Review, 79,* 1306–1374.

Chin, A., & Peterson, M.A. (1985). *Deep pockets, empty pockets: Who wins in Cook county jury trials*. Santa Monica, CA: Rand/Institute for Civil Justice.

Clark, J., Boccaccini, M.T., Caillouet, B., & Chaplin, W. (2007). Five factor model personality traits, jury selection and case outcomes in criminal and civil cases. *Criminal Justice and Behavior, 34*, 641–660.

Clary, E.G., & Shaffer, D.R. (1980). Effects of evidence withholding and a defendant's prior record on juridic decisions. *Journal of Social Psychology, 112*, 237–245.

Cohen, J. (1992). A power primer. *Psychological Bulletin, 112*, 155–159.

Colgrove v. Battin, 413 U.S. 149 (1973).

Conley, J.M., Turnier, W.J., & Rose, M.R. (2000). The racial ecology of the courtroom: An experimental study of juror response to the race of criminal defendants. *Wisconsin Law Review, 2000*, 1185–1220.

Cooper, J., Bennett, E., & Sukel, H. (1996). Complex scientific testimony: How do jurors make decisions? *Law and Human Behavior, 20*, 379–394.

Cooper, J., & Neuhaus, I. (2000). The hired gun effect: Assessing the effect of pay, frequency of testifying, and credentials on the perception of expert testimony. *Law and Human Behavior, 24*, 149–172.

Costanzo, M., & Krauss, D. (2012). *Forensic and legal psychology: Psychological science applied to law*. New York: Worth Publishers.

Couch, J.V., & Sigler, J.N. (2002). Gender of an expert witness and the jury verdict. *Psychological Record, 52*, 281–287.

Cox, M., & Tanford, S. (1989). An alternative method of capital jury selection. *Law and Human Behavior, 13*, 167–183.

Crott, H.W., & Werner, J. (1994). The norm-information-distance model: A stochastic approach to preference change in group interaction. *Journal of Experimental Social Psychology, 30*, 68–95.

Crowley, M.J., O'Callaghan, M.G., & Ball, P.J. (1994). The juridical impact of psychological expert testimony in a simulated child sexual abuse trial. *Law and Human Behavior, 18*, 89–105.

Culhane, S.E., & Hosch, H.M. (2004). Crime victims serving as jurors: Is there bias present? *Law and Human Behavior, 28*, 649–659.

Cutler, B.L., & Hughes, D.M. (2001). Judging jury service: Results of the North Carolina administrative office of the courts survey. *Behavioral Science and the Law, 19*, 305–320.

Cutler, B.L., & Kovera, M.B. (2011). Expert psychological testimony. *Current Directions in Psychological Science, 20*, 53–57.

Cutler, B.L., Moran, G., & Narby, D.J. (1992). Jury selection in insanity cases. *Journal of Research in Personality, 26*, 165–182.

Cutler, B.L., & Penrod, S.D. (1995). *Mistaken identifications: The eyewitness, psychology, and the law*. New York: Cambridge University Press.

Cutler, B.L., Penrod, S.D., & Stuve, T.E. (1988). Juror decision making in eyewitness identification cases. *Law and Human Behavior, 12*, 41–55.

Daftary-Kapur, T., Groscup, J., O'Connor, M., Coffaro, F., & Galietta, M. (2011). Measuring knowledge of the insanity defense: Scale construction and validation. *Behavioral Sciences and the Law, 29*, 40–63.

Dane, F.C. (1985). In search of reasonable doubt: A systematic examination of selected quantification approaches. *Law and Human Behavior, 9*, 141–158.

Daniels, S., & Martin, J. (1990). Myth and reality in punitive damages. *Minnesota Law Review, 75*, 1–64.

Dann, B.M., Hans, V.P., & Kaye, D.H. (2006; November). Can jury trial innovations improve juror understanding of DNA evidence? *NIJ Journal #255*, 2–7.

Daudistel, H.C., Hosch, H.M., Holmes, M.D., & Graves, J.B. (1999). Effects of defendant ethnicity on juries' dispositions of felony cases. *Journal of Applied Social Psychology, 29*, 317–336.

Davis, J.H. (1973). Group decision and social interaction: A theory of social decision schemes. *Psychological Review, 80*, 97–125.

———. (1996). Group decision making and quantitative judgments: A consensus model. In E. Witte & J.H. Davis (Eds.), *Understanding group behavior: Consensual action by small groups* (pp. 35–59). Mahwah, NJ: Erlbaum.

Davis, J.H., Bray, R.M., & Holt, R.W. (1977). The empirical study of decision processes in juries: A critical review. In J.L. Tapp and F.J. Levine (Eds.), *Law, justice and the individual in society: Psychological and legal issues* (pp. 326–361). New York: Holt.

Davis, J.H., Au, W.T., Hulbert, L.G., Chen, X., & Zarnoth, P. (1997). Effects of group size and procedural influence on consensus judgments of quantity: The examples of damage award and mock civil juries. *Journal of Personality and Social Psychology, 73*, 703–718.

Davis, J.H., Kameda, T., Parks, C., Stasson, M., & Zimmerman, S. (1989). Some social mechanics of group decision making: The distribution of opinion, polling sequence, and implications for consensus. *Journal of Personality and Social Psychology, 57*, 1000–1012.

Davis, J.H., Kerr, N.L., Atkin, R.S., Holt, R., & Meek, D. (1975). The decision processes of 6- and 12-person mock juries assigned unanimous and two-thirds majority rules. *Journal of Personality and Social Psychology, 32*, 1–14.

Davis, J.H., Kerr, N.L., Stasser, G., Meek, D., & Holt, R. (1977). Victim consequences, sentence severity, and decision processes in mock juries. *Organizational Behavior and Human Performance, 18*, 346–365.

Davis, J.H., Spitzer, C.E., Nagao, D.H., & Stasser, G. (1978). Bias in social decisions by individuals and groups—An example from mock juries. In H. Brandstatter, J.H. Davis, & H. Schuler (Eds.), *Dynamics of group decisions* (pp. 33–52). Beverly Hills, CA: Sage.

Davis, J.H., Stasser, G., Spitzer, C.E., & Holt, R.W. (1976). Changes in group members' decision preferences during discussion: An illustration with mock juries. *Journal of Personality and Social Psychology, 34*, 1177–1187.

Davis, J.H., Stasson, M., Ono, K., & Zimmerman, S. (1988). Effects of straw polls on group decision making: Sequential voting pattern, timing, and local majorities. *Journal of Personality and Social Psychology, 55*, 918–926.

Davis, J.H., Stasson, M., Parks, C.D., Hulbert, L., Kameda, T., Zimmerman, S.K., & Ono, K. (1993). Quantitative decisions by groups and individuals: Voting procedures and monetary awards by mock civil juries. *Journal of Experimental Social Psychology, 29*, 326–346.

Davis, J.H., Tindale, R.S., Nagao, D.H., Hinsz, V.B., & Robertson, B. (1984). Order effects in multiple decisions by groups: A demonstration with mock juries and trial procedures. *Journal of Personality and Social Psychology, 47*, 1003–1012.

De la Fuente, L., De la Fuente, E.I., & Garcia, J. (2003). Effects of pretrial juror bias, strength of evidence and deliberation process on juror decisions: New validity evidence of the Juror Bias Scale scores. *Psychology, Crime and Law, 8*, 197–209.

De la Fuente Solana, E., Garcia, J., & Tamayo, I.M. (1998). Some individual differences in perception of the evidence and the verdict choice. *Psychology, Crime and Law, 4*, 361–373.

Deosaran, R. (1981). The jury system in a post-colonial, multi-racial society: Problems of bias. *British Journal of Criminology, 21,* 305–323.

Deutsch, M., & Gerard, H.B. (1955). A study of normative and informational social influences upon individual judgment. *Journal of Abnormal and Social Psychology, 51,* 629–636.

Devine, D.J., Buddenbaum, J., Houp, Stolle, D.P., & S., Studebaker, N. (2007). Deliberation quality: A preliminary examination in real juries. *Journal of Empirical Legal Studies, 4,* 273–303.

Devine, D.J., Buddenbaum, J., Houp, S., Stolle, D.P. & Studebaker, N. (2009). Strength of evidence, extraevidentiary influence and the liberation hypothesis: Data from the field. *Law and Human Behavior, 33,* 136–148.

Devine, D.J., Clayton, L.D., Dunford, B.B., Seying, R., & Pryce, J. (2001). Jury decision making: 45 years of empirical research on deliberating groups. *Psychology, Public Policy, and Law, 7,* 622–727.

Devine, D.J., Olafson, K.M., Jarvis, L., Bott, J.L., Clayton, L.D., & Wolfe, J.T. (2004). Explaining jury verdicts: Is leniency bias for real? *Journal of Applied Social Psychology, 34,* 2069–2098.

DeWitt, J.S., Richardson, J.T., & Warner, L.G. (1997). Novel scientific evidence and controversial cases: A social psychological examination. *Law and Psychology Review, 21,* 1–28.

Dexter, H.R., Cutler, B.L., & Moran, G. (1992). A test of voir dire as a remedy for the prejudicial effects of pretrial publicity. *Journal of Applied Social Psychology, 22,* 819–832.

Diamond, S.S., & Casper, J.D. (1992). Blindfolding the jury to verdict consequences: Damages, experts, and the civil jury. *Law and Society Review, 26,* 513–557.

Diamond, S.S., & Levi, J.N. (1996). Improving decisions on death by revising and testing jury instructions. *Judicature, 79,* 224–232.

Diamond, S.S., & Rose, M.R. (2005). Real juries. *Annual Review of Law and Social Science, 1,* 255–284.

Diamond, S.S., & Vidmar, N. (2001). Jury ruminations on forbidden topics. *Virginia Law Review, 87,* 1857–1915.

Diamond, S.S., Vidmar, N., Rose, M., Ellis, L., & Murphy, B. (2003). Juror discussions during civil trials: Studying an Arizona innovation. *Arizona Law Review, 45,* 1–82.

Diamond, S.S., & Zeisel, H. (1974). A courtroom experiment on juror selection and decision-making. *Proceedings of the Division of Personality and Social Psychology, 1,* 276–277.

Dillehay, R.C., & Nietzel, M.T. (1985). Juror experience and jury verdicts. *Law and Human Behavior, 9,* 179–191.

Dion, K., Berscheid, E., & Walster, E. (1972). What is beautiful is good. *Journal of Personality and Social Psychology, 24,* 285–290.

Dixon, T., & Linz, D. (2002). Television news, prejudicial pretrial publicity and the depiction of race. *Journal of Broadcasting and Electronic Media, 46,* 112–136.

Doob, A.N., & Kirschenbaum, H.M. (1973). Bias in police lineups: Partial remembering. *Journal of Police Science and Administration, 1,* 287–293.

Douglas, K.S., Lyon, D.R., & Ogloff, J.R.P. (1997). The impact of graphic photographic evidence on mock juror decisions in a murder trial: Probative or prejudicial. *Law and Human Behavior, 21,* 485–501.

Duggan, L.M., Aubrey, M., Doherty, E., Isquith, P., Levine, M., & Scheiner, J. (1989). The credibility of children as witnesses in a simulated child sex abuse trial. In S.J. Ceci, D.F. Ross, & M.P. Toglia (Eds.), *Perspectives on children's testimony* (pp. 71–99). New York: Springer-Verlag.

Dumit, J. (1999). Objective brains, prejudicial images. *Science in Context, 12,* 173–201.

Dunn, M.A., Salovey, P., & Feigenson, N. (2006). The jury persuaded (and not): Computer animation in the courtroom. *Law and Policy, 28*, 228–248.

Durham v. United States, 214 F.2d 862 (D.C. Cir. 1954).

Efran, M.G. (1974). The effect of physical appearance on the judgment of guilt, interpersonal attraction, and severity of recommended punishment in a simulated jury task. *Journal of Research in Personality, 8*, 45–54.

Eimermann, T.E., & Simon, R.J. (1970). Newspaper coverage of crimes and trials: Another empirical look at the free press–fair trial controversy. *Journalism Quarterly, 47*, 142–144.

Eisenberg, T., Garvey, S.P., & Well, M.T. (2001). Forecasting life and death: Juror race, religion, and attitude toward the death penalty. *Journal of Legal Studies, 30*, 277–312.

Eisenberg, T., Goerdt, J., Ostrom, B., & Rottman, D. (1996). Litigation outcomes in state and federal courts: A statistical portrait. *Seattle University Law Review, 19*, 433–453.

Eisenberg, T., Hannaford-Agor, P.L., Hans, V.P., Waters, N.L., Munsterman, G.T., Schwab, S.J., & Wells, M.T. (2005). Judge–jury agreement in criminal cases: A partial replication of Kalven and Zeisel's *The American Jury. Journal of Empirical Legal Studies, 2*, 171–206.

Ellsworth, P.C. (1989). Are twelve heads better than one? *Law and Contemporary Problems, 52*, 207–224.

Ellsworth, P.C., Bukaty, R.M., Cowan, C.L., & Thompson, W.C. (1984). The death qualified jury and the defense of insanity. *Law and Human Behavior, 8*, 81–93.

Ellsworth, P.C., & Mauro, R. (1998). Psychology and law. In D.T. Gilbert, S.T. Fiske, & G. Lindzey (Eds.), *The handbook of social psychology* (Vol 2; pp. 684–731). Boston: McGraw-Hill.

Elwork, A., Alfini, J.J., & Sales, B. (1982). Towards understandable jury instructions. *Judicature, 65*, 432–443.

Elwork, A., Sales, B.D., & Alfini, J.J. (1977). Juridic decisions: In ignorance of the law or in light of it? *Law and Human Behavior, 1*, 163–189.

Eno Louden, J., & Skeem, J.L. (2007). Constructing insanity: Jurors' prototypes, attitudes, and legal decision-making. *Behavioral Sciences and the Law, 25*, 449–470.

Espinoza, R.K.E., & Willis-Esqueda, C. (2008). Defendant and defense attorney characteristics and their effects on juror decision making and prejudice against Mexican Americans. *Cultural Diversity and Ethnic Minority Psychology, 14*, 364–371.

Erian, M., Lin, C., Patel, N., Neal, A., & Geiselman, R.E. (1998). Juror verdicts as a function of victim and defendant attractiveness in sexual assault cases. *American Journal of Forensic Psychology, 16*, 25–40.

Faigman, D.L. (2008). Expert psychological testimony. In B.L. Cutler (Ed.), *Encyclopedia of psychology and law: Volume 1* (pp. 267–271). Thousand Oaks, CA: Sage.

Faigman, D.L., & Baglioni, A.J. (1988). Bayes' theorem in the trial process: Instructing jurors on the value of statistical evidence. *Law and Human Behavior, 12*, 1–17.

Faigman, D., Kaye, D., Saks, M., & Sanders, J. (1997). *Modern scientific evidence: The law and science of expert testimony.* St. Paul: West Publishing Co.

Feigenson, N., Park, J., & Salovey, P. (1997). Effect of blameworthiness and outcome severity on attributions of responsibility and damage awards in comparative negligence cases. *Law and Human Behavior, 21*, 597–617.

Filkins, J.W., Smith, C.M., & Tindale, R.S. (1998). An evaluation of the biasing effects of death qualification. In R.S. Tindale et al. (Eds.), *Theory and research on small groups* (pp. 153–175). New York: Plenum Press.

Finkel, N.J. (1989). The Insanity Reform Act of 1984: Much ado about nothing. *Behavioral Sciences and the Law, 7,* 403–419.

———. (1991). The insanity defense: A comparison of verdict schemas. *Law and Human Behavior, 15,* 533–555.

———. (1995). *Commonsense justice: Jurors' notions of the law.* Cambridge, MA: Harvard University Press.

———. (2000). But it's not fair! Commonsense notions of unfairness. *Psychology, Public Policy, and Law, 6,* 898–952.

Finkel, N.J., & Duff, K.B. (1989). The insanity defense: Giving jurors a third option. *Forensic Reports, 2,* 235–263.

Finkel, N.J., & Groscup, J.L. (1997). Crime prototypes, objective versus subjective culpability, and a commonsense balance. *Law and Human Behavior, 21,* 209–230.

Finkel, N.J., & Handel, S.F. (1989). How do jurors construe "insanity." *Law and Human Behavior, 13,* 41–59.

Finkel, N.J., Meister, K.H., & Lightfoot, D.M. (1991). The self-defense defense and community sentiment. *Law and Human Behavior, 15,* 585–602.

Finkel, N.J., Shaw, R., Bercaw, S., & Koch, J. (1985). Insanity defenses: From the jurors' perspective. *Law and Psychology Review, 2,* 435–449.

Finkelstein, R., & Bastounis, M. (2010). The effect of the deliberation process and jurors' prior legal knowledge on the sentence: The role of psychological expertise and crime scene photo. *Behavioral Sciences and the Law, 28,* 426–441.

Fitzgerald, J.M. (2000). Younger and older jurors: The influence of environmental supports on memory performance and decision making in complex trials. *Journal of Gerontology: Psychological Sciences, 55B,* 323–331.

Flango, V.E. (1980). Would jurors do a better job if they could take notes? *Judicature, 63,* 436–443.

Flowers, S.M. (2008). *Disparities in jury outcomes: Baltimore city vs. three surrounding jurisdictions—an empirical examination.* Baltimore, MD: The Abell Foundation. Retrieved from http://www.abell.org/Pubsitems/Disparities-cj.908.pdf.

Foley, L.A., & Pigott, M.A. (1997a). Race, age and jury decisions in a civil rape trial. *American Journal of Forensic Psychology, 15,* 37–55.

———. (1997b). The influence of forepersons and nonforepersons on mock jury decisions. *American Journal of Forensic Psychology, 15,* 5–17.

———. (2000). Belief in a just world and jury decisions in a civil rape trial. *Journal of Applied Social Psychology, 30,* 935–951.

Follingstad, D.R., Polek, D.S., Hause, E.S., Deaton, L.H., Bulger, M.W., & Conway, Z.D. (1989). Factors predicting verdicts in cases where battered women kill their husbands. *Law and Human Behavior, 13,* 253–269.

Forgas, J.P., O'Connor, K.V., & Morris, S.L. (1983). Smile and punishment: The effects of facial expression on responsibility attribution by groups and individuals. *Personality and Social Psychology Bulletin, 9,* 587–596.

ForsterLee, L., & Horowitz, I.A. (1997). Enhancing juror competence in a complex trial. *Applied Cognitive Psychology, 11,* 305–319.

ForsterLee, L., Horowitz, I.A., & Bourgeois, M.J. (1993). Juror competence in civil trials: The effects of preinstruction and evidence technicality. *Journal of Applied Psychology, 78,* 14–21.

———. (1994). Effects of notetaking on verdicts and evidence processing in a civil trial. *Law and Human Behavior, 18,* 567–578.

ForsterLee, L., Kent, L., & Horowitz, I.A. (2005). The cognitive effects of jury aids on decision-making in complex civil litigation. *Applied Cognitive Psychology, 19,* 867–884.

Foss, R.D. (1981). Structural effects in simulated jury decision making. *Journal of Personality and Social Psychology, 40,* 1055–1062.

Frank, J., & Applegate, B.K. (1998). Assessing juror understanding of capital-sentencing instructions. *Crime and Delinquency, 44,* 412–433.

Frederick, J.T. (1984). Social science involvement in voir dire: Preliminary data on the effectiveness of "scientific jury selection." *Behavioral Sciences and the Law, 2,* 375–394.

Freedman, J.L., Krismer, K., MacDonald, J.E., & Cunningham, J.A. (1994). Severity of penalty, seriousness of the charge and mock jurors' verdicts. *Law and Human Behavior, 18,* 189–202.

Fulero, S.M., & Penrod, S.D. (1990). Attorney jury selection folklore: What do they think and how can psychologists help? *Forensic Reports, 3,* 233–259.

Furnham, A., & Procter, E. (1989). Belief in a just world: Review and critique of the individual difference literature. *British Journal of Social Psychology, 28,* 365–384.

Gastil, J., Burkhalter, S., & Black, L.W. (2007). Do juries deliberate? A study of deliberation, individual difference, and group member satisfaction at a municipal courthouse. *Small Group Research, 38,* 337–359.

Gerbasi, K.C., Zuckerman, M., & Reis, H.T. (1977). Justice needs a new blindfold: A review of mock jury research. *Psychological Bulletin, 84,* 323–345.

Givelber, D.J., & Farrell, A.S. (2008). Judge and juries: The defense case and differences in acquittal rates. *Law of Social Inquiry, 33,* 31–52.

Gold, G., & Weiner, B. (2000). Remorse, confession, group identity and expectancies about repeating a transgression. *Basic and Applied Social Psychology, 22,* 291–300.

Golding, J.M., Stewart, T.L., Yozwiak, J.A., Djadali, Y., & Sanchez, R.P. (2000). The impact of DNA evidence in a child sexual assault trial. *Child Maltreatment, 5,* 373–383.

Goodman, G.S., Golding, J.M., & Haith, M.M. (1984). Jurors' reactions to child witnesses. *Journal of Social Issues, 40,* 139–156.

Goodman, J. (1992). Jurors' comprehension and assessment of probabilistic evidence. *American Journal of Trial Advocacy, 16,* 363–389.

Graziano, S.J., Panter, A.T., & Tanaka, J.S. (1990). Individual differences in information processing strategies and their role in juror decision making and selection. *Forensic Reports, 3,* 279–301.

Greene, E. (1988). Judge's instruction on eyewitness testimony: Evaluation and revision. *Journal of Applied Social Psychology, 18,* 252–276.

———. (1989). On juries and damage awards: The process of decision making. *Law and Contemporary Problems, 52,* 225–246.

Greene, E., & Bornstein, B.H. (2003). *Determining damages: The psychology of jury awards.* Washington, DC: American Psychological Association.

Greene, E., Chopra, S., Kovera, M., Penrod, S., Rose, V.G., Schuller, R., & Studebaker, C. (2002). Jurors and juries: A review of the field. In J. Ogloff (Ed.), *Taking psychology and law into the twenty-first century* (pp. 225–284). New York: Kluwer/Plenum.

Greene, E., & Dodge, M. (1995). The influence of prior record evidence on juror decision making. *Law and Human Behavior, 19,* 67–78.

Greene, E., Downey, C., & Goodman-Delahunty, J. (1999). Juror decisions about damages in employment discrimination cases. *Behavioral Sciences and the Law, 17,* 107–121.

Greene, E., Hayman, K., & Motyl, M. (2008). "Shouldn't we consider…?" Jury discussions of forbidden topics and effects on damage awards. *Psychology, Public Policy, and Law, 14,* 194–222.

Greene, E., & Johns, M. (2001). Jurors' use of instructions on negligence. *Journal of Applied Social Psychology, 31,* 840–859.

Greene, E., Johns, M., & Bowman, J. (1999). The effects of injury severity on jury negligence decisions. *Law and Human Behavior, 23,* 675–693.

Greene, E., & Loftus, E.F. (1985). When crimes are joined at trial. *Law and Human Behavior, 9,* 193–207.

Greene, E., Woody, W.D., & Winter, R. (2000). Compensating plaintiffs and punishing defendants: Is bifurcation necessary? *Law and Human Behavior, 24,* 187–205.

Gregg v Georgia, 428 U.S. 1543 (1976).

Gunnell, J.J., & Ceci, S.J. (2010). When emotionality trumps reason: A study of individual processing style and juror bias. *Behavioral Sciences & the Law, 28,* 850–877.

Gurley, J.R., & Marcus, D.K. (2008). The effects of neuroimaging and brain injury on insanity defense. *Behavioral Sciences & the Law, 26,* 85–97.

Guy, L.S., & Edens, J.F. (2003). Juror decision-making in a mock sexually violent predator trial: Gender differences in the impact of divergent types of expert testimony. *Behavioral Sciences & the Law, 21,* 215–237.

———. (2006). Gender differences in attitudes toward psychopathic sexual offenders. *Behavioral Sciences & the Law, 24,* 65–85.

Hamilton, V.L. (1978). Obedience and responsibility: A jury simulation. *Journal of Personality and Social Psychology, 36,* 126–146.

Haney, C. (1984). On the selection of capital juries: The biasing effects of death-qualification process. *Law and Human Behavior, 8,* 121–132.

———. (2005). *Death by design: Capital punishment as a social psychological system.* New York: Oxford University Press.

Haney, C., & Lynch, M. (1997). Clarifying life and death matters: An analysis of instructional comprehension and penalty phase closing arguments. *Law and Human Behavior, 21,* 575–595.

Hannaford, P.L., Hans, V.P., & Munsterman, G.T. (2000). Permitting jury discussions during trial: Impact of the Arizona reform. *Law and Human Behavior, 24,* 359–382.

Hannaford-Agor, P.L., & Hans, V.P. (2003). Nullification at work? A glimpse from the national center for state courts study of hung juries. *Chicago–Kent Law Review, 78,* 1249–1277.

Hannaford-Agor, P.L., Hans, V.P., Mott, N.L., & Munsterman, G.T. (September 2002). *Are hung juries a problem?* Williamsburg, VA: National Center for State Courts. Retrieved from http://www.ncsconline.org/wc/Publications/Res_Juries_HungJuriesProblemPub.pdf

Hans, V.P., & Doob, A.N. (1976). Section 12 of the Canada Evidence Act and the deliberation of simulated juries. *Criminal Law Quarterly, 18,* 235–253.

Hans, V.P., & Ermann, M.D. (1989). Responses to corporate versus individual wrongdoing. *Law and Human Behavior, 13,* 151–166.

Hans, V.P., Hannaford-Agor, P.L., Mott, N.L., & Munsterman, G.T. (2003). The hung jury: The American Jury's insights and contemporary understanding. *Criminal Law Bulletin, 39,* 33–51.

Hans, V.P., Kaye, D.H., Dann, M.B., Farley, E.J., & Albertson, S. (2011). Science in the jury box: Jurors' comprehension of mitochondrial DNA evidence. *Law and Human Behavior,* 35, 60–71.

Hans, V.P., & Lofquist, W.S. (1992). Jurors' judgments of business liability in tort cases: Implications for the litigation explosion debate. *Law and Society Review,* 26, 85–115.

Hans, V.P., & Vidmar, N. (1986). *Judging the jury.* New York: Plenum Press.

Hastie, R. (1993). Introduction. In R. Hastie (Ed.), *Inside the juror: The psychology of juror decision making* (pp. 2–41). New York: Cambridge University Press.

Hastie, R., Penrod, S.D., & Pennington, N. (1983). *Inside the jury.* Cambridge, MA: Harvard University Press.

Hastie, R., Schkade, D.A., & Payne, J.W. (1998). A study of juror and jury judgments in civil cases: Deciding liability for punitive damages. *Law and Human Behavior,* 22, 287–314.

———. (1999). Juror judgments in civil cases: Effects of plaintiff's requests and plaintiff's identity on punitive damage awards. *Law and Human Behavior,* 23, 445–470.

Hawkins, C.H. (1962). Interaction rates of jurors aligned in factions. *American Sociological Review,* 27, 689–691.

Hester, R.K., & Smith, R.E. (1973). Effects of a mandatory death penalty on the decisions of simulated jurors as a function of heinousness of the crime. *Journal of Criminal Justice,* 1, 319–326.

Heuer, L., & Penrod, S. (1988). Increasing jurors' participation in trials: A field experiment with jury notetaking and question asking. *Law and Human Behavior,* 12, 231–261.

———. (1989). Instructing jurors: A field experiment with written and preliminary instructions. *Law and Human Behavior,* 13, 409–430.

———. (1994a). Trial complexity: A field investigation of its meaning and its effects. *Law and Human Behavior,* 18, 29–51.

———. (1994b). Juror notetaking and question asking during trials: A national field experiment. *Law and Human Behavior,* 18, 121–150.

Holcomb, M., & Jacquin, K.M. (2007). Juror perceptions of child eyewitness testimony in a sexual abuse trial. *Journal of Child Sexual Abuse,* 16, 79–95.

Holstein, J.A. (1985). Jurors' interpretations and jury decision making. *Law and Human Behavior,* 9, 83–99.

Homant, R.J., & Kennedy, D.B. (1987). Subjective factors in clinicians' judgments of insanity: Comparison of a hypothetical case and an actual case. *Professional Psychology: Research and Practice,* 5, 439–446.

Honess, T.M., Charman, E.A., & Levi, M. (2003). Factual and affective/evaluative recall of pretrial publicity: Their relative influence on juror reasoning and verdict in a simulated fraud trial. *Journal of Applied Social Psychology,* 30, 1404–1416.

Hope, L., Greene, E., Memon, A., Gavisk, M., & Houston, K. (2008). The third verdict: Examining the availability of a not proven verdict on mock juror decision making. *Law and Human Behavior,* 32, 241–252.

Hope, L., Memon, A., & McGeorge, P. (2004). Understanding pretrial publicity: Predecisional distortion of evidence in mock jurors. *Journal of Experimental Psychology: Applied,* 10, 111–119.

Horowitz, I.A. (1980). Juror selection: A comparison of two methods in several criminal cases. *Journal of Applied Social Psychology,* 10, 86–99.

———. (1985). The effect of jury nullification instruction on verdicts and jury functioning in criminal trials. *Law and Human Behavior,* 9, 25–36.

———. (1988). Jury nullification: The impact of judicial instructions, arguments, and challenges on jury decision making. *Law and Human Behavior, 12*, 439–453.

———. (1997). Reasonable doubt instructions: Commonsense justice and standard of proof. *Psychology, Public Policy, and Law, 3*, 285–302.

———. (2008). Jury nullification. In B. Cutler (Ed.), *Encyclopedia of psychology and law, Volume 1* (pp. 412–415). Thousand Oaks, CA: Sage.

Horowitz, I.A., & Bordens, K.S. (1990). An experimental investigation of procedural issues in complex tort trials. *Law and Human Behavior, 14*, 269–285.

———. (2002). The effects of jury size, evidence complexity and note taking on jury process and performance in a civil trial. *Journal of Applied Psychology, 87*, 121–130.

Horowitz, I.A., Bordens, K.S., & Feldman, M.S. (1980). A comparison of verdicts obtained in separate and joined criminal trials. *Journal of Applied Social Psychology, 10*, 444–456.

Horowitz, I.A., & ForsterLee, L. (2001). The effects of note-taking and trial transcript access on mock jury decisions in a complex civil trial. *Law and Human Behavior, 25*, 373–391.

Horowitz, I.A., Kerr, N.L., Park, E.S., & Gockel, C. (2006). Chaos in the courtroom reconsidered: Emotional bias and juror nullification. *Law and Human Behavior, 30*, 163–181.

Horowitz, I.A., & Kirkpatrick, L.C. (1996). A concept in search of a definition: The effects of reasonable doubt instructions on certainty of guilt standards and jury verdicts. *Law and Human Behavior, 20*, 655–670.

Horowitz, I.A., & Seguin, D.G. (1986). The effects of bifurcation and death qualification on assignment of penalty in capital crimes. *Journal of Applied Social Psychology, 16*, 165–185.

Hulbert, L.G., Parks, C.D., Chen, X., Nam, K., & Davis, J.H. (1999). The plaintiff bias in mock civil jury decision making: Consensus requirements, information format and amount of consensus. *Group Processes and Intergroup Relations, 2*, 59–77.

Huntley, J.E., & Costanzo, M. (2003). Sexual harassment stories: Testing a story-mediated model of juror decision-making in civil litigation. *Law and Human Behavior, 27*, 29–51.

Imrich, D.I., Mullin, C., & Linz, D. (1995). Measuring the extent of prejudicial pretrial publicity in major American newspapers: A content analysis. *Journal of Communication, 45*, 94–117.

Jacquin, K.M., & Hodges, E.P. (2007). The influence of media messages on mock juror decisions in the Andrea Yates trial. *American Journal of Forensic Psychology, 25*, 21–40.

James, R. (1959). Status and competence of jurors. *American Journal of Sociology, 64*, 563–570.

Jehle, A., Miller, M.K., & Kemmelmeier, M. (2009). The influence of accounts and remorse on mock jurors' judgments of offenders. *Law and Human Behavior, 33*, 393–404.

Jenkins, G., & Schuller, R.A. (2007). Drug-facilitated sexual assault: The impact of negative forensic evidence on juror decision making. *Law and Human Behavior, 31*, 369–380.

Johnson, C., & Haney, C. (1994). Felony voir dire: An exploratory study of its content and effect. *Law and Human Behavior, 18*, 487–504.

Johnson v. Louisiana, 406 U.S. 356 (1972).

Johnson-Laird, P.N. (1983). *Mental models: Towards a cognitive science of language, inference, and consciousness*. Cambridge, MA: Harvard University Press.

Jonakait, R.N. (2003). *The American jury system*. New Haven, CT: Yale University Press.

Jones, S., & Harrison, M. (2009). To testify or not to testify—that is the question: Comparing the advantages and disadvantages of testifying across situations. *Applied Psychology in Criminal Justice, 5*, 165–181.

Kagehiro, D.K., & Stanton, W.C. (1985). Legal vs. quantified definitions of standards of proof. *Law and Human Behavior, 9*, 159–178.

Kahneman, D., & Tversky, A. (1982). The simulation heuristic. In D. Kahneman, P. Slovic & A. Tversky (Eds.), *Judgment under uncertainty: Heuristics and biases* (pp. 201–208). New York: Cambridge University Press.

Kalven, H., & Zeisel, H. (1966). *The American jury.* Chicago: University of Chicago Press.

Kameda, T. (1991). Procedural influence in small-group decision making: Deliberation style and assigned decision rule. *Journal of Personality and Social Psychology, 61,* 245–256.

Kameda, T., & Sugimori, S. (1995). Procedural influence in two-step group decision making: Power of local majorities in consensus formation. *Journal of Personality and Social Psychology, 69,* 865–876.

Kaplan, M.F., & Krupa, S. (1986). Severe penalties under the control of others can reduce guilt verdicts. *Law and Psychology Review, 10,* 1–18.

Kaplan, M.F., & Martin, A.M. (Eds.). (2006). *Understanding world jury systems through social psychological research.* New York: Psychology Press.

Kaplan, M.F., & Miller, L.E. (1978). Reducing the effects of juror bias. *Journal of Personality and Social Psychology, 36,* 1443–1455.

Kaplan, M.F., & Miller, C.E. (1987). Group decision making and normative v. informational influence: Effects of type of issue and decision rule. *Journal of Personality and Social Psychology, 53,* 306–313.

Kaplan, J.K., & Simon, R.I. (1972). Latitude of severity of sentencing options, race of the victim, and decisions of simulated jurors: Some issues arising from the "Algiers motel" trial. *Law and Society Review, 7,* 87–98.

Kasian, M., Spanos, N.P., Terrance, C.A., & Peebles, S. (1993). Battered women who kill: Jury simulation and legal defenses. *Law and Human Behavior, 17,* 289–312.

Kassin, S.M., & Dunn, M.A. (1997). Computer-animated displays and the jury: Facilitative and prejudicial effects. *Law and Human Behavior, 21,* 269–281.

Kassin, S.M., & Garfield, D.A. (1991). Blood and guts: General and trial-specific effects of videotaped crime scenes on mock jurors. *Journal of Applied Social Psychology, 21,* 1459–1472.

Kassin, S.M., & Neumann, K. (1997). On the power of confession evidence: An experimental test of the "fundamental difference" hypothesis. *Law and Human Behavior, 21,* 469–484.

Kassin, S.M., Reddy, M.E., & Tulloch, W.F. (1990). Juror interpretations of ambiguous evidence: The need for cognition, presentation order and persuasion. *Law and Human Behavior, 14,* 43–55.

Kassin, S.M., & Sukel, H. (1997). Coerced confessions and the jury: An experimental test of the "harmless error" rule. *Law and Human Behavior, 21,* 27–46.

Kassin, S.M., & Wrightsman, L.S. (1983). The construction and validation of a juror bias scale. *Journal of Research in Personality, 17,* 423–442.

Kassin, S.M., & Wrightsman, L.S. (1988). *The American jury on trial: Psychological perspectives.* New York: Taylor & Francis.

Kerr, N.L. (1978). Severity of prescribed penalty and mock jurors' verdicts. *Journal of Personality and Social Psychology, 36,* 1431–1442.

———. (1981). Social transition schemes: Charting the group's road to agreement. *Journal of Personality and Social Psychology, 41,* 684–702.

———. (1982). Social transition schemes: Model, method, and applications. In H. Brandstatter, J.H. Davis, & G. Stocker-Kreichgauer (Eds.), *Group decision making* (pp. 59–80). London: Academy Press.

Kerr, N.L., Atkin, R.S., Stasser, G., Meek, D., Holt, R.W., & Davis, J.H. (1976). Guilt beyond a reasonable doubt: Effects of concept definition and assigned decision rule on the judgments of mock jurors. *Journal of Personality and Social Psychology, 34*, 282–294.

Kerr, N.L., Harmon, D.L., & Graves, J.K. (1982). Independence of verdicts by jurors and juries. *Journal of Applied Social Psychology, 12*, 12–29.

Kerr, N.L., Hymes, R.W., Anderson, A.B., & Weathers, J.E. (1995). Defendant-juror similarity and mock juror judgments. *Law and Human Behavior, 19*, 545–567.

Kerr, N.L., Kramer, G.P., Carroll, J.S., & Alfini, J. (1991). On the effectiveness of voir dire in criminal cases with prejudicial pretrial publicity: An empirical study. *American University Law Review, 40*, 665–701.

Kerr, N.L., & MacCoun, R.J. (1985). The effects of jury size and polling method on the process and product of jury deliberation. *Journal of Personality and Social Psychology, 48*, 349–363.

Kerr, N.L., Niedermeier, K.E., & Kaplan, M.F. (1999). Bias in jurors vs bias in juries: New evidence from the SDS perspective. *Organizational Behavior and Human Decision Processes, 80*, 70–86.

Kerr, N.L., & Sawyers, G.W. (1979). Independence of multiple verdicts within a trial by mock jurors. *Representative Research in Social Psychology, 10*, 16–27.

Kerwin, J., & Shaffer, D.R. (1991). The effects of jury dogmatism on reactions to jury nullification instructions. *Personality and Social Psychology Bulletin, 17*, 140–146.

———. (1994). Mock jurors versus mock juries: The role of deliberations in reactions to inadmissible testimony. *Personality and Social Psychology Bulletin, 20*, 153–162.

Klettke, B., Graesser, A.C., & Powell, M.B. (2010). Expert testimony in child sexual abuse cases: The effects of evidence, coherence and credentials on juror decision making. *Applied Cognitive Psychology, 24*, 481–494.

Kline, F.G., & Jess, P.H. (1966). Prejudicial publicity: Its effect on law school mock juries. *Journalism Quarterly, 43*, 113–116.

Koch, C.M., & Devine, D.J. (1999). Effects of reasonable doubt and inclusion of a lesser charge on jury verdicts. *Law and Human Behavior, 23*, 653–674.

Koehler, J.J. (1996). On conveying the probative value of DNA evidence: Frequencies, likelihood ratios and error rates. *University of Colorado Law Review, 67*, 859–886.

———. (2001). The psychology of numbers in the courtroom: How to make DNA-match statistics seem impressive or insufficient. *University of Southern California Law Review, 74*, 1275–1305.

Koehler, J.J., Chia, A., & Lindsey, J.S. (1995). The random match probability (RMP) in DNA evidence: Irrelevant and prejudicial? *Jurimetrics Journal, 35*, 201–219.

Koehler, J.J., & Macchi, L. (2004). Thinking about low-probability events: An exemplar cuing theory. *Psychological Science, 15*, 540–546.

Koffler, J. (1957). The lie detector: A critical appraisal of the technique as a potential undermining factor in the judicial process. *New York Law Forum, 123*, 138–146.

Kovera, M.B. (2002). The effects of general pretrial publicity on juror decision: An examination of moderators and mediating mechanisms. *Law and Human Behavior, 26*, 43–72.

Kramer, G.P., Kerr, N.L., & Carroll, J.S. (1990). Pretrial publicity, judicial remedies, and jury bias. *Law and Human Behavior, 14*, 409–438.

Krauss, D., & Lee, D. (2003). Deliberating on dangerousness and death: Jurors' ability to differentiate between expert actuarial and clinical predictions of dangerousness. *International Journal of Law and Psychiatry, 26*, 113–137.

Krauss, D.A., Lieberman, J.D., & Olson, J. (2004). The effects of rational and experiential information processing on expert testimony in death penalty cases. *Behavioral Sciences & the Law, 22,* 801–822.

Krauss, D.A., & Sales, B.D. (2001). The effects of clinical and scientific expert testimony on juror decision making in capital sentencing. *Psychology, Public Policy and Law, 7,* 267–310.

Kravitz, D.A., Cutler, B.L., & Brock, P. (1993). Reliability and validity of the original and revised legal attitudes questionnaire. *Law and Human Behavior, 17,* 661–667.

Kulynych, J. (1997). Psychiatric neuroimaging evidence: A high-tech crystal ball? *Stanford Law Review, 49,* 1249–1270.

Lamberth, J., Krieger, E., & Shay, S. (1982). Juror decision making: A case of attitude change mediated by authoritarianism. *Journal of Research in Personality, 16,* 419–434.

Landsman, S., Diamond, S., Dimitropoulos, L., & Saks, M.J. (1998). Be careful what you wish for: The paradoxical effects of bifurcating claims for punitive damages. *Wisconsin Law Review, 1998,* 297–342.

Landwehr, P.H., Bothwell, R.K., Jeanmard, M., Luque, L.R., Brown III, R.L., & Breaux, M. (2002). Racism in rape trials. *Journal of Social Psychology, 142,* 667–669.

Landy, D., & Aronson, E. (1969). The influence of the character of the criminal and his victim on the decisions of simulated jurors. *Journal of Experimental Social Psychology, 5,* 141–152.

Latane, B., & Wolf, S. (1981). The social impact of majorities and minorities. *Psychological Review, 88,* 438–453.

Lecci, L., & Myers, B. (2002). Examining the construct validity of the original and revised JBS: A cross-validation of sample and method. *Law and Human Behavior, 26,* 455–463.

———. (2008). Individual differences in attitudes relevant to juror decision making: Development and validation of the Pretrial Juror Attitude Questionnaire (PJAQ). *Journal of Applied Social Psychology, 38,* 2010–2038.

Leippe, M.R. (1985). The influence of eyewitness nonidentifications on mock-jurors' judgments of a court case. *Journal of Applied Social Psychology, 15,* 656–672.

Leippe, M.R., & Eisenstadt, R. (2009). The influence of eyewitness expert testimony on jurors' beliefs and judgments. In B.L. Cutler (Ed.), *Expert testimony on the psychology of eyewitness identification* (pp. 169–199). New York: Oxford University Press.

Leippe, M.R., Eisenstadt, D.E., Rauch, S.M., & Seib, H. (2004). Timing of eyewitness expert testimony, jurors' need for cognition and case strength as determinants of trial verdicts. *Journal of Applied Psychology, 89,* 524–541.

Leippe, M.R., & Romanczyk, A. (1989). Reactions to child eyewitnesses: The influence of jurors' preconceptions and witness behavior. *Law and Human Behavior, 13,* 103–132.

Lempert, R.O. (1975). Uncovering "nondiscernible" differences: Empirical research and the jury-size cases. *Michigan Law Review, 73,* 644–708.

Lerner, M.J. (1970). The desire for justice and reactions to victims. In J. Macaulay & L. Berkowitz (Eds.), *Altruism and helping behavior.* New York: Academic Press.

———. (1980). *The belief in a just world: A fundamental delusion.* New York: Plenum Press.

Levett, L.M., Danielsen, E.M., Kovera, M.B., & Cutler, B.L. (2005). The psychology of jury and juror decision making. In N. Brewer and K.D. Wilson (Eds.), *Psychology and law: An empirical perspective* (pp. 365–406).

Levett, L.M., & Kovera, M.B. (2008). The effectiveness of opposing expert witnesses for educating jurors about unreliable expert evidence. *Law and Human Behavior, 32,* 363–374.

———. (2009). Psychological mediators of the effects of opposing expert testimony on juror decisions. *Psychology, Public Policy, and Law, 15,* 124–148.

Lieberman, J.D. (2002). Head over the heart or heart over the head? Cognitive-experiential self-theory and extra-legal heuristics in juror decision-making. *Journal of Applied Social Psychology, 32,* 2526–2553.

———. (2009). The psychology of the jury instruction process. In J.D. Lieberman & D.A. Krauss (Eds.), *Jury psychology: Social aspects of trial processes: Psychology in the courtroom, Vol. 1* (pp. 129–155). Burlington, VT: Ashgate Publishing.

———. (2011). The utility of scientific jury selection: Still murky after 30 years. *Current Directions in Psychological Science, 20,* 48–52.

Lieberman, J.D., Carrell, C.A., Miethe, T.D., & Krauss, D.A. (2008). Gold vs. platinum: Do jurors recognize the superiority and limitations of DNA evidence compared to other types of forensic evidence? *Psychology, Public Policy and Law, 14,* 27–62.

Lieberman, J.D., & Sales, B.D. (2007). *Scientific jury selection.* Washington, DC: American Psychological Association.

Lindsay, R.C., Lim, R., Marando, L., & Cully, D. (1986). Mock juror evaluations of eyewitness testimony: A test of metamemory hypotheses. *Journal of Applied Social Psychology, 16,* 447–459.

Lloyd-Bostock, S.M.A. (2000). The effects on juries of hearing about the defendant's previous criminal record: A simulation study. *Criminal Law Review, 2000,* 734–755.

London, K., & Nunez, N. (2000). The effect of jury deliberation on jurors' propensity to disregard inadmissible evidence. *Journal of Applied Psychology, 85,* 932–39.

Lorge, I., & Solomon, H. (1955). Two models of group behavior in the solution of eureka-type problems. *Psychometrika, 20,* 139–148.

Luginbuhl, J. (1992). Comprehension of judges' instructions in the penalty phase of a capital trial. *Law and Human Behavior, 16,* 203–218.

Lykken, D.T. (1998). *A tremor in the blood: Uses and abuses of the lie detector* (2nd ed.). New York: Plenum.

Lynch, M. (2009). The social psychology of capital cases. In J.D. Lieberman & D.A. Krauss (Eds.), *Jury psychology: Social aspects of trial processes: Psychology in the courtroom, Volume 1* (pp. 157–181). Burlington, VT: Ashgate Publishing.

Lynch, M., & Haney, C. (2000). Discrimination and instructional comprehension: Guided discretion, racial bias, and the death penalty. *Law and Human Behavior, 24,* 337–358.

———. (2009). Capital jury deliberation: Effects on death sentencing, comprehension, and discrimination. *Law and Human Behavior, 33,* 481–496.

———. (2011). Mapping the racial bias of the white male juror: Jury composition and the "empathic divide." *Law and Society Review, 45,* 69–101.

MacCoun, R.J. (1996). Differential treatment of corporate defendants by juries: An examination of the "deep-pockets" hypothesis. *Law & Society Review, 30,* 121–161.

MacCoun, R.J., & Kerr, N.L. (1988). Asymmetric influence in mock jury deliberation: Jurors' bias for leniency. *Journal of Personality and Social Psychology, 54,* 21–33.

MacLin, K.M., Downs, C., MacLin, O.H., & Caspers, H.M. (2009). The effect of defendant facial expression on mock juror decision-making: The power of remorse. *North American Journal of Psychology, 11,* 323–332.

Mancini, D.E. (2011). The CSI effect reconsidered: Is it moderated by need for cognition? *North American Journal of Psychology, 13,* 155–174.

Marcus, D.K., Lyons, Jr., P.M., & Guyton, M.R. (2000). Studying perceptions of juror influence in vivo: A social relations analysis. *Law and Human Behavior, 24*, 173–186.

Markwart, A., & Lynch, B.E. (1979). The effect of polygraph evidence on mock jury
decision-making. *Journal of Police Science and Administration, 7*, 324–332.

Marques, J.M. (1990). The black sheep effect: Outgroup homoteneity in social comparison
settings. In D. Abrams & M. Hogg (Eds.), *Social identity theory: Constructive and critical
advances* (pp. 131–151). London: Harvester Wheatsheaf.

Marques, J.M., Yzerbyt, V.Y., & Leyens, J.P. (1988). The black sheep effect: Extremity of judgment towards in-group members as a function of group identification. *European Journal
of Social Psychology, 18*, 1–16.

Marston, W.M. (1924). Studies in testimony. *Journal of Criminal Law and Criminology, 15*,
5–31.

Martin, T.A., & Cohn, E.S. (2004). Attitudes toward the criminal legal system: Scale development and predictors. *Psychology, Crime and Law, 10*, 367–391.

Martire, K.A., & Kemp, R.I. (2011). Can experts help jurors to evaluate eyewitness evidence?
A review of eyewitness expert effects. *Legal and Criminological Psychology, 16*, 24–36.

Mazzella, R., & Feingold, A. (1994). The effects of physical attractiveness, race, socioeconomic status and gender of defendants and victims on judgments of mock jurors: A
meta-analysis. *Journal of Applied Social Psychology, 24*, 1315–1344.

McAuliff, B.D., & Duckworth, T.D. (2010). I spy with my little eye: Jurors' detection of internal validity threats in expert evidence. *Law and Human Behavior, 34*, 489–500.

McAuliff, B.D., & Kovera, M.B. (2008). Juror need for cognition and sensitivity to methodological flaws in expert evidence. *Journal of Applied Social Psychology, 38*, 385–408.

McAuliff, B.D., Kovera, M.B., & Nunez, G. (2009). Can jurors recognize missing control
groups, confounds, and experimenter bias in psychological science? *Law and Human
Behavior, 33*, 247–257.

McCabe, S., & Purves, R. (1972). *The jury at work.* Oxford: Blackwell.

———. (1974). *The shadow jury at work.* Oxford: Blackwell.

McCauley, M.R., & Parker, J.F. (2001). When will a child be believed? The impact of the victim's age and juror's gender on children's credibility and verdict in a sexual-abuse case.
Child Abuse and Neglect, 25, 523–539.

McCauliff, C.M.A. (1982). Burdens of proof: Degrees of belief, quanta of evidence, or constitutional guarantees? *Vanderbilt Law Review, 35*, 1260–1335.

McComas, W.C., & Noll, M.E. (1974). Effects of seriousness of charge and punishment
severity on the judgments of simulated jurors. *Psychological Record, 24*, 545–547.

McCoy, M.L., Nunez, N., & Dammeyer, M.M. (1999). The effect of jury deliberations on
jurors' reasoning skills. *Law and Human Behavior, 23*, 557–575.

McKimmie, B.M., Newton, C.J., Terry, D.J., & Schuller, R.A. (2004). Jurors' responses to
expert witness testimony: The effects of gender stereotypes. *Group Processes and Intergroup Relations, 7*, 131–143.

Meissner, C.A., Brigham, J.C., & Pfeifer, J.E. (2003). Jury nullification: The influence of judicial instruction on the relationship between attitudes and juridic decision-making. *Basic
and Applied Social Psychology, 25*, 243–254.

Memon, A., & Shuman, D. (1998). Juror perception of experts in civil disputes: The role of
race and gender. *Law and Psychology Review, 22*, 179–197.

Miller, M.K., & Hayward, R.D. (2008). Religious characteristics and the death penalty. *Law
and Human Behavior, 32*, 113–123.

Mills, C.J., & Bohannon, W.E. (1980). Juror characteristics: To what extent are they related to jury verdicts? *Judicature, 64*, 23–31.

Mitchell, T.L., Haw, R.M., Pfeifer, J., & Meissner, C.A. (2005). Racial bias in juror decision-making: A meta-analytic review. *Law and Human Behavior, 29*, 621–637.

Mize, G.E., Hannaford-Agor, P., & Waters, N.L. (2007). *The state-of-the-states survey of jury improvement efforts: A compendium report*. Williamsburg, VA: National Center for State Courts. Retrieved from http://www.ncsonline.org/D_Research/cjs/pdf/SosCompendiumFinal.pdf.

Monahan, J. (1981). *The clinical prediction of violent behavior*. Beverly Hills, CA: Sage.

Monahan, J., & Steadman, H. (1994). *Violence and mental disorder: Developments in risk assessment*. Chicago: University of Chicago Press.

Moore, P.J., & Gump, B.B. (1995). Information integration in juror decision making. *Journal of Applied Social Psychology, 25*, 2158–2179.

Moran, G. (2008). Scientific jury selection. In B. Cutler (Ed.), *Encyclopedia of psychology and law, Volume 2* (pp. 705–707). Thousand Oaks, CA: Sage.

Moran, G., & Comfort, J.C. (1982). Scientific juror selection: Sex as a moderator of demographic and personality predictors of impaneled felony juror behavior. *Journal of Personality and Social Psychology, 47*, 1052–1063.

Moran, G., & Comfort, J.C. (1986). Neither "tentative" nor "fragmentary": Verdict preference of impaneled felony jurors as a function of attitude toward capital punishment. *Journal of Applied Psychology, 71*, 146–155.

Morgan v. Illinois, 504 U.S. 719 (1992).

Moscovici, S. (1980). Toward a theory of conversion behavior. In L. Berkowitz (Ed.), *Advances in experimental social psychology, Volume 13* (pp. 209–239). New York: Academic Press.

———. (1985). Social influence and conformity. In G. Lindzey & E. Aronson (Eds.), *The handbook of social psychology, Volume 2* (3rd ed., pp. 347–412). New York: Random House.

Mott, N.L., Hans, V.P., & Simpson, L. (2000). "What's half a lung worth?" Civil juror's accounts of their award decision-making. *Law and Human Behavior, 24*, 401–419.

Mullen, B. (1983). Operationalizing the effect of the group on the individual: A self-attention perspective. *Journal of Experimental Social Psychology, 19*, 295–322.

Munsterman, G.T., Munsterman, J.T., & Penrod, S.D. (1990). *A comparison of the performance of eight- and twelve-person juries*. Arlington, VA: National Center for State Courts, Washington Project Office.

Myers, B., & Arbuthnot, J. (1997). Polygraph testimony and juror judgments: A comparison of the guilty knowledge test and the control question test. *Journal of Applied Social Psychology, 27*, 1421–1437.

Myers, B., & Lecci, L. (1998). Revising the factor structure of the Juror Bias Scale: A method for the empirical evaluation of theoretical constructs. *Law and Human Behavior, 22*, 239–256.

Myers, B., Rosol, A., & Boelter, E. (2003). Polygraph evidence: The impact of corroborating evidence on guilt judgments. *Journal of Applied Social Psychology, 33*, 948–962.

Myers, M.A. (1979). Rule departures and making law: Juries and their verdicts. *Law & Society Review, 13*, 781–797.

Nagao, D.H., & Davis, J.H. (1980). The effects of prior experience on mock juror case judgments. *Social Psychological Quarterly, 43*, 190–199.

Nagel, S., & Weitzman, L. (1972). Sex and the unbiased jury. *Judicature, 56,* 108–111.

Najdowski, C.J., & Bottoms, B.L. (2008). Children's testimony, evaluation by juries. In B.L. Cutler (Ed.), *Encyclopedia of psychology and law: Volume 1* (pp. 82–85). Thousand Oaks, CA: Sage.

Nance, D.A., & Morris, S.B. (2005). Juror understanding of DNA evidence: An empirical assessment of presentation formats for trace evidence with a relatively small random-match probability. *Journal of Legal Studies, 34,* 395–443.

Narby, D.J., & Cutler, B.L. (1994). Effectiveness of voir dire as a safeguard in eyewitness cases. *Journal of Applied Psychology, 79,* 724–729.

Narby, D.J., Cutler, B.L., & Moran, G. (1993). A meta-analysis of the association between authoritarianism and jurors' perceptions of defendant culpability. *Journal of Applied Psychology, 78,* 34–42.

Neil v. Biggers, 409 U.S. 188 (1972).

Nemeth, C. (1977). Interactions between jurors as a function of majority vs. unanimity decision rules. *Journal of Applied Social Psychology, 7,* 38–56.

Nemeth, R.J. (2002). *The impact of gruesome evidence on mock juror decision making: The role of evidence characteristics and emotional response.* Unpublished PhD diss., Louisiana State University, Baton Rouge.

———. (2011). Enhanced persuasion in the courtroom: Visually dynamic demonstrative evidence and juror decision making. In R.L. Wiener & B.H. Bornstein (Eds.), *Handbook of trial consulting* (pp. 203–214). New York: Springer Science + Business Media.

Nemeth, C., Endicott, J., & Wachtler, J. (1976). From the '50s to the '70s: Women in jury deliberations. *Sociometry, 39,* 293–304.

Neuschatz, J.S., Lawson, D.S., Swanner, J.S., Meissner, C.A., & Neuschatz, J.S. (2008). The effects of accomplice witnesses and jailhouse informants on jury decision making. *Law and Human Behavior, 32,* 137–149.

Niedermeier, K.E., Horowitz, I.A., & Kerr, N.L. (1999). Informing jurors of their nullification power: A route to a just verdict or judicial chaos? *Law and Human Behavior, 23,* 331–351.

Nietzel, M.T., McCarthy, D.M., & Kerr, M.J. (1999). Juries: The current state of the empirical literature. In R. Roesch, S.D. Hart & J.R.P. Ogloff (Eds.), *Psychology and law: The state of the discipline* (pp. 23–52). New York: Kluwer Academic/Plenum.

Nietzel, M.T., Dillehay, R.C., & Himelein, M.J. (1987). Effects of voir dire variations in capital trials: A replication and extension. *Behavioral Sciences and the Law, 5,* 467–477.

Nigro, G.N., Buckley, M.A., Hill, D.E., & Nelson, J. (1989). When juries "hear" children testify: The effect of eyewitness age and speech style on jurors' perceptions of testimony. In S.J. Ceci, D.F. Ross, & M.P. Toglia. (Eds.), *Perspectives on children's testimony* (pp. 57–70). New York: Springer-Verlag.

Nikonova, O., & Ogloff, J.R.P. (2005). The impact of judicial instructions on mock jurors' appraisal of child witnesses and accused. *Canadian Journal of Behavioural Science, 37,* 1–19.

Nowicki, S., & Duke, M.P. (1983). Construct validity for the Nowicki-Strickland internal-external control scales. In H. Lefcourt (Ed.), *Research with the locus of control construct: Volume 1* (pp. 3–38). New York: Academic Press.

Ogloff, J.R.P. (1991). A comparison of insanity defense standards on juror decision making. *Law and Human Behavior, 15,* 509–531.

———. (1998). The risk assessment enterprise: Selective incapacitation of increased predictive accuracy. *Law and Human Behavior, 22,* 453–455.

Ogloff, R.P., & Rose, G. (2005). The comprehension of judicial instructions. In N. Brewer and K.D. Wilson (Eds.), *Psychology and law: An empirical perspective* (pp. 407–44). New York: Guilford Press.

Ohtsubo, Y., Masuchi, A., & Nakanishi, D. (2002). Majority influence process in group decision making: Test of the social judgment scheme model in a group polarization context. *Group Processes and Intergroup Relations, 5,* 249–261.

Olczak, P.V., Kaplan, M.F., & Penrod, S. (1991). Attorneys' lay psychology and its effectiveness in selecting jurors: Three empirical studies. *Journal of Social Behavior and Personality, 6,* 431–452.

Oliver, E., & Griffitt, W. (1976). Emotional arousal and objective judgment. *Bulletin of the Psychonomic Society, 8,* 399–400.

O'Neil, K.M., Patry, M.W., & Penrod, S.D. (2004). Exploring the effects of attitudes toward the death penalty on capital sentencing verdicts. *Psychology, Public Policy, and Law, 10,* 443–470.

Osborne, Y.H., Rappaport, N.B., & Meyer, R.G. (1986). An investigation of persuasion and sentencing severity with mock juries. *Behavioral Sciences and the Law, 4,* 339–349.

Ostrom, B.J., Rottman, D.B., & Goerdt, J.A. (1996). A step above anecdote: A profile of the civil jury in the 1990s. *Judicature, 79,* 233–241.

Ostrom, T.M., Werner, C., & Saks, M.J. (1978). An integration theory analysis of jurors' presumptions of guilt or innocence. *Journal of Personality and Social Psychology, 36,* 436–450.

Otto, A.L., Penrod, S., & Dexter, H.R. (1994). The biasing effects of pretrial publicity on juror judgments. *Law and Human Behavior, 18,* 453–469.

Padawer-Singer, A.M., & Barton, A.H. (1975). The impact of pretrial publicity on jurors' verdicts. In R.J. Simon (Ed.), *The jury system in America: A critical overview* (pp. 123–139). Beverly Hills, CA: Sage.

Padawer-Singer, A.M., Singer, A.N., & Singer, R.L.J. (1977). An experimental study of twelve vs. six member juries under unanimous vs. nonunanimous decisions. In B.D. Sales (Ed.), *Psychology in the legal process* (pp. 77–86). New York: Spectrum Publications.

Pansky, A., Koriat, A., & Goldsmith, M. (2005). Eyewitness recall and testimony. In N. Brewer & K.D. Williams (Eds.), *Psychology and law: An empirical perspective* (pp. 93–150). New York: Guilford Press.

Patry, M.W. (2008). Attractive but guilty: Deliberation and the physical attractiveness bias. *Psychological Reports, 102,* 727–733.

Pennington, N., & Hastie, R. (1981). Juror decision making models: The generalization gap. *Psychological Bulletin, 89,* 246–287.

———. (1986). Evidence evaluation in complex decision making. *Journal of Personality and Social Psychology, 51,* 242–258.

———. (1988). Explanation-based decision making: Effects of memory structure on judgment. *Journal of Experimental Psychology: Learning, Memory and Cognition, 14,* 521–533.

———. (1992). Explaining the evidence: Tests of the story model for juror decision making. *Journal of Personality and Social Psychology, 62,* 189–206.

———. (1993). The story model for juror decision making. In R. Hastie (Ed.), *Inside the juror: The psychology of juror decision making* (pp. 192–221). New York: Cambridge University Press.

Penrod, S.D. (1990). Predictors of jury decision making in criminal and civil cases: A field experiment. *Forensic Reports, 3,* 261–277.

Penrod, S.D., & Cutler, B.L. (1999). Preventing mistaken convictions in eyewitness identi-
fication trials: The case against traditional safeguards. In R. Roesch, S.D. Hart, & J.R.P.
Ogloff (Eds.), *Psychology and law: The state of the discipline* (pp. 89–118). New York:
Kluwer.

Penrod, S., Groscup, J.L., & O'Neil, K. (2002). Report filed on behalf of Elizabeth Grubman,
November 6, 2002.

Penrod, S., & Hastie, R. (1979). Models of jury decision making: A critical review. *Psychological Bulletin, 86,* 462–492.

———. (1980). A computer simulation of jury decision making. *Psychological Review, 87,*
133–159.

Penrod, S., & Heuer, L. (1997). Tweaking commonsense: Assessing aids to jury decision
making. *Psychology, Public Policy, and Law, 3,* 259–284.

———. (1998). Improving group performance: The case of the jury. In R.S. Tindale et al.
(Eds.), *Theory and research on small groups* (pp. 127–152). New York: Plenum Press.

Perez, D.A., Hosch, H.M., Ponder, B., & Trejo, G.C. (1993). Ethnicity of defendants and
jurors as influences on jury decisions. *Journal of Applied Social Psychology, 23,* 1249–1262.

Perlin, M. (1994). *The jurisprudence of the insanity defense.* Durham, NC: Carolina Press.

Peterson, M.A. (1987). *Civil juries in the 1980s: Trends in jury trials and verdicts in California
and Cook county, IL.* Santa Monica, CA: RAND.

Petty, R.E., & Cacioppo, J.T. (1986). *Communication and persuasion: Central and peripheral
routes to attitude change.* New York: Springer-Verlag.

Pfeifer, J., & Bernstein, D. (2003). Expressions of modern racism in judgments of others: The
role of task and target specificity on attributions of guilt. *Social Behavior and Personality:
An International Journal, 31,* 749–765.

Pfeifer, J., Brigham, J.C., & Robinson, T. (1996). Euthanasia on trial: Examining public attitudes toward non physician-assisted death. *Journal of Social Issues, 52,* 119–129.

Phares, E.J., & Wilson, K.G. (1972). Responsibility attribution: Role of outcome severity,
situational ambiguity and internal-external control. *Journal of Personality, 40,* 392–406.

Pickel, K.L., Karam, T.J., & Warner, T.C. (2009). Jurors' responses to unusual inadmissible
evidence. *Criminal Justice and Behavior, 36,* 466–480.

Pope, J., & Meyer, R. (1999). An attributional analysis of jurors' judgments in a criminal
case: A preliminary investigation. *Social Behavior and Personality: An International
Journal, 27,* 563–574.

Poulson, R.L. (1990). Mock-juror attribution of criminal responsibility: Effects of race and
the guilty but mentally ill (GBMI) verdict option. *Journal of Applied Social Psychology,
20,* 1596–1611.

Poulson, R., Brondino, M., Brown, H., & Braithwaite, R. (1998). Relations among mock
jurors' attitudes, trial evidence and their selections of an insanity defense verdict: A path
analytic approach. *Psychological Reports, 82,* 3–16.

Pozzulo, J.D., & Dempsey, J.L. (2009). The effect of eyewitness testimonial consistency and
type of identification decision on juror decision making. *American Journal of Forensic
Psychology, 27,* 49–68.

Pozzulo, J.D., Lemieux, J.M.T., Wilson, A., Crescini, C., & Girardi, A. (2009). The influence of identification decision and DNA evidence on juror decision making. *Journal of
Applied Social Psychology, 39,* 2069–2088.

Radvansky, G.A., Spieler, D.H., & Zacks, R.T. (1993). Mental model organization. *Journal of
Experimental Psychology: Learning, Memory and Cognition, 19,* 94–114.

Read, J.D., Connolly, D.A., & Welsh, A. (2006). Archival analysis of actual cases of HCSA: A comparison of jury and bench trials. *Law and Human Behavior, 30,* 259–285.

Reed, J.P. (1965). Jury deliberations, voting, and verdict trends. *Southwestern Social Science Quarterly, 45,* 361–370.

Reifman, A., Gusick, S.M., & Ellsworth, P.C. (1992). Real jurors' understanding of the law in real cases. *Law and Human Behavior, 16,* 539–554.

Rendell, J.A., Huss, M.T., & Jensen, M.L. (2010). Expert testimony and the effects of a biological approach, psychopathy, and juror attitudes in cases of insanity. *Behavioral Sciences and the Law, 28,* 411–425.

Reskin, B.F., & Visher, C.A. (1986). The impacts of evidence and extralegal factors in jurors' decisions. *Law and Society Review, 20,* 423–438.

Roberts, C., & Golding, S. (1991). The social construction of criminal responsibility and insanity. *Law and Human Behavior, 15,* 349–376.

Roberts, C., Golding, S., & Fincham, F. (1987). Implicit theories of criminal responsibility: Decision making and the insanity defense. *Law and Human Behavior, 11,* 207–232.

Robinson, D.T., Smith-Lovin, L., & Tsoudis, O. (1994). Heinous crime or unfortunate accident? The effects of remorse on responses to mock criminal confessions. *Social Forces, 73,* 175–190.

Rokeach, M. (1960). *The open door and the closed mind.* New York: Basic Books.

Rosenhan, D.L., Eisner, S.L., & Robinson, R.J. (1994). Notetaking can aid juror recall. *Law and Human Behavior, 18,* 53–61.

Rotenberg, K.J., Hewlett, M.G., & Siegwart, C.M. (1998). Principled moral reasoning and self-monitoring as predictors of jury functioning. *Basic and Applied Social Psychology, 20,* 167–173.

Rotter, J.B. (1966). Generalized expectancies for internal vs. external control of reinforcement. *Psychological Monographs: General & Applied, 80, 1–28.* (Whole No. 609).

Rotundo, M., Nguyen, D., & Sackett, P.R. (2001). A meta-analytic review of gender differences in perceptions of sexual harassment. *Journal of Applied Psychology, 86,* 914–922.

Rubin, Z., & Peplau, L.A. (1975). Who believes in a just world? *Journal of Social Issues, 31,* 65–89.

Rumsey, M.G. (1976). Effects of defendant background and remorse on sentencing judgments. *Journal of Applied Social Psychology, 6,* 64–68.

Ruva, C.L., & Bryant, J.B. (2004). The impact of age, speech style and question form on perceptions of witness credibility and trial outcome. *Journal of Applied Social Psychology, 34,* 1919–1944.

Ruva, C.L., & McEvoy, C. (2008). Negative and positive pretrial publicity affect juror memory and decision making. *Journal of Experimental Psychology: Applied, 14,* 226–235.

Ruva, C.L., McEvoy, C., & Bryant, J.B. (2007). Effects of pretrial publicity and collaboration on juror bias and source monitoring errors. *Applied Cognitive Psychology, 21,* 45–67.

Saks, M. (1977). *Jury verdicts: The role of group size and decision rule.* Washington, D.C.: Lexington Books.

———. (1998). Merlin and Solomon: Lessons from the law's formative encounters with forensic identification science. *Hastings Law Journal, 49,* 1069–1141.

———. (2008). Jury size and decision rule. In B.L. Cutler (Ed.), *Encyclopedia of psychology and law: Volume 1* (pp. 423–426). Thousand Oaks, CA: Sage.

Saks, M.J., & Kidd, R.F. (1980–81). Human information processing and adjudication: Trial by heuristics. *Law and Society Review, 15,* 123–159.

Saks, M.J., & Marti, M.W. (1997). A meta-analysis of the effects of jury size. *Law and Human Behavior, 21,* 451–466.

Salerno, J.M., & Diamond, S.S. (2010). The promise of a cognitive perspective on jury deliberation. *Psychonomic Bulletin and Review, 17,* 174–179.

Sand, L.B., & Reiss, S.A. (1985). A report on seven experiments conducted by district court judges in the second circuit. *New York University Law Review, 60,* 423–497.

Sandoval v. California, 114 S. Ct. 1239 (1994).

Sandys, M., & Dillehay, R.C. (1995). First-ballot votes, predeliberation dispositions, and final verdicts in jury trials. *Law and Human Behavior, 19,* 175–195.

Sannito, T., & Arnolds, E.B. (1982). Jury study results: The factors at work. *Trial Diplomacy Journal, Spring,* 6–11.

Savitsky, J.C., & Lindblom, W.D. (1986). The impact of the guilty but mentally ill verdict on juror decisions: An empirical analysis. *Journal of Applied Psychology, 16,* 686–701.

Saxton, B. (1998). How well do jurors understand jury instructions? A field test using real juries and real trials in Wyoming. *Land and Water Law Review, 33,* 59–189.

Schklar, J., & Diamond, S.S. (1999). Juror reaction to DNA evidence: Errors and expectancies. *Law and Human Behavior, 23,* 159–184.

Schuller, R.A. (1992). The impact of battered woman syndrome evidence on jury decision-processes. *Law and Human Behavior, 16,* 597–620.

———. (2003). Self defense and battered women who kill. *Duke Journal of Gender, Law and Policy, 10,* 223–244.

Schuller, R.A., & Cripps, J. (1998). Expert evidence pertaining to battered women: The impact of gender of expert and timing of testimony. *Law and Human Behavior, 22,* 17–31.

Schuller, R.A., & Jenkins, G. (2007). Expert evidence pertaining to battered women: Limitations and reconceptualizations. In M. Costanzo, D. Krauss, & K. Pedzek (Eds.), *Expert psychological testimony for the courts* (pp. 203–225). Mahwah, NJ: Erlbaum.

Schuller, R.A., McKimmie, B., & Janz, T. (2004). Trials of battered women who kill: The impact of expert testimony on jurors' decisions. *Psychiatry, Psychology and Law, 11,* 1–12.

Schuller, R.A., & Rzepa, S. (2002). Expert testimony pertaining to battered woman syndrome: Its impact on jurors' decisions. *Law and Human Behavior, 26,* 655–673.

Schuller, R.A., Terry, D., & McKimmie, B. (2001). The impact of an expert's gender on jurors' decisions. *Law and Psychology Review, 25,* 59–79.

———. (2005). The impact of expert testimony on jurors' decisions: Gender of the expert and testimony complexity. *Journal of Applied Social Psychology, 35,* 1266–1280.

Schuller, R.A., Wells, E., Rzepa, S., & Klippenstine, A. (2004). Re-thinking battered woman syndrome evidence: The impact of alternative forms of expert testimony on mock jurors' decisions. *Canadian Journal of Behavioural Sciences, 36,* 127–136.

Schuller, R.A., & Yarmey, M. (2001). The jury: Deciding guilt and innocence. In R.A. Schuller & J.R.P. Ogloff (Eds.), *An introduction to law and psychology: Canadian perspectives* (pp. 157–187). Toronto: University of Toronto Press.

Schulman, J., Shaver, P., Colman, R., Emrich, B., & Christie, R. (1973; May). Recipe for a jury. *Psychology Today, 77,* 37–44; 77–84.

Schumann, E.L., & Thompson, W.C. (1989). *Effects of attorneys' arguments on jurors' use of statistical evidence* (unpublished manuscript).

Schutte, J.W. (1994). Repressed memory lawsuits: Potential verdict predictors. *Behavioral Sciences and the Law, 12,* 409–416.

Schutte, J.W., & Hosch, H.M. (1997). Gender differences in sexual assault verdicts: A meta-analysis. *Journal of Social Behavior and Personality, 12,* 759–772.

Schweitzer, N.J., & Saks, M.J. (2009). The gatekeeper effect: The impact of judges' admissibility decisions on the persuasiveness of expert testimony. *Psychology, Public Policy, and Law, 15,* 1–18.

Schweitzer, N.J., Saks, M.J., Murphy, E.R., Roskies, A.L., Sinnott-Armstrong, W., & Gaudet, L.M. (2011). Neuroimages as evidence in a mens rea defense: No impact. *Psychology, Public Policy, and Law, 17,* 357–393.

Sealy, A.P., & Cornish, W.R. (1973). Juries and the rules of evidence. *Criminal Law Review, April,* 208–223.

Seltzer, R. (2006). Scientific jury selection: Does it work? *Journal of Applied Social Psychology, 36,* 2417–2435.

Seltzer, R., Venuti, M.A., & Lopes, G.M. (1991). Juror honesty during the voir dire. *Journal of Criminal Justice, 19,* 451–462.

Semmler, C., & Brewer, N. (2002). Effects of mood and emotion on juror processing and judgments. *Behavioral Sciences and the Law, 20,* 423–436.

Severance, L.J., Greene, E., & Loftus, E.F. (1984). Criminology: Toward criminal jury instructions that jurors can understand. *Journal of Criminal Law and Criminology, 75,* 198–233.

Severance, L.J., & Loftus, E.F. (1982). Improving the ability of jurors to comprehend and apply criminal jury instructions. *Law and Society Review, 17,* 153–198.

———. (1984). Improving criminal justice: Making jury instructions understandable for American jurors. *International Review of Applied Psychology, 33,* 97–119.

Shaffer, D.R., & Case, T. (1982). On the decision to testify in one's own behalf: Effects of withheld evidence, defendant's sexual preferences, and juror dogmatism on juridic decisions. *Journal of Personality and Social Psychology, 42,* 335–346.

Shaffer, D.R., Plummer, D., & Hammock, G. (1986). Hath he suffered enough? Effects of jury dogmatism, defendant similarity, and defendant's pretrial suffering on juridic decisions. *Journal of Personality and Social Psychology, 50,* 1059–1067.

Shaffer, D.R., & Wheatman, S.R. (2000). Does personality influence reactions to judicial instructions? Some preliminary findings and possible implications. *Psychology, Public Policy, and Law, 6,* 655–676.

Shaw, J.I., & Skolnick, P. (2004). Effects of prejudicial pretrial publicity from physical and witness evidence on mock jurors' decision making. *Journal of Applied Social Psychology, 34,* 2132–2148.

Sheppard v. Maxwell, 384 U.S. 333.

Shestowsky, D.T., & Horowitz, L.M. (2004). How the need for cognition of scale predicts behavior in mock jury deliberations. *Law and Human Relations, 28,* 305–337.

Shestowsky, D.T., Wegener, D.T., & Fabrigar, L.R. (1998). Need for cognition and interpersonal influence: Individual differences in impact on dyadic decisions. *Journal of Personality and Social Psychology, 74,* 1317–1328.

Silver, E., Cirincione, C., & Steadman, H.J. (1994). Demythologizing inaccurate perceptions of the insanity defense. *Law and Human Behavior, 18,* 63–70.

Simon, D., Snow, C., & Read, S.J. (2004). The redux of cognitive consistency theories: Evidence judgments by constraint satisfaction. *Journal of Personality and Social Psychology, 86,* 814–837.

Simon, R.J. (1967). *The jury and the defense of insanity.* Boston: Little, Brown & Co.

Simon, R.J., & Mahan, L. (1971). Quantifying burdens of proof: A view from the bench, the jury and the classroom. *Law and Society Review, 5,* 319–330.

Skeem, J., Eno Louden, J., & Evans, J. (2004). Venireperson's attitudes toward the insanity defense: Developing, refining, and validating a scale. *Law and Human Behavior, 28,* 623–648.

Skeem, J.L., & Golding, S.L. (2001). Describing jurors' personal conceptions of insanity and their relationship to case judgments. *Psychology, Public Policy, and Law, 7,* 561–621.

Smith, V.L (1991a). Prototypes in the courtroom: Lay representation of legal concepts. *Journal of Personality and Social Psychology, 61,* 857–872.

———. (1991b). Impact of pretrial instructions on jurors' information processing and decision making. *Journal of Applied Psychology, 76,* 220–228.

———. (1993). When prior knowledge and law collide: Helping jurors use the law. *Law and Human Behavior, 17,* 507–536.

Smith, A.C., & Greene, E. (2005). Conduct and its consequences: Attempts at debiasing jury judgments. *Law and Human Behavior, 29,* 505–526.

Smith, B., Penrod, S., Otto, A., & Park, R. (1996). Jurors' use of probabilistic evidence. *Law and Human Behavior, 20,* 49–82.

Smith, V.L., & Studebaker, C.A. (1996). What do you expect? The influence of people's prior knowledge of crime categories on fact-finding. *Law and Human Behavior, 20,* 517–532.

Smithson, M., Deady, S., & Gracik, L. (2007). Guilty, not guilty, or . . . ? Multiple verdict options in jury verdict choices. *Journal of Behavioral Decision Making, 20,* 481–498.

Sommers, S.R. (2006). On racial diversity and group decision-making: Identifying multiple effects of racial composition on jury deliberations. *Journal of Personality and Social Psychology, 90,* 597–612.

Sosis, R. (1974). Internal-external control and the perception of responsibility of another for an accident. *Journal of Personality and Social Psychology, 30,* 393–399.

Spano, L.M., Groscup, J.L., & Penrod, S.D. (2011). Pretrial publicity and the jury: Research and methods. In R.L. Wiener and B.H. Bornstein (Eds.), *Handbook of trial consulting* (pp. 217–244). New York: Springer Science + Business Media.

Spanos, N.P., Myers, B., DuBreuil, S.C., & Pawlak, A.E. (1992–1993). The effects of polygraph evidence and eyewitness testimony on the beliefs and decisions of mock jurors. *Imagination, Cognition and Personality, 12,* 103–113.

Sporer, S.L., Penrod, S., Read, D., & Cutler, B. (1995). Choosing, confidence, and accuracy: A meta-analysis of the confidence-accuracy relation in eyewitness identification studies. *Psychological Bulletin, 118,* 315–327.

Stalans, L.J. (1993). Citizens' crime stereotypes, biased recall, and punishment preferences in abstract cases: The educative role of interpersonal sources. *Law and Human Behavior, 17,* 451–470.

Stasser, G. (1988). Computer simulation as a research tool: The DISCUSS model of group decision making. *Journal of Experimental Social Psychology, 24,* 393–422.

———. (1992). Information salience and the discovery of hidden profiles by decisionmaking groups: A "thought experiment." *Group Decision Making, 52,* 156–181.

Stasser, G., & Davis, J.H. (1981). Group decision making and social influence: A social interaction sequence model. *Psychological Review, 88,* 523–551.

Stasser, G., Kerr, N.L., & Davis, J.H. (1989). Influence processes and consensus models in decision-making groups. In P.B. Paulus (Ed.), *Psychology of group influence* (2nd ed.; pp. 279–326). Hillsdale, NJ: Erlbaum.

Stasser, G., Stella, N., Hanna, C., & Colella, A. (1984). The majority effect in jury delibera-tions: Number of supporters versus number of supporting arguments. *Law and Psychology Review, 8,* 115–127.

Steblay, N.M., Besirevic, J., Fulero, S.M., & Jimenez-Lorente, B. (1999). The effects of pretrial publicity on juror verdicts: A meta-analytic review. *Law and Human Behavior, 23,* 219–235.

Steblay, N., Hosch, H.M., Culhane, S.E., & McWethy, A. (2006). The impact on juror verdicts of judicial instruction to disregard inadmissible evidence: A meta-analysis. *Law and Human Behavior, 30,* 469–542.

Steele, W.W., & Thornburg, E.G. (1988–1989). Jury instructions: A persistent failure to com-municate. *North Carolina Law Review, 67,* 77–119.

Stephan, C. (1972). Sex prejudice in jury simulation. *Journal of Psychology, 88,* 305–312.

Stewart, J.E. (1980). Defendant's attractiveness as a factor in the outcome of criminal trials: An observational study. *Journal of Applied Social Psychology, 10,* 348–361.

———. (1985). Appearance and punishment: The attraction–leniency effect in the court-room. *Journal of Social Psychology, 125,* 373–378.

Strawn, D.J., & Buchanan, R.W. (1976). Jury confusion: A threat to justice. *Judicature, 59,* 478–483.

Strodtbeck, F.L., James, R.M., & Hawkins, C. (1957). Social status in jury deliberations. *American Sociological Review, 22,* 713–719.

Strodtbeck, F.L., & Lipinski, R.M. (1985). Becoming first among equals: Moral consid-erations in jury foreman selection. *Journal of Personality and Social Psychology, 49,* 927–936.

Strodtbeck, F.L., & Mann, R.D. (1956). Sex role differentiation in jury deliberations. *Sociom-etry, 19,* 3–11.

Studebaker, C.A., & Penrod, S.D. (2005). Pretrial publicity and its influence in juror decision making. In N. Brewer & K.D. Williams (Eds.), *Psychology and law: An empirical perspec-tive* (pp. 254–275). New York: Guilford Press.

Studebaker, C.A., Robbennolt, J.K., Pathak-Sharma, M.K., & Penrod, S.D. (2000). Assessing pretrial publicity effects: Integrating content analytic results. *Law and Human Behavior, 24,* 317–336.

Studebaker, C.A., Robbennolt, J.K., Penrod, S.D., Pathak-Sharma, M.K., Groscup, J.L., & Devenport, J.L. (2002). Studying pretrial publicity effects: New methods for improving ecological validity and testing external validity. *Law and Human Behavior, 26,* 19–41.

Summers, A., Hayward, R.D., & Miller, M.K. (2010). Death qualification as systematic exclu-sion of jurors with certain religious and other characteristics. *Journal of Applied Social Psychology, 40,* 3218–3234.

Sunstein, C.R., Hastie, R., Payne, J.W., Schkade, D.A., & Viscusi, K. (2002). *Punitive dam-ages: How juries decide.* Chicago: University of Chicago Press.

Sweeney, L.T., & Haney, C. (1992). The influence of race on sentencing: A meta-analytic review of experimental studies. *Behavioral Sciences and the Law, 10,* 179–195.

Swenson, R.A., Nash, D.L., & Roos, D.C. (1984). Source credibility and perceived expertness of testimony in a simulated child-custody case. *Professional Psychology: Research and Practice, 15,* 891–898.

Tanford, S., & Cox, M. (1988). The effects of impeachment evidence and limiting instruc-tions on individual and group decision making. *Law and Human Behavior, 12,* 477–496.

Tanford, S., & Penrod, S. (1982). Biases in trials involving defendants charged with multiple offenses. *Journal of Applied Social Psychology, 12,* 453–480.

———. (1984). Social inference processes in juror judgments of multiple-offense trials. *Journal of Personality and Social Psychology, 47,* 749–765.

———. (1986). Jury deliberations: Discussion content and influence processes in jury decision making. *Journal of Applied Social Psychology, 16,* 322–347.

Tanford, S., Penrod, S., & Collins, R. (1985). Decision making in joined criminal trials: The influence of charge similarity, evidence similarity and limiting instructions. *Law and Human Behavior, 9,* 319–337.

Tang, C.M., & Nunez, N. (2003). Effects of defendant age and juror bias on judgment of culpability: What happens when a juvenile is tried as an adult? *American Journal of Criminal Justice, 28,* 37–52.

Tankard, J.W., Middleton, K., & Rimmer, T. (1979). Compliance with American Bar Association fair trial–free press guidelines. *Journalism Quarterly, 56,* 464–468.

Taylor, T.S., & Hosch, H.M. (2004). An examination of jury verdicts for evidence of a similarity-leniency effect, an out-group punitiveness effect, or a black sheep effect. *Law and Human Behavior, 28,* 587–599.

Tenney, E.R., MacCoun, R.J., Spellman, B.A., & Hastie, R. (2007). Calibration trumps confidence as a basis for witness credibility. *Psychological Science, 18,* 46–50.

Thomas, E.A., & Hogue, A. (1976). Apparent weight of evidence, decision criteria and confidence ratings in juror decision making. *Psychological Review, 83,* 442–465.

Thompson, W.C. (1989). Death qualification after *Wainwright v. Witt* and *Lockhart v. McCree. Law and Human Behavior, 13,* 185–215.

Thompson, W.C., Fong, G.T., & Rosenhan, D.L. (1981). Inadmissible evidence and juror verdicts. *Journal of Personality and Social Psychology, 40,* 453–463.

Thompson, W.C., & Schumann, E.L. (1987). Interpretation of statistical evidence in criminal trials: The prosecutors' fallacy and the defense attorney's fallacy. *Law and Human Behavior, 11,* 167–187.

Tindale, R.S., Davis, J.H., Vollrath, D.A., Nagao, D.H., & Hinsz, V.B. (1990). Asymmetrical social influence in freely interacting groups: A test of three models. *Journal of Personality and Social Psychology, 58,* 438–449.

Tindale, R.S., & Nagao, D.H. (1986). An assessment of the potential utility of "scientific jury selection": A "thought experiment" approach. *Organizational Behavior and Human Decision Processes, 37,* 409–425.

United States v. Brawner, 471 F.2d 969 (1973).

Velasco, P.D.P. (1995). The influence of size and decision rule in jury decision-making. In G. Davies et al. (Eds.), *Psychology, law, and criminal justice: International developments in research and practice* (pp. 344–348). Berlin, Germany: Walter De Gruyter.

Victor v. Nebraska (92–8894), 511 U.S. 1 (1994).

Vidmar, N. (1972). Effects of decision alternatives on the verdicts and social perceptions of simulated juries. *Journal of Personality and Social Psychology, 22,* 211–218.

———. (1997). Generic prejudice and the presumption of guilt in sex abuse trials. *Law and Human Behavior, 21,* 5–25.

———. (1998). The performance of the American civil jury: An empirical perspective. *Arizona Law Review, 40,* 849–899.

———. (2002). Case studies of pre- and mid-trial prejudice in criminal and civil litigation. *Law and Human Behavior, 26,* 73–105.

———. (2003). When all of us are victims: Juror prejudice and "terrorist" trials. *Chicago-Kent Law Review, 78*, 1143–1178.

Vidmar, N., & Hans, V.P. (2007). *American juries: The verdict.* New York: Prometheus.

Vinson, K.V., Costanzo, M.A., & Berger, D.E. (2008). Predictors of verdict and punitive damages in high-stakes civil litigation. *Behavioral Sciences and the Law, 26*, 167–186.

Visher, C.A. (1987). Juror decision making: The importance of evidence. *Law and Human Behavior, 11*, 1–17.

Vondergeest, L., Honts, C.R., & Devitt, M.K. (1993). Effects of juror and expert witness gender on jurors' perceptions of an expert witness. *Modern Psychological Studies, 1*, 1–6.

Wainwright v. Witt, 469 U.S. 412 (1985).

Walker, L. (1979). *The battered woman.* New York: Harper and Row.

Warling, D., & Peterson-Badali, M. (2003). The verdict on jury trials for juveniles: The effects of defendant's age on trial outcomes. *Behavioral Sciences and the Law, 21*, 63–82.

Wasserman, D.T., & Robinson, J.N. (1980). Extra-legal influences, group processes, and jury decision-making: A psychological perspective. *North Carolina Central Law Journal, 12*, 96–151.

Wegner, D.M. (1994). Ironic processes of mental control. *Psychological Review, 101*, 34–52.

Weir, J.A., & Wrightsman, L.S. (1990). The determinants of mock jurors' verdicts in a rape case. *Journal of Applied Social Psychology, 20*, 901–919.

Weld, H.P., & Danzig, E.R. (1940). A study of the way in which a verdict is reached by a jury. *American Journal of Psychology, 53*, 518–536.

Weld, H.P., & Roff, M. (1938). A study in the formation of opinion based on legal evidence. *American Journal of Psychology, 51*, 609–623.

Werner, C.M., Strube, M.J., Cole, A.M., & Kagehiro, D.K. (1985). The impact of case characteristics and prior jury experience on jury verdicts. *Journal of Applied Social Psychology, 15*, 409–427.

Whalen, D.H., & Blanchard, F.A. (1982). Effects of photographic evidence on mock juror judgment. *Journal of Applied Social Psychology, 12*, 30–41.

Wheatman, S.R., & Shaffer, D.R. (2001). On finding for defendants who plead insanity: The crucial impact of dispositional instructions and opportunity to deliberate. *Law and Human Behavior, 25*, 167–183.

Whittemore, K.E., & Ogloff, J.R. (1995). Factors that influence jury decision making. *Law and Human Behavior, 19*, 283–303.

Wiener, R.L., Habert, K., Shkordriani, G., & Staebler, C. (1991). The social psychology of jury nullification: Predicting when jurors disobey the law. *Journal of Applied Social Psychology, 21*, 1379–1401.

Wiener, R.L., Richmond, T.L., Seib, H.M., Rauch, S.M., & Hackney, A.A. (2002). The prototypes of telling murder stories: Do we think in scripts, exemplars, or prototypes? *Behavioral Sciences and the Law, 20*, 119–139.

Wiener, R.L., Rogers, M., Winter, R., Hurt, L., Hackney, A., Kadela, K., Seib, H., Rauch, S., Warren, L., & Morasco, B. (2004). Guided jury discretion in capital murder cases: The role of declarative and procedural knowledge. *Psychology, Public Policy, and Law, 10*, 516–576.

Williams v. Florida, 90 S. Ct. 1893 (1970).

Willis Esqueda, C., Espinoza, R.K., & Culhane, S.E. (2008). The effects of ethnicity, SES, and crime status on juror decision making. *Hispanic Journal of Behavioral Sciences, 30*, 181–199.

Winter, R.J., & Greene, E. (2007). Juror decision-making. In F. Durso (Ed.), *Handbook of applied cognition* (2nd ed.; pp. 739–761). Hoboken, NJ: Wiley.

Wissler, R.L., & Saks, M.J. (1985). On the inefficacy of limiting instructions: When jurors use prior conviction evidence to decide on guilt. *Law and Human Behavior, 9,* 37–48.

Wissler, R., Rector, K., & Saks, M. (2001). The impact of jury instructions on the fusion of liability and compensatory damages. *Law and Human Behavior, 25,* 125–139.

Witherspoon v. Illinois, 391 U.S. 510 (1968).

Wuensch, K.L., & Moore, C.H. (2004). Effects of physical attractiveness on evaluations of a male employee's allegation of sexual harassment by his female employer. *Journal of Social Psychology, 144,* 207–217.

Wyer, Jr., R.S. (2007). Principles of mental representation. In A. Kruglanski & E.T. Higgins (Eds.), *Social psychology: Handbook of basic principles* (2nd ed.; pp. 285–307). New York: Guilford Press.

York, E., & Cornwell, B. (2006). Status on trial: Social characteristics and influence in the jury room. *Social Forces, 85,* 455–477.

Young, W., Cameron, N., & Tinsley, Y. (2001). *Juries in Criminal Trials, Report 69.* Wellington, NZ: New Zealand Law Commission.

Zeisel, H. (1971). And then there were none: The diminution of the federal jury. *University of Chicago Law Review, 38,* 710–724.

Zeisel, H., & Callahan, T. (1963). Split trials and time saving: A statistical analysis. *Harvard Law Review, 76,* 1606–1625.

Zeisel, H., & Diamond, S.S. (1974). "Convincing empirical evidence" on the six member jury. *University of Chicago Law Review, 41,* 281–295.

———. (1978). The effects of peremptory challenges on jury and verdict: An experiment in a federal district court. *Stanford Law Review, 30,* 491–531.

INDEX

ABA. *See* American Bar Association

Abramson, J., 5, 19

ad damnum, 175

Adler, F., 102

Adler, S., 19

aggravating circumstances, 56, 123, 230

Alfini, J., 48, 55, 57, 178

Algebraic models of juror decision making, 23–25

Allen, M., 50

alternative stories, defense, 196–199, 210, 217, 219–220

alternative verdict options, 82–84

American Bar Association (ABA), 16, 72, 74

American Jury, The (Kalven & Zeisel), 16, 159–160

American Jury on Trial, The (Kassin & Wrightsman), 18

American Law Institute (ALI), 85

American Psychological Association, 20

American Psychology-Law Society, 20

Anderson, N., 24

Antonio, M., 95–96

Apodaca v. Oregon, 17, 44

Arbuthnot, J., 73, 137

Arizona Jury Reform Project, 227, 231; Diamond et al. (2003), 19, 65–66, 122, 154, 157, 176; Diamond & Vidmar (2001), 177

Asch, S., 42

ATCLS. *See* Attitudes Toward the Criminal Legal System

attitudes toward legal system, juror, 106–108

Attitudes Toward the Criminal Legal System (ATCLS) measure, 107, 214

attraction-leniency bias, 93–95

Australia, 6, 143

authoritarianism, juror, 103–105, 107, 121, 183, 192, 214

awards. *See* damage awards

Baldus, D., 18, 118, 120, 123

Baldwin, J., 17, 112, 114, 117

Ballew v. Georgia, 42

Battered Woman Syndrome (BWS), 134–135

Bayes, T., 22

Bayesian model, 22–23, 138–140, 145, 151

belief in a just world (BJW), juror, 107, 110–111, 121, 224

Bennett, W., 28, 135

Bentele, U., 56

Berman, G., 127–129

beyond reasonable doubt. *See* standard of proof

bias. *See* attraction-leniency bias; black-sheep effect; ingroup bias; outgroup bias; racial bias; similarity-leniency effect

bifurcation, 18, 62–63, 183–184

BJW: *See* belief in a just world

Black male presence effect, 119

black-sheep effect, 113, 117–120, 191

Boehm, V., 17, 103

Bohannon, W., 114, 166

Bordens, K., 43, 59–64

Bornstein, B., 20, 62, 76, 95, 102, 109, 175–176

Bottoms, B., 124

Bourgeois, M., 62–63, 66

Bowers, W., 55–56, 119–120

Bray, R., 7, 17, 104

Brehm, S., 78

Brewer, N., 119, 125–126, 128, 133

ABOUT THE AUTHOR

DENNIS J. DEVINE is Associate Professor in the Department of Psychology at Indiana University–Purdue University Indianapolis. He has conducted research on juries for over a decade, and his work has been published in numerous professional journals, including *Law and Human Behavior*; *Psychology, Public Policy, and Law*; *Journal of Empirical Legal Studies*; and *Journal of Applied Social Psychology*.

Made in the USA
Middletown, DE
03 March 2021

34724541R00170